Gender and Diplomacy

This volume provides a detailed discussion of the role of women in diplomacy and a global narrative of their current and historical role within it.

The last century has seen the Ministries of Foreign Affairs (MFAs) experience seismic shifts in their policies concerning the entry, role, and agency of women within their institutional make-up. Despite these changes, and the promise that true gender equality offers to the diplomatic craft, the role of women in the diplomatic sphere continues to remain overlooked, and placed on the fringes of diplomatic scholarship. This volume brings together established scholars and experienced diplomatic practitioners in an attempt to unveil the story of women in diplomacy, in a context which is historical, theoretical, and empirical. In line with feminist critical thought, the objective of this volume is to theorise and empirically demonstrate the understanding of diplomacy as a gendered practice and study. The aims of are three-fold: 1) expose and confront the gender of diplomacy; 2) shed light on the historical involvement of women in diplomatic practice in spite of systemic barriers and restrictions, with a focus on critical junctures of diplomatic institutional formation and the diplomatic entitlements which were created for women at these junctures; 3) examine the current state of women in diplomacy and evaluate the rate of progress towards a gender-even playing field on the basis thereof.

This book will be of much interest to students of diplomacy studies, gender studies, foreign policy, and international relations.

Jennifer A. Cassidy is a Doctoral Candidate in International Development at the University of Oxford, UK.

Routledge New Diplomacy Studies
Series Editors: Corneliu Bjola
University of Oxford
and
Markus Kornprobst
Diplomatic Academy of Vienna

This series publishes theoretically challenging and empirically authoritative studies of the traditions, functions, paradigms, and institutions of modern diplomacy. Taking a comparative approach, the New Diplomacy Studies series aims to advance research on international diplomacy, publishing innovative accounts of how 'old' and 'new' diplomats help steer international conduct between anarchy and hegemony, handle demands for international stability vs international justice, facilitate transitions between international orders, and address global governance challenges. Dedicated to the exchange of different scholarly perspectives, the series aims to be a forum for inter-paradigm and interdisciplinary debates, and an opportunity for dialogue between scholars and practitioners.

International Law, New Diplomacy and Counter-Terrorism
An Interdisciplinary Study of Legitimacy
Steven J. Barela

Theory and Practice of Paradiplomacy
Subnational Governments in International Affairs
Alexander S. Kuznetsov

Digital Diplomacy
Theory and Practice
Edited by Corneliu Bjola and Marcus Holmes

Chinese Public Diplomacy
The Rise of the Confucius Institute
Falk Hartig

Diplomacy and Security Community-Building
EU Crisis Management in the Western Mediterranean
Niklas Bremberg

Diplomatic Cultures and International Politics
Translations, Spaces and Alternatives
Edited by Jason Dittmer and Fiona McConnell

Secret Diplomacy
Concepts, Contexts and Cases
Edited by Corneliu Bjola and Stuart Murray

Diplomatic Style and Foreign Policy
A Case Study of South Korea
Jeffrey Robertson

Gender and Diplomacy
Edited by Jennifer A. Cassidy

Gender and Diplomacy

Edited by
Jennifer A. Cassidy

Routledge
Taylor & Francis Group
LONDON AND NEW YORK

First published 2017
by Routledge
2 Park Square, Milton Park, Abingdon, Oxon OX14 4RN

and by Routledge
711 Third Avenue, New York, NY 10017

Routledge is an imprint of the Taylor & Francis Group, an informa business

© 2017 selection and editorial matter, Jennifer A. Cassidy; individual chapters, the contributors

The right of the editor to be identified as the author of the editorial matter, and of the authors for their individual chapters, has been asserted in accordance with sections 77 and 78 of the Copyright, Designs and Patents Act 1988.

All rights reserved. No part of this book may be reprinted or reproduced or utilised in any form or by any electronic, mechanical, or other means, now known or hereafter invented, including photocopying and recording, or in any information storage or retrieval system, without permission in writing from the publishers.

Trademark notice: Product or corporate names may be trademarks or registered trademarks, and are used only for identification and explanation without intent to infringe.

British Library Cataloguing in Publication Data
A catalogue record for this book is available from the British Library

Library of Congress Cataloging in Publication Data
Names: Cassidy, Jennifer A., editor.
Title: Gender and diplomacy / edited by Jennifer A. Cassidy.
Description: Abingdon, Oxon ; New York, NY : Routledge, [2017] | Series: Routledge new diplomacy studies | Includes bibliographical references and index.
Identifiers: LCCN 2016058258| ISBN 9781138234307 (hbk) | ISBN 9781315270777 (ebk)
Subjects: LCSH: International relations–Social aspects. | Diplomacy–Social aspects. | Women diplomats. | Women ambassadors. | Women international relations specialists.
Classification: LCC JZ1253.2 .G444 2017 | DDC 327.2082–dc23
LC record available at https://lccn.loc.gov/2016058258

ISBN: 978-1-138-23430-7 (hbk)
ISBN: 978-1-315-27077-7 (ebk)

Typeset in Times New Roman
by Wearset Ltd, Boldon, Tyne and Wear

Dedicated to Siobhan Cassidy:
my mother, my light, and the strongest woman I know.
I would be nothing without her.

Contents

List of illustrations	ix
Notes on contributors	x
Foreword	xiv
MARY ROBINSON	
Acknowledgements	xvi

Introduction: analysing the dynamics of modern diplomacy through a gender lens   1
JENNIFER A. CASSIDY AND SARA ALTHARI

PART I
Getting to the table: historical challenges and reflections   13

1 **Women, gender, and diplomacy: a historical survey**   15
HELEN McCARTHY AND JAMES SOUTHERN

2 **Alison Palmer's fight for sex and gender equity in the twentieth-century United States Foreign Service**   32
BEATRICE McKENZIE

3 **From marriage bar towards gender equality: the experience of women in Ireland's Department of Foreign Affairs 1970–2000**   48
ANNE BARRINGTON

4 **Women of the South: engaging with the UN as a diplomatic manoeuvre**   65
DEVAKI JAIN

PART II
At the table: broken boundaries and persisting institutional challenges 81

5 Towards a feminist US foreign policy? Secretary of State Hillary Clinton's metaphorical diplomacy 83
ERIC M. BLANCHARD

6 Gender, status, and ambassador appointments to militarized and violent countries 100
BIRGITTA NIKLASSON AND ANN TOWNS

7 Women in foreign lands: women diplomats and host-country cultures 120
JANE MARRIOTT OBE

8 Women in global economic governance: scaling the summits 140
SUSAN HARRIS RIMMER

9 Becoming UN Women: a journey in realizing rights and gaining global recognition 170
PHUMZILE MLAMBO-NGCUKA

10 Unprecedented: women's leadership in twenty-first century multilateral diplomacy 187
JESSICA FLIEGEL

11 Conclusion: progress and policies towards a gender-even playing field 210
JENNIFER A. CASSIDY

Index 219

Illustrations

Figures

1.1	Timeline of women's admission to selected diplomatic services	24
8.1	2015 labour participation in G20 countries by gender	162

Tables

2.1	FSO distribution by sex within each job function (cone) (June 1974, percent of total)	39
6.1	Descriptive statistics of included variables	106
6.2	Share of women and men (percent) of different regions' ambassador appointments	108
6.3	Share of women and men (percent) of the ambassadors received by different regions	109
6.4	The extent (percent) to which female and male ambassadors are sent to countries of high economic status	110
6.5	The extent (percent) to which female and male ambassadors are sent to countries of high military status	111
6.6	Degree of militarism of the receiving countries to which female and male ambassadors are sent	112
6.7	Share of female and male ambassadors (percent) that are sent to countries with different levels of armed conflict	113
6.8	Share of female and male ambassadors (percent) in receiving countries of different GPI rank	114
6.9	Average GPI score and rank of the receiving countries to which female and male ambassadors are sent (means)	114
9.1	What is UN Women? Policy objectives in the twenty-first century	176

Contributors

Sara Althari is a Radcliffe Department of Medicine Scholar in Genetics and Genomics at the University of Oxford. She is one of the first Saudi women to attend the University of Oxford as a doctoral student, and is fully sponsored by the Saudi Arabian Ministry of Higher Education. In 2013, Althari graduated magna cum laude with a Bachelors of Arts in Biological Sciences and Anthropology from Wellesley College, and was awarded membership to Phi Beta Kappa. She has acquired biological research training at the Broad Institute of Harvard and MIT, Harvard Medical School, and Brigham and Women's Hospital in Boston.

Anne Barrington joined Ireland's Department of Foreign Affairs in 1977. She is currently Ambassador to Japan. Prior to taking up that position in 2014 Anne held successive positions as Director General Europe and Strategy and Performance Divisions Dublin, Joint Secretary at the North South Ministerial Council in Armagh, Northern Ireland and Ambassador to Tanzania, Kenya, and Burundi. As well as serving at headquarters, with periods seconded to the Department of the Taoiseach (Prime Minister's Office) Anne served in the Permanent Mission to the United Nations in New York and in Washington DC. Anne has a degree in History and Politics and a Diploma in European Law from University College Dublin, a Certificate in Public Administration from the Institute of Public Administration and is completing a Doctorate in Governance in Queen's University Belfast. She is married with two adult children.

Eric M. Blanchard is currently Assistant Professor in the Political Science Department at SUNY Oswego in Oswego, New York. He holds a PhD from the University of Southern California in Los Angeles and has research interests in gender and world politics, international security, US foreign policy, Sino-American relations, East Asian security, International Relations theory, and the intersection of technology and politics. He was recognised as an American Council of Learned Societies New Faculty Fellow in 2011 and his work has been published in the journals *International Studies Quarterly, International Studies Review, Review of International Studies, Journal of International Relations and Development,* and *Signs: Journal of Women in*

Culture and Society. Blanchard has also taught International Relations at the University of Southern California and at Columbia University in New York City.

Jennifer A. Cassidy is a Doctoral Candidate in International Development at the University of Oxford. She has served as a political attaché to Ireland's Permanent Mission to the United Nations (New York), the European External Action Service to the Kingdom of Cambodia, and Ireland's Department of Foreign Affairs and Trade during its 2013 Presidency of the Council of the European Union. Her research interests cover digital diplomatic communication during times of political crisis, the construction of strategic narratives and their impact on diplomatic communication, and theories of gender in international politics.

Jessica Fliegel is a consultant who implements people-focused solutions for United States federal government agencies in Washington, DC. Prior to consulting, Ms. Fliegel worked for an international democracy-building non-profit organisation where she supported the organisation's global women's empowerment initiative by designing and implementing programs to increase women's political participation and inclusion in peacebuilding and negotiations globally. Over the course of her tenure, Ms. Fliegel facilitated programming reaching beneficiaries in 61 countries throughout the world and led in-country activities in Bosnia and Herzegovina, Indonesia, Mongolia, Turkey, Qatar, and Sweden. Ms. Fliegel holds an MSc in Global Governance and Diplomacy from the University of Oxford.

Devaki Jain is a feminist economist and writer on public affairs, with special focus on poverty removal, and has published many books as well as essays on gender and development in the context of India and global spaces. She founded a Third World Network of women social scientists called Development Alternatives for Women Networks [DAWN] in 1985 – which continues to bring the voice of women in the former colonies into the global domain. Over the decades she has been a Visiting Fellow at Harvard University, Boston University, University of Sussex, the Scandinavian Institute for Asian Studies, Copenhagen, and Oxford University. She has received several awards, the most prestigious being the Padma Bhushan by the President of India in the Honours List of 2006 and an Honorary Doctorate from the University of Westville, Durban South Africa for her contribution to international development.

Jane Marriott OBE is currently the Director for the Joint International Counter Terrorism Unit, a joint Foreign and Commonwealth and Home Office unit. Previously, she was co-director for the Middle East and North Africa. She has served as Ambassador to Sana'a, Yemen and Deputy and Acting Ambassador to Tehran, Iran. She was a special advisor to the US Special Representative to Afghanistan and Pakistan, Richard C. Holbrooke, and worked for then US CENTCOM Commander, General Petraeus, as part of the CENTCOM

Assessment Team. She was one of the first civilians into southern Iraq in 2003, followed by a role as a political advisor to the US Central Forces Command – Afghanistan, and then political-military counsellor at the British Embassy in Baghdad. London postings have included head of nuclear non-proliferation and deputy head of Afghanistan Department.

Helen McCarthy is Reader in Modern British History at Queen Mary University of London. She is the author of two books, *The British People and the League of Nations: Democracy, Citizenship and Internationalism, 1918–1945* (Manchester University Press 2011) and *Women of the World: The Rise of the Female Diplomat* (Bloomsbury 2014) which won Best Book on International Affairs at the 2015 Political Book Awards She is currently writing a history of working motherhood in the twentieth century (Bloomsbury, 2019). Helen is Managing Editor of *Twentieth Century British History*, a Fellow of the Royal Historical Society and a member of the Public Policy Committee of the British Academy.

Beatrice McKenzie is Associate Professor and Chair of the History Department at Beloit College in Wisconsin. McKenzie has two research areas: American women acting inside and outside official diplomatic channels and the history of US birthright citizenship law. Recent articles on gender and diplomacy were published in *Gender and History* and in the *European Journal of American Studies*. Her chapter, "To Know a Citizen: Birthright Citizenship Documents Regimes in US History," is included in *Citizenship in Question: Evidentiary Birthright and Statelessness* (Duke University Press 2016). McKenzie has an MA in US foreign policy from Johns Hopkins' School of Advanced International Studies and a PhD in US history from the University of Oregon. She served in the US Foreign Service in Uganda and Hong Kong and as a Peace Corps Volunteer in Burkina Faso.

Phumzile Mlambo-Ngcuka is United Nations Under-Secretary-General and Executive Director of UN Women. Ms. Mlambo-Ngcuka has worked in government and civil society, and with the private sector, and was actively involved in the struggle to end apartheid in her home country of South Africa. From 2005 to 2008, she served as Deputy President of South Africa, overseeing programmes to combat poverty and bring the advantages of a growing economy to the poor, with a particular focus on women. Prior to this, she served as Minister of Minerals and Energy from 1999 to 2005 and Deputy Minister in the Department of Trade and Industry from 1996 to 1999. She was a Member of Parliament from 1994 to 1996 as part of South Africa's first democratic government. She has completed her PhD on education and technology at the University of Warwick, United Kingdom.

Birgitta Niklasson is an Assistant Professor in political science at the University of Gothenburg. Her research focuses on bureaucratic structures and gender, more specifically on the politicisation of public administration and career paths of politicians and civil servants. She is currently working on a large research project on gender and diplomacy in the Swedish Ministry for Foreign Affairs, funded by the Swedish Research Council. Niklasson is the author of a large number of chapters and articles that appear in journals such as *Public Administration, West European Politics, Foreign Policy Analysis, Policy and Society, Politica,* and *Comparative Social Research.*

Susan Harris Rimmer is an Associate Professor and Australian Research Council future fellow at Griffith Law School, and an adjunct reader in the Asia-Pacific College of Diplomacy at the Australian National University. Susan was selected as an expert for the official Australian delegation to the 58th session of the UN Commission on the Status of Women in New York in March 2014, and is one of two Australian representatives to the W20 in Turkey and China. In 2014 she was named one of the Westpac and Australian Financial Review's 100 women of influence in the global category. She has served in voluntary roles as a board member of UN Women National Committee Australia, Australian Lawyers for Human Rights, the Refugee Council of Australia and International Women's Development Agency.

James Southern is a PhD Candidate in History at Queen Mary University of London. His current project examines social diversity and recruitment at the British Foreign Office since 1945. His research is funded by an AHRC Collaborative Doctoral Award, and is based both at QMUL and with the Foreign and Commonwealth Office Historians. He has published in *Twentieth Century British History* and various FCO publications. Previously he studied at the University of Manchester.

Ann Towns is Associate Professor in political science at the University of Gothenburg and a Wallenberg Academy Fellow. Her research centres on questions of norms, hierarchies, and resistance in international politics, generally with a focus on gender. She is currently conducting a large research project on gender norms, gender practices and hierarchies in diplomacy with generous funding from the Knut and Alice Wallenberg Foundation and the Swedish Research Council. Towns is the author of *Women and States: Norms and Hierarchies in International Society* (Cambridge University Press 2010). Her research has also appeared in journals such as *International Organization, European Journal of International Relations, Millennium*, and *Party Politics* and in many other venues. She is associate editor of *International Studies Quarterly* and a member of the editorial boards of *Cambridge Studies in Gender and Politics, Politics* and *Internasjonal Politikk.*

Foreword

Achieving gender equality across all spheres of political engagement remains one of the great challenges of our time. I understand all too well the pervasive structural barriers, entrenched within political systems, that serve to limit the role of women in decision making. Tackling obstacles to women's participation is not merely an act of ensuring more women have greater access to roles in governance. The empowerment of women in political life requires that women can reach the decision making table in greater numbers, while also ensuring that their participation is meaningful, their voices are heard and they are enabled to play an active role in shaping outcomes.

Part of the problem is the issue, which still lingers, of whether women are capable of holding high office successfully. When I was elected President of Ireland in December 1990, I made a point of explaining that I felt being a woman added to my ability to understand the challenges of the position, and to carry them through with particular empathy.

Diplomacy serves as the heartbeat of international relations, yet the social inequalities with which women struggle in day to day life are mirrored in the instruments of international negotiations. Careful analysis of the current state of diplomacy is required to disentangle the ubiquitous gender dimension present in diplomatic roles in order to advance the participation of women in governance and policy making. Drawing on the substantial expertise and experience of the authors, this volume of essays provides a rigorous analysis of the gendered nature of diplomacy. The common themes that emerge in the essays, coupled with the concrete recommendations put forward by the authors, offer fertile ground from which academics and policy makers can analyse and improve women's empowerment in the field of diplomacy.

Today, we are living through challenging times, amid shifting geopolitical dynamics, increasing inequality, and serious environmental instabilities. Perhaps more than ever before, we are relying on our diplomats to chart a course to a safer and fairer world for present and future generations. Should current gender inequality in diplomacy persist, the resulting policy development will not adequately consider the needs of women – or worse, will be completely gender blind. Allowing this unequal, gendered landscape to persist would be immoral and ill-conceived. Immoral because all people have the right to equal participation in political and public affairs, regardless of gender. Ill-conceived because we already understand that policies and decisions that respond to the needs of all genders will have a better chance of success. My hope would be that this volume of work inspires others, and that increasing awareness of the gender dimensions of international negotiations can be transformed into enhanced action to address gender imbalances in diplomacy.

Mary Robinson
Former President of Ireland

Acknowledgements

This volume was born out of an initial quest to find literature on the topic of women in diplomacy for the production of an academic paper. The quest was halted when it became clear that there was a distinct lack of literature within the field. Having worked for a brief number of years in the diplomatic realm, and under some of the most formidable female Ambassadors and colleagues, it seemed obvious that there should exist a volume where these women could express their experiences, both historical and present, and where others could learn from them. And so, the volume was born.

Here, I would like to thank, in particular, Dr Corneliu Bjola who guided me throughout this process, and stood with me every step of the journey, providing support and invaluable advice. Without him this volume would not have been created, or possible. In addition, I would like to thank Katie Washington who gave countless hours of her time in editing and reworking chapters and providing insightful feedback and comments on the volume overall. She played an enormous role in this project, and I am so grateful for her support, generosity, and friendship. Also to Georgina Brett, who took on a number of editing roles, and provided hours of support for an entire year. The volume would not have been the same without her. Also to Tristan Parker and Sara Althari, who gave so generously of their time to review and edit a number of chapters. I would also like to thank the two anonymous reviewers who provided useful criticisms and constructive suggestions, which have undoubtedly resulted in a stronger volume. Last, special thanks to the editorial team at Routledge, including Hannah Ferguson and Andrew Humphrys, who provided superb support and guidance throughout the publication process.

Finally, I would also like to express my deepest gratitude towards my friends and family, both here at Oxford, and abroad. You stand and fight for what is right and just in this world, especially during these tumultuous and uncertain times. You continually inspire me, and keep me strong. You bring new meaning to the words of Hillary R. Clinton, 'stronger together', and for that I thank you.

Introduction
Analysing the dynamics of modern diplomacy through a gender lens

Jennifer A. Cassidy and Sara Althari

It is beyond dispute that various sociocultural, ideological, economic, and institutional barriers have historically ensured the exclusion of women from the political arena: the professional space in which the most consequential decisions are made. From Kings, Sultans, Princes, Emirs, Prime Ministers, to their governments, envoys, and representatives, men have functioned as the primary authors and facilitators of the geopolitical order since the beginnings of human history. Indeed, the culture and structure of diplomacy has been defined and constructed by the chronicles of men. Whilst modernity continues to challenge archaic patriarchal infrastructures, the practice of diplomacy remains adherent to conventional notions of gender. As a result, diplomacy continues as a sphere rife with power dynamics, which serve to reinforce gender inequality and perpetuate the historical 'otherisation' of women.

It is important to preface further support of a claim that positions of political leadership, authority, and decision-making are gendered with a definition of gender and a demonstration of its utility as an analytic tool. To those unfamiliar with feminist theory, the distinction between sex and gender may not immediately be self-evident: 'sex' referring to biological differences between 'women' and 'men' (Youdell 2006; Haraway 1988), while 'gender' describes socially constructed differences between those biologically perceived to be women or men (Childs 2006). In other words, 'sex' is a technical distinction whereas 'gender' represents the totality of social perceptions derived from those biological variations.

Gender, however, need not overlap with biological sex. Social gender categories can be classified as masculinities and femininities, where the former encompasses characteristics associated with perceived manhood and the latter with perceived womanhood. Whilst the precise constitution of gender categories is dynamic, depending on shifting sociocultural and political contexts, gender subordination – defined as the subordination of femininities to masculinities – remains a constant feature of social and political life across time and space (Risman 2004; Hey 2006).

For the purposes of this analysis, this volume views gender as 'a set of discourses which can set, change, enforce and represent meaning on the basis of perceived membership in or relation to sex categories' (Sjoberg 2009; Connell

1995; Gibson-Graham 1994). In these discourses, characteristics associated with masculinity include strength, objectivity, power and autonomy, independence, rationality, and aggressiveness, whilst feminine characteristics are drawn from those which include, *inter alia*, weakness, sympathy, marginality, dependence, and passivity. Indeed, in this view, men are associated with the public sphere (professional and public life) while women are associated with the private sphere (motherhood, the household, and the bedroom). These gender tropes influence the expectations that we have of people (including diplomatic agents) and societal institutions (including the diplomatic space itself) and ultimately how we choose to analyse and interpret their behaviour.

This volume examines diplomacy through a 'gender' lens: an approach that identifies gender in the phenomenon that it studies, and uses the identified gender to guide the conceptual analysis (Runyan and Peterson 1999). As Jill Steans explains, using a gender lens as an analytical tool for examination allows the reader and researcher to:

> focus on gender as a particular kind of power relation, or to trace out the ways in which gender is central to understanding international processes. Gender lenses also focus on the everyday experiences of women as women and highlight the consequences of their unequal social position.
>
> (Steans 1998: 5)

This choice of methodology helps reveal the gender subordination embedded in our conceptualisation of political phenomena, and our studies of political events, and enables this volume to reconstruct models of diplomacy which are more conceptually and causally accurate. Such an analytical approach is not only important for understanding the gendered nature of diplomacy, both theoretical and practical, but also for exposing the locus of power and the shifting contours of political sovereignty and statecraft over time. Using gender as a lens through which to study diplomacy opens up a rich vein of scholarship that does not take the participation of men in diplomacy for granted; rather, it interrogates how conventionally masculine norms and values have shaped diplomacy, enabling students of diplomacy to conduct near-objective assessments of the extent to which normative ideas about manhood inform policymakers and decision making in both academic and political contexts.

By examining the historical and institutional scarcity of female diplomats through a gender lens, it becomes clear that diplomacy has been, and remains, decidedly masculine. When asked about her views on a career in politics, Nancy Pelosi, the 52nd Speaker of the United States House of Representatives, and the first women to serve as Speaker in American history, responded 'this is not for the faint of heart'. Yet, men have traditionally perceived women as being inherently faint of heart, and have indeed relied on a number of sexist and redundant arguments to justify gender disparity in politics. Over centuries, noted diplomats from Niccolò Machiavelli to Sir Harold Nicholson have preached that, by their very nature, women are ill-equipped for diplomatic practice as they lack the uniquely masculine characteristics required to steer a career in diplomacy. Machiavelli, one of the earliest diplomatic pioneers, placed much emphasis on the importance of masculine characteristics in conducting state relations. His inner beliefs were that, empirically, states are run and defended by men, and therefore advance only the interest of men (Falco 2010). Nicholson declared that '... women are prone to qualities of zeal, sympathy and intuition which, unless kept under the firmest control, are dangerous qualities in international affairs' (Sylvester 1994: 82). Not only were women viewed as too weak, passive, and conciliatory for the rough and tumble of internal relations, their exclusion has also, to some degree, been justified by their lack of military experience. It was assumed that women must be incapable of fully understanding the stakes involved in foreign policy without proper exposure to the realities of combat. Moreover, for some time, there has been a significant shortage of women formally trained in political science, economics, and international relations; rather than being interpreted as a direct consequence of systemic gender discrimination, this has been largely regarded as a direct reflection of an absence of interest in these fields. Furthermore, some nations are simply not ready to accept women in policy-making positions of high visibility. This creates an obstacle in the face of practical translation within progressive governments, more accepting of female inclusion theoretically and in practice, perhaps out of fear of offending more conservative allies or compromising international reputation.

The gender of diplomacy: a feminist approach

The aforementioned arguments centred on the sex and gender composition of diplomatic agents demonstrate that, in these agents, we value the traits of strength, power, autonomy, independence, and rationality, all traditionally associated with masculinity and the male sex. However, across various disciplines, these arguments are now considered as frail and antiquated as the very dichotomisation of masculinity and femininity. In fact, feminist scholarship has long scrutinised the degree to which International Relations (IR), both as an academic discipline and a practice, has been, and continues to be, dominated by perspectives based solely on the experiences of men. As such, feminists politicise what they view as the androcentrism of IR: a reflection of the standpoint of white, Western males by whom the field is dominated (Runyan and Peterson 2013). Feminists critique the masculinist biases within IR by demonstrating how the field silences women (and minorities), and rids them of their agency, via the expression of hegemonic forms of masculinity. Anne Marie Goetz (1995) has argued, for example, that gendered public sector institutional failures cannot be seen simply as the result of 'discriminatory attitudes or irrational choices on the part of individuals, or unintended oversight in policy. Nor are they deliberate policy outcomes. They are embedded in the norms, structures and practices of institutions'. Further, as Sjoberg (2011: 110) illustrates, gender is not simply an individual or group attribute, meaning that 'institutions, organizations, and even states' can become gendered. Because 'gendering is about the distribution of power and regard based on perceived association with sex-based characteristics', the interaction of gender with these entities has profound effects on how they act and are perceived within IR. Feminist IR has thus moved beyond the simplistic study of masculinity as a social phenomenon existing only in individual agents.

However, scholars operating within more traditional IR paradigms have voiced scepticism regarding these feminist critiques. Such scepticism emerges from the belief that gendered critiques challenge the assumptions of IR scholars at a foundational level, rejecting much of their work as androcentric or masculinised and therefore rejecting its usefulness in understanding the totality of the social world. As such, it is unsurprising that these scholars view the critiques of feminists as originating from a politics of grievance, which seeks to threaten a legitimate science. However, as the work of Enloe (1989) and other scholars demonstrates, foregrounding gender (and especially women and other marginalised voices) provides important empirical insights about global politics, regardless of whether one agrees with their political or epistemological claims. Furthermore, analytic neglect of the role of gender within diplomacy comes at a high price; namely the inability to conduct near-objective assessments of the extent to which normative ideas about masculinity inform policymakers and decision making in both academic and political contexts, and to gain a true understanding of how and why diplomacy works and acts the way it does in the twenty-first century.

In line with feminist critical thought, the objective of this volume is to theorise and empirically demonstrate the understanding of diplomacy as a gendered practice and study. The aim of this contribution to the domains of diplomatic studies is three-fold: (1) to expose and confront the gender *of* diplomacy; (2) to shed light onto the overlooked historical involvement of women in diplomatic practice in spite of systemic barriers and restrictions, with a focus on critical junctures of diplomatic institutional formation and the diplomatic entitlements which were created for women at these junctures; (3) to examine the current state of women in diplomacy and evaluate the rate of progress towards a gender-even playing field on the basis thereof.

By bringing together established scholars and seasoned practitioners of diplomacy, this volume therefore seeks to provide a detailed discussion of the role of women in diplomacy and to craft for its readers a global narrative of understanding relating to their current and historical role within it. At its centre, the volumes endeavours to move beyond the simple perception of women entering the diplomatic corps as a 'novel' or 'unique' act, and begin a necessary discussion regarding the type of role women play, or are provided with, once they enter the diplomatic sphere. Through a diverse cadre of contributors and chapter topics, this volume explores the individual and collective power women hold within their respective ministries and international diplomatic bodies at large, their agency for change within them, and the obstacles they continue to face – both institutional and normative – as they continue the battle for gender parity while they serve the diplomatic corps. To achieve this, this volume chooses to view and frame the experiences of women, and the institutions they served and serve, through a number of timely, relevant, and inter-related concepts; *gender, institutional power*, and *leadership roles*. These concepts provide a set of unique analytical lenses in which the reader can view and examine the historical and present experiences of women in the diplomatic sphere, and do so in a manner which is structured and conceptual. This overarching framework is then used by contributors to discuss, analyse, and project on the relationship between gender and diplomacy, and on the gender of diplomacy itself.

With that said, this book does not attempt to advocate for the mandatory involvement of women in the diplomatic sphere. It is not meant to serve as a persuasive tool, as there is no necessity for persuasion. By all measures, we are on a steady path towards non-gendered diplomacy despite various obstacles, which persist to this day. These play a wide-ranging prohibitive role which spans everything from complete absence of female participation in some countries to an absence from highest political office in other nations and virtually every scenario in between. While eliminating these obstacles is one way towards achieving equal involvement and representation of women in the diplomatic sphere, such a strategy would depend largely on the open-mindedness of men, by whom the barriers were set up in the first place. This volume does not represent a form of appeal to those who would prefer a state of perpetual isolation of women from diplomacy. Rather, this volume attempts to bring to the mainstream the often downplayed and underreported role of women in governance and policymaking. More importantly, it strives to showcase the inevitability of increased female representation in the realm of diplomacy despite deep-seated doubt, resentment, sexism, and misogyny.

In an attempt to tell some of this unfinished story of women in diplomacy, this volume brings together established scholars and experienced diplomatic practitioners, in a context which is historical, theoretical, and empirical. The contributors to the work are varied both in terms of their style of writing and professional experiences, with this variation reflecting the diversity of contributors as a whole. This diversity is deemed essential to the fabric of the work, and is a highly important aspect in bridging the academic–practitioner divide – so often an obstacle to coherent and connected discussion within the realm of diplomatic studies. Indeed, it is only by bringing together the global and diverse voices of women within the diplomatic sphere – voices which represent different cultural perspectives, diverse national priorities, and individual challenges – that we can begin to appreciate and reimagine women as equal participants in the structures, processes and outcomes of twenty-first century diplomatic practice.

Helen McCarthy and James Southern open the first section of the book, with an in-depth historical survey of women's place in the history of diplomacy. They acknowledge that the history of diplomacy is one dominated by a story of great men – of kings, generals, envoys, and traders – and challenge us to now turn our attention to the place of women in this story and to reconstruct the roles they played within it: as queens with political power in their own right, as consorts, wives, and mistresses with influence over high-ranking men, as explorers, writers, experts, and activists who advised or lobbied governments on matters of foreign policy, and, finally, as professional diplomats representing their nations. Building on this, their chapter provides an overview of the ancient and medieval periods as far as sources allow, with greater emphasis given to the early modern era, when queens regnant and noblewomen were major diplomatic players, and to the post-1800 period, when democratisation and feminist agitation began to reshape the possibilities for women's public activism and professional employment. Using gender as an analytical tool, McCarthy and Southern demonstrate how beliefs about sexual difference shaped the roles that women were able to play in the diplomatic space and international affairs in different places and at different times in history. Furthermore, their discussion identifies the factors which enabled women to exercise power in this sphere either formally or informally, as well as those which served to marginalise and exclude women from decision-making processes and foreign policy debates. Overall, this chapter provides a solid foundation on which to begin the historical reconstruction of women's roles, formal or informal, within the diplomatic sphere.

Beatrice McKenzie's chapter builds firmly upon the historical narrative introduced by McCarthy and Southern, offering an examination of the life and career of a notable, yet overlooked, United States Foreign Service Officer – Alison Palmer. Palmer, who served as a Foreign Service Officer between 1959 and 1981, offers a fascinating case study in which to examine the institutional and societal challenges women faced as they began their initial entry into the diplomatic service. McKenzie's chapter highlights the sizeable literature gap in the study of the gender in the United States Foreign Service, and notes that where literature does exist in this field, it focuses on women in extra-governmental and informal structures rather than their involvement in government service – partly because so few women served prior to 1970 but also due in part to the State Department itself successfully initiating a history about women's participation. McKenzie's discussion of Palmer's career and activism in the second half of the twentieth century is both pertinent and consistent with the lenses used by this volume to explore and dissect the gender of diplomacy: in particular, that of agency and institutional structures, serving to reveal the gendered labour stratification which has existed since World War II, as well as elucidating changes in the participation of women in the twentieth century US Foreign Service.

Current Ambassador of Ireland to Japan, and long-serving diplomat with Ireland's Department (Ministry) of Foreign Affairs, Anne Barrington, speaks to the experiences of female diplomats who entered the Department from 1970 to the year 2000 onwards. Her chapter illuminates the varying, but continuous, barriers and challenges these women faced during this period, crafting a historical narrative of their diplomatic journeys both at headquarter level and whilst serving abroad. Barrington's use of the Irish historical paradigm provides an extremely interesting case study for analysis, as there are still women working in the system, or recently retired, who were junior diplomats before the issue of gender inequality in the service was even acknowledged, let alone addressed. Barrington weaves together the voices of these women into a narrative, which represents their experiences concerning recruitment, early careers obstacles, sexism, the challenges to, and of, family life, and their perception of progress in the Department itself. The chapter concludes by highlighting a number of key developments the Department has undertaken to work towards the promotion of gender equality within their Ministry at large, and highlights potential routes for further progress towards ensuring the achievement of full gender equality within the Foreign Service. Such developments enacted within the Irish Service will prove useful to policy makers and other Ministries of Foreign Affairs (MFAs) as they seek to initiate similar changes.

Although firmly placed within the historical narrative construction on the gender of diplomacy itself, Devaki Jain's chapter is the first to construct it through the lens of an international institution, the United Nations. Set firmly within this overarching framework, Jain's chapter traces some of the major ideas that shaped the UN's engagement with women over the decades, beginning in the 1940s. Through the construction of a detailed historical narrative, Jain's chapter describes and discusses the various strategies the international women's movement used to negotiate their ideas and proposals in an international bureaucratic system which consistently overlooked their calls for equality. A welcome distinction is drawn in her chapter between the women of the South and the North, who – while both working for the international women's movement of the day – came to the movement with substantially different experiences, and views of the world order. Furthermore, this skewed distribution of power between the North and South resulted in the dismissal of many Southern countries' initiatives post-World War II. This persists in historical reflections on the UN's beginnings, particularly on the role and impact of the women of the South, not only in the respect to the women's movement, but also in relation to their position within the United Nations institution at large. Framed by her analytical contribution, Jain concludes that international institutions such as the UN are no longer able to serve the ideas and proposals which arise from constituencies such as women, and other excluded groups, such as ethnic and other minorities. Jain therefore concludes that the theatre of diplomatic negotiations and outcomes must now shift away from the inner workings of the UN, and other intergovernmental negotiations and institutions, towards global and regional, subject and identity based associations, better able to represent the aims and outcomes of these constituencies.

The second section of the book turns our attention to the current (or recent past) institutional, societal, and normative challenges women face when serving their national Ministries and international diplomatic institutions at large. Eric M. Blanchard questions the prospects for a 'feminist' US foreign policy. Analysing Hillary Clinton's rhetoric and policy during her tenure as US Secretary of State, and using constructivist metaphor theory in concert with gender analysis, Blanchard seeks to address the question of the difference gender makes in US diplomacy and foreign policy. Clinton as Secretary of State is a significant figure in the history of both American gender politics and US diplomacy, as, amongst other things, she has been credited with the formulation of the 'Hillary Doctrine', an effort to place gender at the heart of US foreign policy by explicitly tying the global subjugation of women to American national security. Existing mainstream assessments of Clinton's tenure as top diplomat have rated it solid but not spectacular, but this chapter argues that the view changes in interesting ways when approached through a gender lens. While the specialist feminist International Relations literature often focuses on structural or systematic effects of gender in global politics, and the processes entailed in the workings of femininities and masculinities across time, space, and culture, this approach can leave the impact of individual (feminist) leaders' agency oddly understudied. With careful attention to Clinton's discursive record as US Secretary of State, the chapter analyses Clinton's construction of women's leadership and her gendered expression of American power as it was deployed to promote an 'investing in women' strategy. This chapter ties into the intrinsic thesis of this volume: that diplomacy has a gender, and that gender is masculine.

Focusing on ambassador appointments, Birgitta Niklasson and Ann Towns begin their discussion by addressing some fundamental questions about where men and women are positioned in diplomacy. The chapter speaks to the increasing interest in gender in the burgeoning and dynamic literature on diplomacy, as well as the international relations scholarship on gender and international hierarchies. Viewing diplomatic practice from an aggregate level, the chapter poses a number of critical questions: how many female ambassadors are there in the world? Where are they posted, geographically and with respect to positions of economic and military power and prestige? Are there gender patterns in ambassador appointments? In answering these basic questions, this chapter broadens our knowledge about men, women, and diplomacy on a fundamental level. Their analysis is based on a unique data set containing all ambassador appointments made by the 50 highest ranked countries in terms of GDP in 2014, with a total of almost 7,000 ambassador appointments coded for the analysis.

Building on these conclusions, Jane Marriott, the current Director for the Joint International Counter Terrorism Unit, a joint Foreign and Commonwealth and Home Office unit, draws on her own experiences as a FCO diplomatic officer (notably as Ambassador to Sana'a, Yemen and Acting Ambassador to Tehran, Iran) and that of her colleagues, to provide a welcome insight into the experiences of female diplomatic officers when posted abroad, and the societal and professional challenges they face whilst serving there. To date, there has been a distinct lack of analyses focusing on the role of the female diplomat abroad and how she is received by the country to which she is posted. This chapter provides a unique contribution to the existing literature by identifying the type and range of challenges faced by female representatives of Her Britannic Majesty's Government when they operate in an overseas environment in the present day, specifically in host countries where the political and legal status, and cultural understandings of women in society differ significantly from their own. Interestingly, in identifying the ways in which women working in the British Diplomatic Service overcame these issues and challenges, Marriott demonstrates through her primary sources that there can be specific advantages to working in particularly difficult host-country cultures as women. The UK's female diplomats who were interviewed within this chapter overwhelmingly concluded that in spite of the challenges along the way, including hurdles that others may not have to face, they had ultimately been able to turn most situations to the UK's advantage, particularly when it came to building trust and managing diplomatic relationships with all members of the host country's community, including local women.

Susan Harris Rimmer describes the role and narrative of women who participate in the sphere of global economic governance, with a particular focus on women representing their state in Group of 20 processes. Taking a feminist approach to diplomacy, she examines women's lived experiences of economic summitry, whilst firmly interrogating how masculine values and worldviews, such as the assumptions of mainstream economics, have shaped this area of diplomacy. Indeed, economic diplomacy and trade are an area resistant to the participation of women today, with women making up only 25 per cent of the heads of state of the G20 member countries, and 15 per cent of finance ministers, central bank governors and 'sherpas' (A 'sherpa' is the personal representative of the leader, helping them to reach the 'summit' in G20 negotiations). This ties into the narrative of highly segregated masculine and feminine realms of diplomacy, with matters of the economy falling formally with the former.

Seeking to highlight the journey of the most powerful UN body in support of women and girls – UN Women – particularly in its quest to gain global recognition for the inalienable rights of women and girls worldwide, the current United Nations Under-Secretary-General and Executive Director of UN Women, Phumzile Mlambo-Ngcuka, writes a much-needed chapter, exploring the historical journey of UN Women from its foundation to its current incarnation. Mlambo-Ngcuka first considers and provides a historical context for the women's movement in the United Nations through three primary areas: the foundational Commission on the Status of Women, milestone conferences which have continued to impact the global agenda towards equality, and notable women diplomats whose presence altered the landscape for their successors. Placed within this historical context, the chapter then moves to examine the current role of UN Women, offering positive and concrete examples of its work in the present day. UN Security Council resolution 1325 is an illustrative case in point, which demonstrates how UN Women has successfully propelled gender equality into the top diplomatic channels and the international political sphere at large. The chapter also carries a prescriptive, providing policy recommendations on moving forward and the implementation of the United Nations 2030 Agenda for Sustainable Development, a landmark roadmap that has placed gender equality as a globally accepted key priority.

Using a constitutive theorising approach, Jessica Fliegel, in the final chapter, identifies key characteristics and factors influencing women's ambassadorial leadership in the twenty-first century. Through interviews with fifteen women permanent representatives to the United Nations, Fliegel examines the character, contingency, and contextual dimensions of their appointments and how these dimensions shaped their experiences, as women serving in positions of ambassadorial leadership. Understanding women's ambassadorial leadership in the twenty-first century is essential for analysing if and how women's increased representation is reshaping the way that foreign affairs and diplomacy are conducted. This chapter lays firm groundwork for future research on the effects of women's increased representation in diplomatic leadership, whilst providing practical recommendations for the continued advancement of women's leadership in multilateral diplomacy settings.

Bibliography

Bell, G. 2015. *A Woman in Arabia: The Writings of the Queen of the Desert*. New York, NY: Penguin Classics.

Childs, M. 2006. 'Not through Women's Eyes: Photo-Essays and the Construction of a Gendered Tsunami Disaster', *Disaster Prevention and Management* 12(2): 202–212.

Connell, R. W. 1995. *Masculinities*. Berkeley, CA: University of California Press.

Enloe, C. 1989. *Bananas, Beaches and Bases: Making Feminist Sense of International Politics*. Berkley, CA: University of California Press.

Falco, M. J. 2004. *Feminist Interpretations of Niccolò Machiavelli*. Pennsylvania, PA: Pennsylvania State University Press.

Gibson-Graham, J. K. 1994. ' "Stuffed if I Know": Reflections on Postmodern Feminist Social Research', *Gender, Place and Culture* 1(2): 205–224.

Goetz, A. M. 1995. 'Institutionalising Women's Interests and Gender Sensitive Accountability in Development', *IDS Bulletin* 26(3).

Haraway, D. 1988. 'Situated Knowledges: The Science Question in Feminism and the Privilege of Partial Perspective', *Feminist Studies* 14(3): 575–599.

Hey, V. 2006. 'The Politics of Performative Resignification', *British Journal of the Sociology of Education* 27(4): 439–457.

McCarthy, H. 2009. 'Petticoat Diplomacy: The Admission of Women to the British Foreign Service, c.1919–1946', *Twentieth Century British History* 20(3): 285–321.

McCarthy, H. 2015. *Women of the World: The Rise of the Female Diplomat*. London: Bloomsbury Press and Bell.

Risman, B. J. 2004. 'Gender as Social Structure: Theory Wrestling with Activism', *Gender and Society* 18(4): 429–450.

Runyan, A. S. and V. S. Peterson. 1999. *Global Gender Issues* (2nd edn). Boulder, CO: Westview Press.

Runyan, A. S. and V. S. Peterson. 2013. *Global Gender Issues in the New Millennium*. Boulder, CO: Westview Press.

Sjoberg, L. 2006. 'The Gendered Realities of the Immunity Principle: Why Gender Analysis Needs Feminism', *International Studies Quarterly* 50(4): 889–910.

Sjoberg, L. 2007. 'Agency, Militarized Femininity, and Enemy Others', *International Feminist Journal of Politics* 9(1): 69–74.

Sjoberg, L. 2009. 'Gender, Race, and Imperial Wars', *International Studies Review* 11(2): 368–370.

Sjoberg, L. 2011. 'Gender, the State and War Redux: Feminist International Relations across the Levels of Analysis', *International Relations* 25(1): 108–134.

Steans, J. 1998. *Gender and International Relations: An Introduction*. New Brunswick, NJ: Rutgers University Press.

Steans, J. 2003. 'Engaging from the Margins: Feminist Encounters with the Mainstream of International Relations', *British Journal of Politics and International Relations* 5(3): 428–454.

Sylvester, C. 1994. *Feminist Theory and International Relations in a Postmodern Era.* Cambridge: Cambridge University Press.

Youdell, D. 2006. 'Sex-Gender-Sexuality: How Sex, Gender, and Sexuality Constellations are Constituted in Secondary Schools', *Gender and Education* 17(3): 249–270.

Part I
Getting to the table
Historical challenges and reflections

Part I

1 Women, gender, and diplomacy
A historical survey

Helen McCarthy and James Southern

Diplomacy is as old as human society and, as with other arenas of public and political life, gender has shaped the roles which men and women have played within it. For a long time, the history of diplomacy was a story of great men – of kings, generals, envoys, and traders. More recently, however, historians have turned their attention to the place of women in this story and have begun to reconstruct the agency they exercised: as queens with political power in their own right; as consorts, wives, and mistresses with influence over high-ranking men; as explorers, writers, experts, and activists who advised or lobbied governments on matters of foreign policy; and finally as professional diplomats representing their nations. This latter development – the appointment of women to formal diplomatic posts – took place in the twentieth century and forms part of a larger, and unfinished, story of women's political emancipation and their public and professional advance in modern times. However, it is impossible to make sense of this more recent history, or of the opportunities and challenges that women encounter in the international political arena in the twenty-first century, without looking back at the *longue durée* of early-modern and modern diplomacy (Sluga and James 2015: 1–12). As this chapter reveals, this is a story of continuity as well as change in the forms of agency that women were able to exercise in foreign policy decision-making processes and debates, set against a shifting backdrop of beliefs about sexual difference and its relevance in international politics. The chapter argues that recovering women's agency is not just important for understanding the gendered nature of diplomacy as a profession and political practice, but is valuable for illuminating the locus of power and the shifting contours of political sovereignty and statecraft over time.

The chapter draws on recent research by historians, including the growing body of work on the role of queens consort and regnant, princesses, ladies-in-waiting, chamberers, and wives, which demonstrates conclusively that women were present in, not absent from, diplomacy in the era preceding their formal inclusion in national diplomatic services in the twentieth century. In geographical terms, much of the existing scholarship takes Britain, western Europe and the US for its focus, but this chapter draws on perspectives from elsewhere wherever the literature allows. It is not yet possible to write a survey chapter on the history of *men*, gender, and diplomacy, because few scholars have explored the gendered experiences of male diplomats or the construction of masculine identities in the diplomatic arena in any depth.[1] To date, most gender historians working on diplomacy have addressed the prior empirical task of 'putting women back into the historical picture'. As Glenda Sluga and Carolyn James note in their recent edited collection on women and diplomacy since 1500, this approach was 'a much more primitive phase in the development of gender history, but it was a crucial phase, and one that has been lacking in the renewal of international history' (Sluga and James 2015: 11). This chapter follows their lead, then, by writing the history of gender and diplomacy primarily through the prism of female agency.

Conceptualising women's agency

The historian Emily Rosenberg has argued that efforts to uncover women's contribution to diplomacy in the past have tended to adopt one of two approaches, both of which she regards as problematic (Rosenberg 1990). The first involves the study of 'extraordinary' individuals who transcended the social constraints of gender to make an impact – typically, as Rosenberg put it, 'those exceptional, often slighted, women who influenced foreign policy' (Rosenberg 2015: 116). The difficulty with this approach is twofold: first, it entrenches the assumption that women were marginalised and excluded from diplomacy, and second, it leads to a disproportionate focus on those who were 'atypical' of their sex, thus defeating the object of the exercise to look at *women's* impact on international history. An example of this might be the case of Feng Liao, one of the earliest recorded examples of a female diplomat. In first century BC China, she married an influential general in the province of Wusun. When a new occupant to the throne in that region threatened to destabilise the authority of the regional governor Zheng Ji in 64 BC, he remembered Feng Liao's knowledge of Wusun, and made her the Han Dynasty's official envoy (Goh 1999: 71–82). Such was her success and subsequent veneration, she was celebrated in a contemporary poem by an unknown author:

> A warm send-off for the royal caravan
> moving westward through the pass.
> Resourceful and talented,
> the woman envoy
> studied history and emulates
> Ambassador Su Wu.
> Her sage, heroic deeds will be famous
> down through the ages.
> (Bennett Peterson 2000, 74)

The poem demonstrates that Feng was respected and even lionised for her abilities and achievements. But in calling her 'the woman envoy', it also reveals that her career was very much an anomaly. The reference to her emulation of

Ambassador Su Wu, a famous diplomat (140 BC–60 BC) who also represented the Han Dynasty, indicates the masculine standard against which any exceptional woman would inevitably be judged. There is no doubt that Feng deserves her place in history, but her case offers only limited insight into the wider operations of gender and power in ancient China.

The second approach Rosenberg critiques focuses on groups or communities of women who influenced international relations from *outside* the male-dominated world of conventional diplomacy. Examining phenomena such as women's international peace movements, Rosenberg argues,

> emphasizes that women wielded power in the international arena, not by becoming atypical of their gender, but by pressing the possibilities of the socially constructed women's spheres to the limit, all the while helping redefine their boundaries.
>
> (Rosenberg 1990: 118)

The problem with this approach, Rosenberg contends, is that it implies that there are 'separate spheres' in which men and women operate, and that by working within these gendered spaces – both physical and discursive – women campaigners for peace, suffrage, temperance, or humanitarian reform can 'be blamed for their own restricted opportunities' (Rosenberg 1990: 118). Though they may influence international politics, often indirectly, without compromising their femininity, these groups of women nonetheless reinforce the notion that diplomacy is a man's world. One example of this might be the gathering of feminist pacifists at The Hague in April 1915 to debate ways of ending the war and securing a just peace founded on the values of human rights and democracy. Many of the delegates adopted a 'maternalist' language, emphasising the special moral qualities that women possessed as mothers or potential mothers, and defining their politics in opposition to the militarism and inhumanity of the male-controlled state. As historians have shown, The Hague Congress offers an important insight into the origins of twentieth-century feminist internationalist activism (McCarthy *et al.* 2015). But its significance for wider histories of gender and diplomacy is arguably unclear, given that the event had little direct impact on the progress of the war or the post-war settlement.

This problem raises a larger question of how broadly to conceptualise the diplomatic arena and actors within it. A recent trend in international history is to seek the inclusion of an increasingly diverse cast of 'non-state actors', who contributed to the forging of international relations as travellers, journalists, businessmen, non-governmental campaigners, and family members, including wives. This casting of the net to include actors outside the elites who traditionally formed the focus of diplomatic history offers opportunities for historians of gender, but it also poses risks. Women's agency, like their supposed powerlessness, cannot be simply assumed. Rather, it must be carefully reconstructed and contextualised, and the factors which facilitated or inhibited it in different places and at different times must be identified and judiciously weighed. Diplomatic wives, as we will see, *could* be powerful figures throughout the period covered in this chapter, but the resources and opportunities available to them to exert influence changed quite significantly over time. This chapter aims to offer a brief outline of what this more nuanced history of agency might look like.

Finally, it is important to note that recovering women's voices often relies on a creative use of source material. Women are frequently invisible or silent in the standard sources deployed by diplomatic historians, which tend to neglect female letter-writing (women's correspondence is often filed separately from that of male rulers and politicians), the records of women's organisations, or oral histories (only a handful of the *c.*150 interviews in the British Diplomatic Oral History Project, for instance, are with women). In addition, the conventions of female epistolary networks and autobiography have meant that letters, memoirs, and tracts produced by women have often been regarded as appropriate source material for social and cultural history, but not for the study of politics and diplomacy. In all these ways, women have appeared to stand outside the major narratives of diplomatic history, although recent scholarship is now changing that picture significantly.

Women, gender, and diplomacy before 1800

The starting place for most histories of women and diplomacy in the pre-1800 era is the role of medieval and early modern queens.[2] Queens regnant, consort and regent had to deal with international affairs and shape foreign policy, as Elena Woodacre puts it, 'in a male-dominated and highly gendered political sphere' (Woodacre 2013: 6). Case studies of queens help to illuminate how gender placed constraints upon the possibilities for women to exercise diplomatic influence in different eras. During the Crusades, for example, Alice of Antioch's bold attempt to seize power in her region after the death of her husband Bohemond II continues to provoke debate among historians as to the skill and nature of her diplomatic efforts. According to twelfth-century chronicler William of Tyre, Alice was 'an extremely malicious and wily woman' whose crimes included seeking an alliance with the Muslims, attempting to bribe her foreign enemies to curry favour, and an audacious demand that she be allowed to choose her own husband (Asbridge 2003: 29). Historian Thomas Asbridge, however, contests William of Tyre's account, calling Alice's influence 'quite startling' and labelling her 'one of the most powerful figures in the principality's history' (Asbridge 2003: 39, 41). She eventually failed, Asbridge argues, not because of clumsy or devious diplomacy, but simply because when 'presented with an adult male of high birth', Raymond of Poitiers, as her contender, the population of Antioch turned against Alice (Asbridge 2003: 44). Here, then, is an example of a contemporary chronicler and a twenty-first century historian revealing the nature and limitations of female power in a twelfth-century society through commentaries on a remarkable and diplomatically influential woman.

Through the fifteenth, sixteenth, and seventeenth centuries, the power of queenship offered opportunities for a handful of women to engage in foreign affairs. The best-known example, of course, is Elizabeth I, whose diplomatic skill has attracted extensive attention from historians.³ Regina Schulte has argued that Elizabeth had both a natural, female body and a political, monarchical body, and 'in her initiation into her status as sovereign and into absolute rule ... succeeded in maintaining a high degree of self-determination by continually playing the two sides of the royal body against each other' (Schulte 2006: 4). Above all else, though, it was her education and intellectual and cultural resources that enabled her to engage in diplomacy effectively. When writing to the Russian Tsar Ivan 'the Terrible' in 1561, for example, Elizabeth deliberately wrote in Latin – a language she knew Ivan could not understand – to assert her authority (Sowerby 2015). From an early age, the education that Catherine Parr took care to emphasise and arrange for Elizabeth gave her access to a network of noble and royal families across Europe. As Karen Britland explains:

> International royalty patronised and shared foreign tutors: Elizabeth I was trained in Italian by Baldassare Castiglione; Queen Anna patronized the Anglo-Italian John Florio; Prince Charles in England and Henrietta Maria in France shared the same French dancing master. Noblewomen's education and their cultural and religious awareness, far from being ornamental, were important social and political networking tools.
>
> (Britland 2009: 126)

This network of elites enabled Elizabeth to circulate gifts and letters around the courts of Europe in order to exert political influence. She wrote in French to Catherine de Medici expressing her condolences for the loss of the latter's son, and she wrote a passionate letter, also in French, to Henri IV informing him of her disappointment at his conversion to Catholicism (Britland 2009: 127). Anna of Denmark and Henrietta Maria of France both also made use of such networks to influence diplomatic relations through their letter-writing, and the former was particularly skilful at using her proximity to the king, her husband James VI and I, to conduct his diplomatic affairs on his behalf while leaving him free from implication.⁴ Women often practised these negotiating skills when facilitating royal marriages, which could have major diplomatic implications. Queens Mariana and Maria Theresa of Austria, for instance, cooperated to secure the union of Carlo II of Spain to the French Princess Maria Louisa in the 1670s, a marriage which brought 14 years of Franco-Spanish conflict to a close (Mitchell 2015, 86–106). Capable and educated, these queens regnant and consort demonstrate that women could play an important role in the international affairs of early modern Europe.

Queens were exceptional women whose power derived from their positional authority as occupants of thrones or through proximity to regnant husbands. They were not 'diplomats' in the sense that Garrett Mattingly used the term in *Renaissance Diplomacy*, his classic work on the origins of diplomacy in the fifteenth-century Italian city-state: that is, in terms of states appointing official ambassadors to foreign cities to conduct negotiations and compile intelligence in order to avoid conflict. This form of statecraft was exclusively practised by men

(Mattingly 1955). The question becomes, then, to what extent did women infiltrate and influence these new diplomatic networks and structures?

The answer is, quite considerably. In Elizabethan England, according to historian James Daybell, there were three main ways in which women influenced international politics (Daybell 2011: 101–119). The first of these was via the networks of family newsletters written by women in the sixteenth and seventeenth centuries, which transmitted both personal and political news across Europe. Early-modern aristocratic women increasingly were, like the queens discussed above, given a classical humanist education, providing them with the tools to 'bolster their political networks' and 'legitimate their epistolary advice' (Allen 2013: 7. See also Whitehead 1999). By the sixteenth century, educated women were less and less seen as oddities or outsiders, and could circulate political intelligence with authority – if not as official diplomatists. Lady Elizabeth Russell, for example, of whose letters over 50 survive, was particularly adept at combining personal friendship with political alliance through her writing. She managed to 'mix social niceties with a combination of news, report, and counsel', revealing 'beyond the staged courtesies of social decorum ... an interest in patronage, domestic politics and even foreign policy' (Daybell 2011: 104–105). Similarly, Penelope Lady Rich made use of a large network of contacts across Europe – and even had a codename, 'Ryalta' – to influence her brother's diplomatic relations with James VI of Scotland, and when Thomas Phelippes was imprisoned following the infamous gunpowder plot, his wife Mary took over his intelligence gathering activities. Examples abound of women using information networks to maintain diplomatic relationships, often clandestinely (Daybell 2011: 101, 106).

The second zone of female diplomatic influence was the early-modern court. Ladies-in-waiting and chamberers could hold a great deal of influence because of their proximity to the queens of early modern Europe, and were the subject of a great deal of attention from male suitors as a result (Daybell 2011: 108). Ladies-in-waiting were in a particularly unique position, with exclusive access to the monarch. Lady Carlisle, a Lady of the Bedchamber and a favourite of Queen Henrietta Maria of France, was a crucial link between the queen and the Earl of Carlisle when the two 'shared foreign policy aims' (Wolfson 2014: 326). The gentlewomen of Elizabeth's Privy Chamber, in particular Lady Mary Sidney, were essential to her marriage negotiations with the Spanish ambassador for Archduke Charles in 1559, and were generally involved in all her diplomatic activities, a phenomenon not exclusive to English courts (Mears 2004; Sanchez 1998). For these women, their sex and high birth were a passport to a position of diplomatic privilege, granting access to international political networks without the risk of public failure that came with a conventional ambassadorial role. Their agency reveals how, in the world of early modern diplomacy, power was located in the relatively secluded spaces of the bedchamber as well as in the grand halls and throne-rooms where ambassadors were formally received.

The final way in which women participated in diplomacy in this period, according to Daybell, was through the 'underground Catholic networks' of the time (Daybell 2011: 111). Women were active in hiding priests, and some Catholic women were 'able to wield influence at a more public, diplomatic level' (Daybell 2011: 112). Significantly, these women were technically enemies of the Jacobean state, and they were conducting diplomacy without the insurance of proximity to a monarch. Anne Vaux, for example, daughter of the third Baron Vaux of Harrowden, passed letters to Henry Garnett in the Tower of London (he had been arrested following the gunpowder plot) containing secret messages written in invisible ink made using orange juice (Daybell 2011: 112).

This draws attention to the fact that, whilst women were clearly able to exercise different forms of agency in the early-modern world of diplomacy, that agency was always limited and their position was far from assured. This was true of court insiders, such as ladies-in-waiting, as much as it was of Catholic conspirators. As Cynthia Fry points out:

> The fact that these women had no formal power to enact diplomatic policies meant that if their covert actions were discovered, these women could be separated from official foreign policy and their actions presented as unsanctioned by those in power, whether that was the reality or not.
>
> (Fry 2014: 267)

How, then, did women's position change in the era of 'modern' diplomacy?

Women, gender, and 'modern' diplomacy

Before the nineteenth century, international politics was essentially interdynastic politics, involving men and women of high rank and centred on royal and imperial courts. This aristocratic flavour did not disappear after 1800, but political power became more widely dispersed with the rise of popularly elected legislatures and modern government bureaucracies. A corollary of this was the increasing professionalisation of diplomacy and a clearer codification of its structures, ranks and protocols (Davis Cross 2007). As noted, early-modern ambassadors were always male, but lack of formal diplomatic credentials did not stop women from participating in political argument and debate through their networks of letter-writing and kin. Some historians have argued that the scope for this kind of informal influence diminished in the decades following the French Revolution due to the hardening of gendered divisions between the 'public' and 'private' spheres, categories which, as noted earlier, had little purchase in early-modern political culture. The public sphere became identified with the masculine exercise of political power and reason, whilst the private sphere was a feminised realm associated with family, home and 'sensibility'. Women who were active in the public world of politics were at risk of being accused of seeking 'illegitimate' influence, now commonly identified with aristocratic privilege.[5]

This was the fate of Georgiana, Duchess of Devonshire, whose vigorous public interventions in Whig politics in the 1770s and 1780s attracted hostile press attention, including from political caricaturists like James Gillray (Foreman 1998). Dorothea Lieven, the aristocratic wife of the Russian ambassador and a key figure in London's political and social scene between 1814 and the mid-1830s, was branded a meddling 'intriguer' who transgressed gender norms, as was her near contemporary, the liberal intellectual Germaine de Staël. One Russian envoy described Staël, who used her position as wife of the Swedish ambassador to host highly influential political salons, as a 'monstrous' creature, comporting herself 'like a woman' but speaking and writing 'like a man' (Sluga 2015: 130). Glenda Sluga argues that Lieven and Staël were threatening figures in early nineteenth-century Europe because they flouted the emerging norms of a professionalised and masculinised diplomacy that was 'emotionally disinvested and institutionally procedural and bureaucratically transparent' (Sluga 2015: 132). As diplomacy became established as a stable career for male elites, and the extension of suffrage to adult men defined the political citizen as male, the stage thus appeared to be set for women's marginalisation.

This perspective is supported to some extent by evidence from the lives of diplomatic wives, particularly those who appeared content to reproduce the sexual divisions of the bourgeois family, now becoming culturally dominant in western Europe. Whereas in earlier times a male diplomat might have left his family at home or elect to remain a bachelor, by mid-century it was common practice for ambassadors to set up households in post, presided over by a spouse with the right social and educational credentials (Mori 2011). Wives became partners in the symbolic projection of prestige, participating in formal, carefully-choreographed public occasions, and fostering goodwill through networks of female sociability involving the 'ladies' of the diplomatic corps and philanthropic initiatives for the benefit of the host country (McCarthy 2014: Chapter 2). They also had a pastoral duty towards embassy staff, entertaining young bachelor secretaries for instance, or helping newly-arrived wives to find houses and servants. The lively memoirs and diaries penned by nineteenth-century wives offer colourful portraits of the social whirl of diplomatic life, but are notably silent on politics. This suggests a practice of self-censorship prompted by a wish to avoid any accusation of 'meddling' in affairs outside their womanly sphere. Politics was difficult terrain for 'respectable' middle-class women in the nineteenth century, reflected in the fact that many politically-active feminists of the era left instructions for their letters to be destroyed after death for fear of posthumous scandal or abuse (Richardson 2013).

This tendency towards self-censorship or destruction of personal papers poses a challenge to the historian seeking to reconstruct women's political agency, but it does not make the task impossible. Fragmentary sources point to a more direct role for female kin in the business of diplomacy, in, for instance, the case of Meriel Buchanan, daughter of the British minister in Sofia, who helped out with deciphering telegrams for several months in the British legation following Bulgaria's declaration of independence in 1908 (Buchanan 1958). In other cases, wives acted as private secretaries to their husbands, managing their diaries and copying out confidential correspondence. It might be further argued that, although figures like Staël and Lieven became the target of abuse on account of their political ambitions, the intensity of hostile opinion towards them is itself evidence of the continuing influence of the 'social politics' that they practised. Despite the trend towards professionalisation and bureaucratisation, diplomacy continued to be conducted to a large extent through sociability and talk, and the salon remained a key site for the gathering and spreading of news. Staël's use of 'salon diplomacy' is a prime example of this. Between 1812 and 1815, Staël hosted salons during her travels through Russia, Sweden, England and France, assembling potential allies to bring about Napoleon's demise and promote a liberal future for Europe. Staël actively lobbied the European statesmen involved in setting the terms of the Treaty of Paris and subsequent Congress of Vienna by the same means. The American ambassador to Paris, John Quincy Adams, described Staël's salon as 'a kind of temple of Apollo' where one could 'meet the world' (Sluga 2015: 125). In Sluga's words, Staël stood as 'a 'private' (or non-state) agent of the political ideas that informed the 'transformational' peace-making agenda culminating in the congressing system and the Concert of Europe' (Sluga 2015: 123).

Figures like Staël and Lieven reveal how politically active and ambitious women could model many of the typical behaviours of the accredited diplomat, without earning the title. They gathered, analysed, and spread political information amongst networks of opinion-formers and power-brokers, acted as agents for foreign rulers, and advanced particular sovereign interests. Both women are 'exemplary of the possibilities for transgressive agency', but they were not, to return to Rosenberg's framework, 'extraordinary' women in the sense of transcending the political cultures of their times (Sluga 2015: 132). Rather, their political strategies help us to see the contours of those political cultures in sharper relief, and to appreciate the continuities, as well as discontinuities, with earlier forms of female political agency rooted in sociability and networks of communication.

Women, gender, and diplomacy in the twentieth century

The twentieth century may be regarded as the era in which women's formal inclusion in the world of diplomacy began. Nineteenth-century feminist movements fought for women's suffrage, property rights, access to education, and admission to professions such as medicine and academia, and to branches of the civil service which were felt to be particularly suited to women's expertise, such as factory and school inspection. The demand for equal eligibility for diplomatic careers was not made until much later. In the British case, the first concerted campaign was launched by feminists in the 1930s, several years after women had won full political equality as voters, and their demand was only granted in 1946 following much resistance from the Foreign Office (McCarthy 2014). Establishing exactly how, when, and why women gained access to diplomatic careers in different countries is not straightforward, as every case has a unique history which requires in-depth research to reconstruct in full.[6] Figure 1.1 below

Figure 1.1 Timeline of women's admission to selected diplomatic services.

provides a timeline for countries where the decision to admit women was relatively clear-cut and can be documented, although more research is required to provide a fuller picture.[7]

However, a number of countries, including many new states with embryonic foreign services, made temporary or ad hoc appointments of women in the interwar period or during the Second World War which did not necessarily establish the principle of gender equality for all time. For example, the short-lived First Republic of Armenia (1918–1920) briefly appointed Diana Apcar Honorary Consul to Japan, in recognition of her efforts in persuading the Japanese to recognise the fledging state.[8] Similarly, British feminists reported in 1934 the appointment of a female attaché by the Turkish Ministry of Foreign Affairs, although subsequent inquiries by the Foreign Office revealed that she had been rejected for an overseas posting and shortly resigned (McCarthy 2014: 145).

There are two chief contenders for the title of the world's first fully-accredited female diplomat. One is Rosika Schwimmer, who attended the Labour and Socialist International Conference in February 1919 in Berne, having been appointed Hungary's official 'plenipotentiary' before Mihály Károlyi's short-lived liberal government fell at the end of that year (Sluga 2000: 506–507). The other is Nadeja Stancioff, daughter of a wealthy and well-connected family of diplomats, who was appointed Secretary at the Bulgarian legation in Washington in 1921 (Firkitian, 2008: 224–234). The following year, Bolshevik revolutionary Alexandra Kollontai was posted to the Soviet Union's trade delegation to Norway and became the first woman to head a diplomatic mission when Norway formally recognised the Soviet regime two years later (Porter 1980). The United States followed suit a decade on by appointing Ruth Bryan Owen Head of Mission in Denmark in 1934, and by the late 1930s there was a quartet of female ambassadors across Scandinavia: republican Spain's Isabel de Palencia and the USSR's Kollontai in Stockholm, revolutionary Mexico's Palma Guillén and

Bryan Owen in Copenhagen. The US's Florence Harriman joined the group in 1937, posted as ambassador to Norway (although Bryan Owen had resigned the previous year).

The interwar decades also provided the first opportunities for women to represent their countries at the League of Nations, the peace-keeping machinery created at the Paris Peace Conference of 1919 which opened its operations in Geneva the following year. It became common for women to be included amongst the national delegations to the annual League assembly (Kollontai represented the USSR from 1934), whilst the League Secretariat offered opportunities for aspiring international bureaucrats. British-born Rachel Crowdy served as Head of the League's Social Section from 1919–1931, whilst Canada's Mary McGeachy worked in the Information Section for 12 years before taking up a temporary diplomatic post for the British Foreign Office during the Second World War (Kinnear 2004).

Multiple factors lay behind the growing presence of women diplomats on the world stage. In the cases of Britain and the US, the appointment of women to diplomatic posts was preceded by the feminisation of lower-level clerical grades in the Foreign Office and State Department respectively, and the routine employment of women in overseas embassies as archivists, stenographers, and secretaries. In both cases, vocal women's societies placed pressures on democratically-elected governments to open all avenues of public and professional life to women, although in the US the practice of making political appointments accelerated this possibility. Bryan Owen was a well-connected Democrat and earned her posting to Denmark in 1934 from President Roosevelt following forceful lobbying by the First Lady Eleanor Roosevelt and Molly Dewson, Head of the Women's Division of the Democratic National Committee (Nash 2005: 57–72). By contrast, political appointments were rare at the British Foreign Office, meaning that women's only route into a diplomatic career was through the civil service examination – which they were permitted to take in 1946, the Second World War having finally broken down resistance to feminist demands (McCarthy 2009: 285–321; McCarthy 2014).

In other cases, women diplomats were showcased as a mark of modernity by new and post-revolutionary states. Kollontai's appointment was presented as evidence of women's equality – in theory at least – under Communism, whilst Spain and Mexico were keen, through de Palencia and Guillén's postings, to advertise their advanced attitudes towards the equality of the sexes (Huck 1999). British feminists, when lobbying the Foreign Office in the 1930s, hammered home in a rather chauvinistic fashion the fact that 'lesser' countries were streaking ahead on this front: *even Chile*, they noted, had posted female vice-consuls to London and New York (McCarthy 2014: 132). This association of women diplomats with modern, innovative diplomatic practice was further reinforced by press coverage, which frequently noted the fashionable clothes and refreshing manner of these new faces, contrasting them to the dull, frock-coated males of the old diplomatic corps (Herren 2015).

Nonetheless, women's professional progress was slow, even in countries where the bar against their inclusion was removed at an early date. Although women were, on paper, equally eligible for the US Foreign Service in the 1920s, in practice very few got past the final interview stage, which was conducted by senior male officers who were deeply hostile to the prospect of sending women overseas. In 1924, State Department officials even attempted to exclude women from presenting themselves as candidates. This was unsuccessful, but nonetheless, by the time Bryan Owen was appointed there were just two women serving overseas as diplomats and eight employed as consuls or trade commissioners. The first woman to reach ambassadorial rank through the 'career' route (as opposed to a political appointment, like Bryan Owen's or Harriman's) was Frances Willis, posted to Switzerland in 1953 (Nash 2002: 1–20). A marriage bar, requiring female officers to tender their resignations if they wished to marry, was in place at the State Department until 1971 (and in the British Foreign Office until 1973). Recent research suggests that female diplomats are significantly more likely to be single than their male colleagues, even at the beginning of the twenty-first century.[9]

Women's professional prospects were similarly limited in practice at the League of Nations, despite its progressive equal opportunities policies, which included the absence of a marriage bar and equal pay. Crowdy was the only woman to head a section in the Secretariat, and the vast majority of women were employed at routine clerical or intermediate levels, working as translators, information officers, or research assistants. Women delegates to the annual Assembly often found themselves despatched to its Fifth Committee, which dealt with social or humanitarian issues such as human trafficking or child welfare, on the grounds that these fell within women's 'natural' domain of interest. One British delegate, the pacifist Helena Swanwick, was irritated by this practice, which made it harder for women to speak with authority on matters of security and disarmament, which most saw as the 'real' work of the League (Swanwick 1935).

This alerts us to the fact that the very legitimacy of women's participation in the professional diplomatic arena remained contested throughout the twentieth century. The British Foreign Office's response to feminists' demands for equality in the 1930s is a prime example of the 'ideological work' which, in Sluga and James's words, 'men employed to make [women] irrelevant to the concerns of international politics' (Sluga and James 2015: 9). Foreign Office chiefs referred to women's incapacity for clear, unbiased thought, to the disruptive effects their presence would have upon the smooth functioning of the (male) embassy workforce, to their 'natural' desire for marriage and motherhood, and to the horrified reception they would face from foreign officials when posted overseas. Not only did women lack the right qualities, but they possessed others that were undesirable for diplomacy, such as a tendency, as one official put it, 'to espouse causes', which was 'a matter of their very nature' (McCarthy 2014: 235). Foreign Office men noted with scepticism feminist arguments about the 'special gifts' that women could bring to diplomacy, including an interest and feel for female public opinion and the progress of women's movements globally. Such political intelligence, if required, could be easily supplied by diplomatic wives for free, they replied.

It is significant that the women who entered the British Foreign Office in the 1950s and 1960s once the bar was lifted did not pursue a 'women's agenda' as envisaged by many interwar feminists. They preferred to work hard and pursue their careers without any distinction of sex, although that proved impossible in the light of the marriage bar and unequal access to 'hard' language training.[10] The presence of female officials made no difference to the British Foreign Office's sceptical attitude towards the emerging women's rights agenda at the United Nations in the 1970s, marked by the declaration of International Women's Year in 1975 and the subsequent Decade of Women. Instead, women MPs and NGO representatives took the lead in pressuring the Foreign Office to take women's rights seriously as a foreign policy issue, rather as they had at the League of Nations in the interwar decades.[11] Madeleine Herren has argued that the League represented a 'successful back door to power' for women's civil society organisations because they could leverage its 'multi-lateral, public-oriented' model of international politics much more effectively than the old-style closed systems of national ministries of foreign affairs (Herren 2015: 193). The League's successor body, the UN, played an even more important role as a powerbase for women's campaigning bodies in the second half of the twentieth century, building their power to intervene in debates and reframe global norms.[12]

It is through international bodies like the UN, and political spaces such as those created by the Decade for Women, that the two threads identified by Rosenberg – women as extraordinary political actors and women as political outsiders – arguably came together in the later twentieth century, although we still require more research to understand this relationship in all its complexity. We need to conceptualise a model of diplomacy which can integrate multiple forms of female agency in the twenty-first century, from the professional authority of a woman ambassador, to the grassroots activism of an NGO campaigner, to the cultural power of a celebrity feminist like Angelina Jolie or Emma Watson, to name just a few. We should continue to ask where in this model the diplomatic spouse – a category which today encompasses husbands and same-sex partners as well as wives – might fit in this model. Although an Enlightenment creation, the political salon persisted, as we have seen, through the nineteenth century, and even into the second half of the twentieth. Kenneth Weisbrode has pointed to the legendary gatherings of Vangie Bruce, beautiful and accomplished wife of David Bruce, the American ambassador to London in the 1960s, to demonstrate the longevity of this type of diplomatic sociability facilitated and directed by women with 'regular political effect' (Weisbrode 2015: 250). Vangie's salon, Weisbrode argues, helped to 'define the text of American and European diplomacy at mid-century by ordering its standards of communication and performance' (Weisbrode 2015: 247–248. See also Bilteken 2015; McCarthy 2014). We need more research which can sketch this picture of continuity in women's power to shape the rules of diplomatic discourse over time with greater texture and depth.

Conclusion

The history of women, gender, and diplomacy is undoubtedly a history of change. One cannot fail to be struck by the scale of women's professional advance, including to the highest-ranking diplomatic posts by the end of the twentieth century. But it is also a story of continuity. As Sluga and James observe, the formal, positional authority of a Hillary Clinton (US Secretary of State, 2009–2013) Catherine Ashton (EU High Representative for Foreign Affairs, 2009–2014) or Federica Mogherini (Italian Minister for Foreign Affairs 2014, and Ashton's successor at the EU to date), is 'not simply an anomalous consequence of modernity', but is 'contiguous with practices since the origins of diplomacy; in which women acted as agents of cross-state and cross-cultural information-gathering, alliance-building and networking, and as political negotiators, even if this was somewhat controversial' (Sluga and James 2015: 1). Even if tracing those connections in detail over time remains an unfinished task for historians, we can assert with confidence that it is a story of women's agency, not women's absence.

The larger question is whether gender analysis has the power to transform mainstream histories and understandings of international politics in the longer-term. What this chapter has sought to show is that paying attention to gender not only illuminates women's relationship with diplomacy but how power works more broadly. By writing aristocratic women into histories of early-modern diplomacy, we better understand the dynamics of inter-dynastic politics, the blurring of public and private categories, and the transnational nature of the elite social relations that constituted the international political arena. By exploring women's salon diplomacy from the nineteenth to late twentieth centuries, we better appreciate how professionalisation and bureaucratisation were not all-encompassing processes but co-existed with older forms of diplomatic sociability. By setting women's professional advance alongside their political activism through international bodies like the League and UN, we better comprehend the multiple levels and sites in which women exercise agency and the connections between them. This is why looking back to the past is crucial if we are to understand women's future in diplomacy and international politics.

Notes

1 Exceptions include Dean (1998), Mori (2011), and Hoganson (1998).
2 See, for example, Woodacre (2013); Levin and Bucholz (2009); Campbell Orr (2004).
3 See, for example, Beem (2011); Levin (2013).
4 See Britland (2009); Fry (2014); Wolfson (2014).
5 For the debate on this point, see Clark (2005); Vickery (1993); Richardson (2013).
6 For existing work on the US, see Calkin (1978), and, on Brazil, de Souza Farias (2014).
7 Information has been sourced from existing secondary works or from direct requests to relevant Ministries of Foreign Affairs.
8 Little information is available on Apcar's life and work beyond this short biographical sketch on the website of the Armenian Cultural Foundation; www.armenianculturalfoundation.org/default.aspx?view=article&id=54 [accessed 8 July 2015].

9 Caroline Linse found that while 47 per cent of all US Foreign Service employees were single, the figure rose to 57 per cent for female employees. See Linse (2004) 253–263.
10 Until the 1980s, women were not allowed to learn Arabic, Japanese or other 'hard' languages (requiring a year of more of intense study to master) on the grounds that it was a poor investment of resources were they to resign on marriage – a circular argument of course before 1973, given that the marriage bar left them no choice. See McCarthy (2014).
11 See McCarthy (2015). This is supported by political science research on women as foreign policy decision-makers, on which see Bashevkin (2014).
12 The literature on women's activism and women's rights at the UN is extensive, but see Winslow (1995), and the official UN publication, *The United Nations and the Advancement of Women, 1945–1996* (United Nations 1996).

References

Allen, Gemma. *The Cooke Sisters: Education, Piety and Politics in Early Modern England* (Manchester, 2013).
Armenian Cultural Foundation www.armenianculturalfoundation.org/default.aspx?view=article&id=54 [n.d.: accessed 8 July 2015].
Asbridge, Thomas. 'Alice of Antioch: A Case Study of Female Power in the Twelfth Century', in Peter Edbury and Jonathan Phillips, eds, *The Experience of Crusading: Volume 2 – Defining the Crusader Kingdom* (Cambridge, 2003), 275–296.
Bashevkin, Sylvia. 'Numerical and Policy Representation on the International Stage: Women Foreign Policy Leaders in Western Industrialised Systems', *International Political Science Review* 35 (2014), 409–429.
Beem, Charles, ed. *The Foreign Relations of Elizabeth I* (Basingstoke, 2011).
Bennett Peterson, Barbara, ed. *Notable Women of China: Shang Dynasty to the Early Twentieth Century* (London, 2000).
Britland, Karen. 'Women in the Royal Courts', in Laura Lunger Knoppers, ed., *The Cambridge Companion to Early Modern Women's Writing* (Cambridge, 2009), 124–139.
Buchanan, Meriel. *Ambassador's Daughter* (London, 1958).
Calkin, Homer. *Women in the Department of State: Their Role in American Foreign Affairs* (Washington, DC, 1978).
Campbell Orr, Clarissa. *Queenship in Europe, 1660–1815: The Role of the Consort* (Cambridge, 2004).
Clark, Anna. 'Women in Eighteenth-Century British Politics', in Sarah Knott and Barbara Taylor, eds, *Women, Gender and Enlightenment* (Basingstoke, 2005), 570–586.
Davis Cross, Mai'a K. *The European Diplomatic Corps: Diplomats and International Cooperation from Westphalia to Maastricht* (Basingstoke, 2007).
Daybell, James. 'Gender, Politics and Diplomacy: Women, News and Intelligence Networks in Elizabethan England', in Robyn Adams and Rosanna Cox, eds, *Diplomacy and Early Modern Culture* (Basingstoke, 2011), 101–119.
Dean, Robert. 'Masculinity as Ideology: John F. Kennedy and the Domestic Politics of Foreign Policy', *Diplomatic History* 22(1) (1998), 29–62.
de Souza Farias, Rogerio. *The Admission of Women in Brazilian Professional Diplomacy, 1918–1954* (Institute of International Relations of Universidade de Brasília, 2014).
Firkitian, Mari Agop, *Diplomats and Dreamers: The Stancioff Family in Bulgarian History* (Lanham, MD, 2008).
Foreman, Amanda. *Georgiana Duchess of Devonshire* (London, 1998).

Fry, Cynthia 'Perceptions of Influence: The Catholic Diplomacy of Queen Anna and Her Ladies, 1601–1604', in Nadine Akkerman and Birgit Houben, eds, *The Politics of Female Households: Ladies-in-Waiting Across Early Modern Europe* (Boston, 2014), 267–285.

Goh, Geraldine, trans. *Famous Chinese Diplomats Through the Ages* (Singapore, 1999).

Herren, Madeleine. 'Gender and International Relations through the Lens of the League of Nations', in Glenda Sluga and Carolyn James, eds, *Women, Diplomacy and International Politics since 1500* (London, 2015), 182–201.

Hoganson, Kristin L. *Fighting for American Manhood: How Gender Politics Provoked the Spanish–American and Philippine–American Wars* (New Haven, CT, 1998).

Huck, James D. 'Palma Guillén, Mexico's First Female Ambassador and the International Image of Mexico's Post-Revolutionary Gender Policy', *MACLAS: Latin American Essays* 13 (1999), 159–171.

Kinnear, Mary. *Woman of the World: Mary McGeachy and International Cooperation* (Toronto, 2004).

Levin, Carole. *The Heart and Stomach of a King: Elizabeth I and the Politics of Sex and Power* (Philadelphia, PA, 2013).

Levin, Carole, and Robert Bucholz. *Queens and Power in Medieval and Early Modern England* (Lincoln, 2009).

Linse, Caroline, 'Challenges Facing Women in Overseas Diplomatic Positions', in Hannah Slavik, ed., *Intercultural Communication and Diplomacy* (Malta 2004), 253–263.

Mattingly, Garrett. *Renaissance Diplomacy* (Baltimore, MD, 1955).

McCarthy, Helen. 'Petticoat Diplomacy: The Admission of Women to the British Foreign Service, c1919-1946', *Twentieth Century British History* 20 (2009), 285–321.

McCarthy, Helen. *Women of the World: The Rise of the Female Diplomat* (London, 2014).

McCarthy, Helen. 'The Diplomatic History of Global Women's Rights: The British Foreign Office and International Women's Year, 1975', *Journal of Contemporary History* 50 (2015), 833–853.

McCarthy, Helen, Ingrid Sharp, Laura Beers, Glenda Sluga, and Celia Donert. 'Women, Peace and Transnational Activism, a Century On'. *History and Policy*, online publication March 2015: www.historyandpolicy.org/dialogues/discussions/women-peace-and-transnational-activism-a-century-on.

Mears, Natalie. 'Politics in the Elizabeth Privy Chamber: Lady Mary Sidney and Kat Ashley', in James Daybell, ed., *Women and Politics in Early Modern England, 1450–1700* (Aldershot, 2004), 67–82.

Mitchell, Silvia Z. 'Marriage Plots: Royal Women, Marriage Diplomacy and International Politics and the Spanish, French and Imperial Courts 1665-1679', in Glenda Sluga and Carolyn James, eds, *Women, Diplomacy and International Politics since 1500* (London, 2015), 86–106.

Mori, Jennifer. *The Culture of Diplomacy: Britain in Europe, c.1750–1830* (Manchester, 2011).

Nash, Philip. 'A Woman's Touch in Foreign Affairs? The Career of Ambassador Frances E Willis', *Diplomacy & Statecraft* 13 (2002), 1–12.

Nash, Philip. 'America's First Female Chief of Mission: Ruth Bryan Owen, Minister to Denmark, 1933–36', *Diplomacy and Statecraft* 16 (2005), 57–72.

Porter, Cathy. *Alexandra Kollontai: A Biography* (London, 1980).

Richardson, Sarah. *The Political Worlds of Women: Gender and Politics in Nineteenth-Century Britain* (London, 2013).

Rosenberg, Emily. 'Gender', *Journal of American History* 77 (1990), 116–124.
Sanchez, M. S. *The Empress, the Queen, and the Nun: Women and Power at the Court of Philip III of Spain* (Baltimore, MD, 1998).
Schulte, Regina, ed. *The Body of the Queen: Gender and Rule in the Courtly World 1500–2000* (Oxford, 2006).
Sluga, Glenda. 'Female and National Self-determination: a Gender Re-reading of "the Apogee of Nationalism"', *Nations and Nationalism* 6 (2000), 495–521.
Sluga, Glenda. 'Women, Diplomacy and International Politics before and after the Congress of Vienna', in Glenda Sluga and Carolyn James, eds, *Women, Diplomacy and International Politics since 1500* (London, 2015), 120–136.
Sluga, Glenda and Carolyn James. 'Introduction: the Long International History of Women and Diplomacy', in Glenda Sluga and Carolyn James, eds, *Women, Diplomacy and International Politics since 1500* (London, 2015), 1–12.
Sowerby, Tracey. 'A Letter from Elizabeth I to Tsar Ivan "the Terrible"'. *Textual Ambassadors*. www. Textualambassadors.org/?p+610. Accessed 12 June 2015.
Swanwick, Helena. *I Have Been Young* (London, 1935).
United Nations. *The United Nations and the Advancement of Women, 1945–1996* (New York, NY, 1996).
Vickery, Amanda. 'Golden Age to Separate Spheres? A Review of the Categories and Chronology of English Women's History' *Historical Journal* 36 (1993), 383–414.
Weisbrode, Kenneth. 'Vangie Bruce's Diplomatic Salon', in Glenda Sluga and Carolyn James, eds, *Women, Diplomacy and International Politics since 1500* (London, 2015), 240–253.
Whitehead, Barbara, ed. *Women's Education in Early Modern Europe: A History, 1500–1800* (London, 1999).
Winslow, Anne, ed. *Women, Politics, and the United Nations* (Westport, CT, 1995).
Wolfson, Sara. 'The Female Bedchamber of Queen Henrietta Maria: Politics, Familial Networks and Policy, 1626–40', in Nadine Akkerman and Birgit Houben, eds, *The Politics of Female Households: Ladies-in-Waiting Across Early Modern Europe* (Boston, 2014), 311–341.
Woodacre, Elena, ed. *Queenship in the Mediterranean: Negotiating the Role of the Queen in the Medieval and Early Modern Eras* (Basingstoke, 2013).

2 Alison Palmer's fight for sex and gender equity in the twentieth-century United States Foreign Service

Beatrice McKenzie

This chapter studies the life and career of a Foreign Service Officer, Alison Palmer, as a means of examining changes in the participation of women in the United States Foreign Service. Alison Palmer served as a Foreign Service Officer between 1959 and 1981. After rapid promotions in her first five years, Palmer experienced gender discrimination in assignments. In 1968 she brought an internal complaint, which was settled in her favor in 1975. She used the $25,000 financial settlement from that case to bankroll a class action lawsuit that a group of women officers brought against the State Department the following year. Many administrations fought this lawsuit, which was finally settled in 2010. Although State Department never admitted fault, the lawsuit slowly changed aspects of recruitment and promotion of women, moving in the direction of a meritocratic system.

The chapter offers three chronological arguments. The first addresses change in the participation of women in the US Foreign Service. There were no female Foreign Service officers until 1922; by the end of the twentieth century approximately 30 percent of the agency's officers were women, although gender inequities persisted (President's Interagency Council on Women 2000: 219). Ninety-five years after women officers first joined the service, they are still better represented among junior officers (50 percent) than among senior officers (29 percent) (State Magazine 2015: 2). The first part of the chapter explains the change in the participation of women in US diplomacy in the first half of the twentieth century. To address why inequities persisted after women were admitted, the chapter argues that a system of gendered labor stratification developed at State Department in the second half of the twentieth century. Hiring women into the lower ranks in jobs that had fewer opportunities for promotion served the interests of men, whose careers proceeded more quickly. I use Alison Palmer's story as an example of how the gendered system affected one female officer's career. The final argument engages with women officers' activism. Women officers faced discrimination, including sexual harassment, which worsened when Alison Palmer challenged the system. But Palmer was not alone in the battle. This chapter argues that her activism provided what Joan Freeman has called "a radical flank" against which other women reformers' activities were viewed as more acceptable (Freeman 2008).

My aim is to advance scholarship about women diplomats in the US Foreign Service. What literature exists primarily focuses on women in extra-governmental and informal structures rather than their involvement in government service; this is partly because so few women served prior to 1970 but also because the State Department itself successfully initiated a history about women's participation.[1] Recent scholarship has focused on American women's involvement in international women's organizations in the early decades of the twentieth century and on the participation of Foreign Service wives and non-career women diplomats.[2] The only book that exists on women's role in the Department of State is a landmark volume written by Homer Calkin in 1978. The work makes a case that women have been integral to the Department since the early 1800s—its inclusion of hard-to-acquire sources, stories, and statistics makes it a valuable tool for researchers. Yet its publication in the early years of the class action lawsuit by a historian who had served for 37 years in the research and reference division of the Department of State makes its message political at best.[3] It is an example of the ability of the Department of State to control the messaging about women's service by controlling access to information, access that was key to arguing the plaintiffs' case in the class action lawsuit. Along with a number of other scholars, my work has begun to examine women career officers and the significance of gender in the US Foreign Service (Nash 2001; Wood 2007; Epstein 2008; McKenzie 2015). My work also studies women's activism in State Department in the 1970s. An examination of Alison Palmer's career and activism in the second half of the twentieth century reveals the gendered labor stratification that has existed since World War II, as well as elucidating changes in the participation of women in the twentieth-century US Foreign Service.

Changes in women's participation in US Foreign Service, 1922–1947

Early in the twentieth century, the Foreign Service Officer corps was an elite group of white, male professional diplomats who staffed the Department of State, United States embassies, and United States consulates overseas.[4] Executive branch administrations in the early twentieth century passed reforms, including entry by a written and an oral exam, to professionalize the corps (Foreign Service Journal 1999). The agency has its own culture, with norms that have changed little over the years. After 1924, most officers entered these corps in their twenties as junior officers, having studied history, political science, economics, languages, and/or law at prestigious Ivy League universities such as Harvard, Yale, Brown, and Columbia. Most were in their twenties and possessed bachelor's degrees. To pass the exams, prospective applicants took a short course or were tutored by experts to gain knowledge in diplomatic history and law. The hierarchy was managed from within the agency with some oversight by the Department of State and Congress. Senior Foreign Service officers directed the agency, wrote, administered, and scored the written and oral exams, and served on assignments and promotions boards. Successful applicants served a probationary period as unclassified officers before being assigned a job function and, as in the US military, the career was "up or out": officers who were not promoted in a certain period of time were dismissed from the service. The most senior officers were eligible to be selected as ambassadors, although Presidents maintained the prerogative to select ambassadors from outside the service. Yet, more than half of all ambassadorships, virtually all other officers in overseas posts, and many positions in the Department of State were filled by professional officers.

The Foreign Service justified the exclusion of women from its ranks in the early twentieth century for reasons of women's health and propriety. The idea that women's weaker constitutions made them unable to serve in mainly hot or tropical overseas posts was cited for decades, even after women worked in the same posts as secretaries and code clerks (Calkin 1978: 67). A second barrier to women's service was the idea that they would be exposed to inappropriate people. In 1917, a woman applicant was informed that "only men are admitted to the foreign service examination and commissioned as officers in that service" (Calkin 1978: 58). When debating women's participation in the early 1920s, the Director General of the Foreign Service named climatic conditions, duties that required "mingling freely with persons from whom information is to be obtained," and handling issues relating to seamen and immigration as reasons the career should be closed to women applicants (Calkin 1978: 67). A related barrier to women's service was whether foreign governments would find them acceptable representatives. Since relations depended so heavily on discussions carried out in parlors and offices, and relations in the diplomatic corps were so important to success as an officer, a nation's representative needed to be able to integrate in that community. Men in the agency asked how a woman officer could adjourn to the smoking parlor after dinner, for example. In early discussions, Foreign Service directors also found it appalling to imagine the awkward position in the diplomatic community of the male spouse of a female officer. The Foreign Service resolved this issue by requiring women officers who married to resign their diplomatic posts; this unwritten rule remained in place for decades (Women's Action Organization Oral History Project Final Transcripts 1974–1977: 1–2; Calkin 1978: 144).

An increased number of young women applied to take the exams after women won the right to vote in 1920, and Foreign Service directors faced political pressure to admit them to the exam. The Department of State announced in 1921 that women would be "admitted to future examinations for career officers upon the same terms that are applicable to men" (Calkin 1978: 60). The first woman who passed the exam, Lucile Atcherson, had completed university at age 18 and worked as a paid organizer for woman suffrage prior to acting as secretary to the female president of the American Committee for Devastated France from 1919–1921. Fluent in French, she followed her male peers' lead by being tutored in political science and economics at University of Chicago, prior to taking the exam. She received the third-highest score on the exam and joined the service in

1922 (Wood 2007). Foreign Service directors instructed Atcherson on appropriate behavior and sent her to a climatically suitable post, Berne, Switzerland.

Atcherson's successful integration did not quell senior officers' concerns about women officers. While rumors flew that Atcherson was only accepted due to high level political pressure, the Executive Committee of the Foreign Service met to discuss whether they could lobby for an executive order to exclude women—along with African Americans and naturalized citizens. The Secretary General of the Foreign Service wrote in 1922 that "the most feasible way to deal with the question" would be "to defeat (women, African American, and naturalized citizens) in the examination" (Calkin 1978: 69). When four of eight women passed the first written exam in 1924, the Executive Committee quickly met to make the oral exam "more thorough" so that "no one not clearly possessing fitness for the Service should be certified as eligible." Only one white woman (and one African American man) passed the first oral exam (Calkin 1978: 69).[5] Four additional women passed the exams in the decade of the 1920s, a period of time the agency later referred to as "as experiment" with women officers. When four of the six women officers resigned, three to marry and one (Atcherson) to enter a different profession, Under Secretary of State Grew deemed the experiment a failure (Calkin 1978: 81). No other woman passed the exam to enter as a junior officer until 1947.[6]

A shortage of male officers during World War II, however, required the Department to hire officers from other governmental agencies to staff overseas posts and positions in the Department. During and immediately following the war, the number of women who worked as officers increased dramatically.[7] In fact, the Department crowed in 1951 that the number of women had grown nearly tenfold since prior to the war, from two officers to 17 (out of 1,275).[8] As in other government agencies, a large number of women and men changed positions during the war; these transfers, too, were inequitable by gender (McKenzie 2015). The war required the military service of men ages 18–35, exactly the age of junior and mid-ranking Foreign Service officers. The shortage of male officers required the Department of State to make "lateral hires" from other government agencies, and this method of filling low-ranking positions was used through the remainder of the twentieth century, playing into the gendering of the service, discussed in the next section. Because there remained only two women who had entered as junior officers in the 1920s, the Department of State tokenized them, touting their success for decades as evidence of equal treatment for women officers. Frances Willis, with a PhD in political science from Stanford University, fought her way into a career as a political officer and Constance Harvey, fluent in French, German, and Italian, served as a consular officer. Both women performed heroic deeds in wartime Europe but privately lamented their lackluster promotions records.[9] In the 1950s, however, their careers began to take off; Willis served as the first female career Ambassador, to Switzerland in 1953, and Harvey served as the first female Consul, to Strasburg in 1959. With many low-ranking women and the two high-achieving token women, Foreign Service appeared to be a viable career for women. Yet what emerged out of the wartime labor program was a gendered labor organization in which, by 1960, though women officers made up nearly 7 percent of the service and served all over the world, those who were promoted to Senior Foreign Service were nearly all male. This is the service Alison Palmer joined in 1959.

Alison Palmer in a career stratified by gender, 1955–1981

Women began to pass the Foreign Service exams after 1947, entering an agency that increasingly became stratified by gender. Using some of the same justifications—women's weaker constitutions and propriety—the agency steered women into jobs with fewer opportunities for advancement, a system that benefitted white male officers. Thus a discriminatory system operated to enhance white men's access to higher level positions while it kept most women, all of whom were white, at the bottom of the hierarchy. The system was also racialized in similar ways, although racial discrimination is not the focus of this chapter. When Alison Palmer graduated from college in 1955, she eagerly answered a call for women to apply.[10] She very quickly came up against the systematic gender discrimination operating at State, a system that involved discrimination against women in recruitment, job function, assignments, and promotion.

Although she shared a similar background to male officers who joined the Foreign Service in the 1950s, and might have therefore expected to pass the exams, Alison Palmer only passed the officer exam after stellar performance as a Foreign Service secretary for four years. Palmer's class and educational backgrounds were similar to that of many entering officers. She came from an educated family, she attended Pembroke College, the women's college affiliated with the Ivy-League institution, Brown University, where she studied journalism.[11] Although she passed the written exam in 1955, Palmer failed at the oral. Here Palmer ran up against the first of many barriers that women faced. As a personnel officer testified at a discrimination hearing in 1971, in the mid-1950s, it was State Department's unofficial policy that examiners admit only one white female officer OR one African American male officer each year. The officer added, "Miss Palmer must have taken the exam in the wrong year."[12] As predicted in 1922, the rest were "defeated" by the oral exam.

Women and African American employees did enter the Foreign Service in higher numbers in this era, but they entered through the less prestigious lateral programs as Foreign Service Officers or they entered as Foreign Service Reserve Officers (FSRs) and Foreign Service Specialists (FSSs). The existence of lateral and affiliated programs allowed State Department to address concerns that they denied employment on an equal basis to women and African American employees while they confirmed the belief among Foreign Service personnel that most women and African American applicants were incapable of passing the oral exam. Because they were hired under different circumstances, officers who entered the service laterally were viewed as less capable than those who came in at entry level. Palmer experienced rapid promotions as a Foreign Service Secretary in Ghana and back in Washington, in the Personnel section of State

Department. She knew she needed to take the exam in order to enter the career at entry level, and she passed the oral exam the second time she took it, in 1959.[13]

Although she performed admirably, Palmer's experience in her first tours as an officer exemplify the ways the Foreign Service discriminated against women officers early in their careers. In their first two tours, incoming junior officers were rotated in positions in two different embassies in order to show potential in a particular job function, called a "cone." Palmer's first assignment was as a consular officer in the US Consulate in Leopoldville, in the Congo, which, while she was there, was re-designated as an embassy when the country became independent. This is the point in her career where Palmer's excellence as an officer should have caught the notice of State Department superiors. She landed in the Congo just a month after it formally became independent, in the midst of a crisis in the new nation: Congolese troops were mutinying against postcolonial control by the Belgians. Palmer took her consular role to protect American civilians quite seriously, even defying the Ambassador's order to evacuate with all American women and children. The first incident that brought her international attention happened one day when embassy officials headed to the airport to see off a visiting American dignitary. Driving on the airport road, Palmer came across the terrible scene of an embassy vehicle overturned in a ditch. The vehicle had hit and killed a Congolese cyclist on the road, and villagers were taking vengeance for the death on two young American men who had been in the vehicle. A crowd gathered around, beating and stabbing them. Palmer drove her car into the crowd and pulled the more injured man into her car. A bus then followed, and someone in it picked up the other man. Not knowing whether the man in her car would live or die, Palmer sped him to the airport where, thanks to her efforts, he lived. A second incident occurred the following day. Palmer left work with Canadian Consul General Bill Wood to have a drink at his house. En route they drove by the Ghanaian Consul's house where a dramatic scene was unfolding: the Ghanaian diplomat had been declared *persona non grata* by the Congolese government for over-involvement in domestic affairs, but the diplomat refused to leave. A phalanx of United Nations troops surrounded the Ghanaian's house to prevent the Congolese military from arresting him. Walking with Wood around the side of the house, Palmer spied three of her journalist friends, two Americans and a Briton, under arrest and encircled by Congolese soldiers who seemed ready to execute them. Acting immediately, Palmer called out, "Hi there!" and stepped into the middle of the circle. The effect of Palmer's action was to defuse the situation. According to one of the Americans, "She was unbelievable. The soldiers were so stunned at the nerve of this girl, they just sort of faded away."[14]

Newspapers covered Palmer's actions, and while they initially characterized her as a bit player in these dramas, by the time she left Leopoldville, accounts in the press and in friends' memories emphasized Palmer's central role and bravery. In the initial reports of the airport road incident, journalists emphasized the unruliness of the Congolese mob and the bravery of the American men who had stepped away from the military attaché and his wife to protect them. Palmer "happened by" in her car and one of the men leaped into it (Newport Daily News

1960). By the time she left the post, however, a journalist remembered Palmer as a heroine, "about the most attractive and cheerful fixture of the Congo's first two chaotic years of independence." A friend wrote later, "We remember so vividly your coolness and courage when you saved the lives of two of your colleagues on the road from Kinshasa out to the airport. You were magnificent."[15] Whether she acted differently than a male colleague would have in her position, gender played into the awarding of honors for service in the Congo.

Later accounts played up 30-year-old Palmer's gender, from the headline "Girl is Praised for Bravery in African Post" to specific mentions of her calmness, kindness, and modesty.[16] One story depicted Palmer as naive rather than cool in the face of danger. It described her arrival at work on the morning troops started their revolt "walking crisply to work as the troops were rampaging through the streets" while "male diplomats who had been alerted [huddled] inside the embassy building." Palmer herself played down a separate incident in which she was pushed and shoved by rifle-bearing Congolese soldiers when she protested the mistreatment of a prisoner because she knew it would be blown out of proportion and might cause her to be sent home for her protection. Another article stated that Palmer "manned the official switchboard with girlish gusto" after local employees fled the embassy. Ultimately, as a female vice consul, Palmer's life-saving actions were merely part of the job while the actions of political officer Frank Carlucci, who "plunged in among mutinying and rioting Congolese troops ... to get at the reasons for their disorder" won him an individual award (State Department Publicity Bulletin 1962: 59: Alison Palmer's personal papers).

Palmer did share a prize awarded to all of the officers at the US embassy in Leopoldville and the US consulate in Elizabethville in Katanga province, and she was promoted, but she was denied the opportunity to rotate in other areas of the embassy and hone her skills as a political officer. In that way, Palmer's early career experiences in the hierarchical system matched those of other women. Women officers faced early career discrimination in job functions in the Foreign Service. The department assigned junior officers to embassies that would rotate the officer between at least two embassy offices to allow them to gain skills and bid, based on those skills, for future positions in the area of the embassy to which their skills were best suited.[17] Junior officers knew that political and economic officer assignments led to longer careers at higher levels, and ambitious officers sought those positions early in their careers. As Palmer hoped to be a political officer, it would have been ideal, for example, to serve for a year in the political office in the embassy in the Congo. In the chaos of that tour, however, she stayed in the consular section through her time at that post and through the next, in British Guiana. Women officers served in the consular function at much higher levels than other functions (see Table 2.1). In spite of the disparity of numbers of women officers in 1974, for example, nearly 20 percent of all consular officers were women, while only 4 percent of all political officers were. After that assignment, however, when Palmer had been promoted three times in five years—the normal promotion rate was once every two or three years—she

Table 2.1 FSO distribution by sex within each job function (cone) (June 1974, percent of total)[18]

	Women	Men
Program Director	0.4	99.6
Political	3.9	96.1
Economic/Commercial	5.8	94.2
Administration	7.9	92.1
Consular	19.7	80.3
Budget and Finance	24	76
Personnel	80	20
General Services	2.6	97.4

received a coveted assignment to political officer training. Buoyed by excellent personnel reviews and promotions, the ambitious Palmer believed she could excel at political work.

It was in assignments at the mid-level of the career that gendered labor stratification most clearly hurt women's careers. In a chart from June 1962, for example, when most women were barred from "substantive" work as political and economic officers, political and economic positions made up two-thirds of the available mid-ranking jobs, while consular and administrative positions made up the remaining one-third.[19] For Palmer, moving from the consular function at the lower rank to the political function at the middle rank meant she would compete for promotions in a field with many more jobs at her level and above.[20] With, moreover, new posts opening every year on the continent, Africa seemed to represent a part of the world with the most opportunity. Palmer was selected in 1964 to attend advanced area studies training in African Studies at Boston University. In 1965 and 1966, however, three US ambassadors in African countries refused her assignments to their staffs as political officer. When the Department put pressure on the third Ambassador, Edward Korry, to accept her, he moved her into a staff position with mainly secretarial tasks for the final year of his service in the US Embassy in Addis Ababa, Ethiopia. Palmer had one year in the political section after that, in which she performed well, but she felt she'd lost years of service and opportunities for promotion: two years trying to be assigned to a political position in Africa and one year in the staff position in Addis. From her next posting in Vietnam in 1968, Palmer filed a sex discrimination complaint against State Department.

Women's activism

In acting individually and publicly, Palmer's demands for gender equity came to be seen as a radical approach against which other female officers' demands seemed more acceptable. Palmer's Equal Employment Opportunity (EEO) grievance hearing marked the first time the department evaluated gender bias on an officer's career. In the public testimony, heard from June 8–25, 1971, the case revealed much information about the State Department's discrimination against women candidates and officers, as well as the Department's efforts to quietly address some of the reforms that women officers demanded (Transcript of Proceedings 1971). Palmer was not alone in the battle against gender discrimination in US diplomacy. Separate from Palmer's efforts, a group of mid-ranking women officers from State Department, US Agency for International Development, and US Information Agency sought reforms in the three Foreign Affairs agencies beginning in 1970. They had realized there was "minimal representation of women" and no discussion at all of women's issues among 14 management tasks under the rubric, "Challenges of the Seventies."[21] They formed a group called the "Ad hoc Committee to Improve the Status of Women in the Foreign Service Agencies," later called the Women's Action Organization. This group aimed to make reforms in recruitment, training opportunities, assignments, and promotion of women candidates and officers. It is clear from the testimony in the 1971 hearing that Palmer was a militant voice against which the demands of the Women's Action Organization seemed moderate (Transcript of Proceedings 1971: 210). Feminist theorist Jo Freeman has explained the value of a "radical flank" to social change (Freeman 1975). "A good radical flank is essential to steady social change," she explained, referring to the feminist movement in the United States in the 1970s. It was important that a person or thing have "nothing to gain by playing the insiders' game" and must "regularly raise new issues ... to pull the mainstream in a progressive direction." Although Alison Palmer did not know it at the time, she became an outsider from the moment she made her EEO claim.

As the 1971 testimony demonstrated, Palmer's complaint immediately cast her as a "troublemaker" and damaged her career.[22] Upon receipt of her letter in 1968, the EEO office investigated the allegations, found she *had* experienced discrimination, and proposed a settlement, but the letter back to Ms. Palmer was delayed by nine months because no senior officer was willing to sign it. Finally the Director of the Equal Opportunity Office drafted and signed a new letter that advised Palmer to drop the complaint. The new letter included a threat that Palmer's career would be hurt if she pursued the claim. "People knowledgeable in how the Foreign Service Selections system works, including the Director of Personnel, have expressed apprehension that your career prospects [will] be damaged by inclusion of reference in your file to this grievance procedure."[23] One of the three ambassadors who had refused to hire Palmer, and was thus named in her complaint, had taken over as Director General of the Foreign Service just a week before the new letter was sent.[24]

Several Senior Foreign Service officers defended inequity to women in assignments; to do so they publicly aired racist and sexist tropes, such as the threat of African counterparts to white women. A woman was unsuitable to serve as political officer in Ethiopia, Ambassador Korry testified, because the "savages" in the Ethiopian labor movement would only be interested in her sexually. Korry referred to African men as "wolves."[25] Yet Palmer testified that in six years serving in Ghana, the Congo, and Ethiopia she never experienced sexual harassment by an African. She did, however, face sexual harassment by colleagues and superior officers. Open discussion of sexual harassment in the workplace marked Alison Palmer as a Women's Libber.[26]

Several other female Foreign Service officers testified about their experiences, including Mary Olmsted, a career economic officer who had served on a selections board that made assignments. Olmsted testified about the routine refusal of assignments to women as well as the way in which the refusals occurred. Most often, a panel mentioned a woman officer's name with two male officers' names. Rather than an explicit denial of the assignment, the woman's name dropped out of consideration. Senior Foreign Service leaders likely considered Olmsted a friendly witness, an insider. Under Secretary of State for Management, William Macomber, had named Olmsted to lead a management-approved organization for gender reform at State Department. Even so, she used her membership of Women's Action Organization to encourage reform on women's issues, once referring to the difficulty she faced in preventing women's "disappointment and militancy" if the office lost a staff member.[27]

In light of the growing complaints, Under Secretary of State Macomber hoped to reform the State Department from within. He noted later, regarding the efficacy of the Women's Action Organization effort, "They presented these things and there wasn't any of them crazy, bra-burning kinds of things. They were sensible, honest, legitimate things that no really sensible person could quarrel with."[28] Macomber went on to describe how much more motivating it was to work with appreciative female employees than it was to make changes women *demanded*:

> When we got something done, even though we hadn't gotten everything done, and there were certain things (Women's Action Organization) hoped would be done that weren't done yet, they said "thank you" for what's been done. Well, that sends you back to the drawing board really trying to get the rest of it done.

Like many other Foreign Service Officers, Macomber worked toward slow, steady reform at State and eschewed the radical approach.

In 1971 Civil Service Commissioner Andrew Beath found a pattern of discrimination existed at State Department that negatively affected Alison Palmer's career. He did not find wilful violation of equal opportunity rules by any ambassador. Palmer appealed this part of the decision to the Civil Service Commission on October 8, 1971, seeking punishment of the Ambassadors—such as a reprimand in their personnel files—who had denied her assignments. In 1973 Palmer's new attorney demanded a retroactive promotion for Palmer, back pay, and legal fees. Although Palmer lost in District Court, she appealed the case in Summer 1975 and won. She invested the court-ordered legal fees of $25,000 in a new campaign for gender equality among Foreign Service Officers, a class action lawsuit.

Using a group action lawsuit popular with civil rights movement leaders, in 1975, Palmer and two other women brought a class action lawsuit charging State

Department with a "pattern and practice" of sex discrimination in recruitment, examination, appointments distribution by job type, performance evaluations, training, assignments, counseling, promotions, retirements, and selections-out.[29] The complaint noted that women made up 40 percent of the nation's labor force and 44 percent of college graduates but only 7 percent of all FSOs in June 1965, a number that dropped to 4.8 percent in June 1970 and rose to only 8.86 percent in June 1975. Complainants relied heavily on State Department statistics and on the testimony of women Foreign Service officers and their managers. Complainants argued, for example, that women's pass rate at the exam was still much lower than men's in 1975 (10.1 percent vs. 16 percent), and that although women now made up 30 percent of written exam applicants, they comprised only 13 percent of the 1975 Foreign Service classes.[30] State Department settled on various elements during the 34 years the lawsuit was fought. Palmer's lawsuit forced State Department to act on reforms in recruitment to the Foreign Service. In 1983, State Department settled on the issue of discrimination against women in recruitment and appointed 75 women as FSOs who had been rejected at the exam.[31]

After settlement of the recruitment issue, the class action case came to trial in the US District Court in 1985. Focusing on the trajectory of the career for women, plaintiffs argued that women were disproportionately assigned to consular work, which attorney Karen Edgecomb said was seen as "social work" that "trapped" them, and under-assigned to the political cone, missing out on "the lion's share of the senior jobs."[32] Appearing as the defendant each time part of the case came to court, State Department consistently recognized discrimination in the past but denied its relevance in the present. In 1985, for example, a spokesman for the Department of State, Stuart Newberger, declared that there had been "no sex discrimination in the Foreign Service since the 1970s." *Palmer et al.* lost in the lower court in 1985, but once again won in the appeal. Yet, the court-ordered remedies saw no action by State, prompting *Palmer et al.* to file again in 1988.[33]

In this piecemeal fashion, gendered policies changed at State Department. Women's Action Organization accepts credit for the same reforms Palmer's case achieved; in truth, the reformers worked hand-in-hand. With Alison Palmer and class action lawsuit members working from the outside, through the courts, and Women's Action Organization working from inside, from within the Department, women saw reforms in recruitment, assignments, and promotions policies. In January 1971, State Department dropped the marriage ban for women officers. State Department issued an equal assignment policy which forbade discrimination against women "for any job, at any level, in any country," and State Department agreed that women with dependents could serve abroad under the same conditions as male officers.[34]

Conclusion

This chapter examined three themes evidenced by Alison Palmer's career and fight for rights as an officer in the United States Foreign Service between 1959 and 1980. In that mid-century era, the number of women officers in the agency grew precipitously, although, in the twenty-first century, equity remains elusive at the senior levels. The first theme regards an institutional shift in the participation of women in United States diplomacy. No women had served as officers prior to 1922; two served regular careers before World War II; and women slowly joined in the latter decades of the twentieth century. As a second theme, the chapter argued that the self-regulated agency incorporated women in the lower and mid-level ranks, cultivating a gendered hierarchy that allowed male officers to rise to the highest levels. Alison Palmer and other women officers fought the discrimination they faced in the Department of State, and Palmer's name is associated with that battle. Palmer fought a series of gender equity lawsuits between 1976 and 2010, leading State Department to settle some aspects of the suit, such as equity in recruitment, and ignore others, such as equity in assignments and promotions. Until very recently, Palmer's activism was denounced by State Department management and officers alike, but it provided a useful element of radicalism against which other female officers' demands seemed acceptable.

This research demonstrates the strides in gender equity by female Foreign Service officers over nearly a century, but it does not definitively answer whether sexism limits women's careers at present. Palmer herself, who retired from the Foreign Service to Cape Cod, Massachusetts in 1981, does not believe the task is complete. She wonders whether anyone at State keeps track of gender equity in job specialization, training, and promotion among Foreign Service Officers. "What a waste," she complains, to hire and train so many women officers who, once they realize the disadvantages of the career, move to careers without such obstacles. State Department has recently asked similar questions. An article in *State Magazine* in June 2015 reported the results of focus groups of women who left the profession early. The women cited feelings of marginalization at State Department and being expected to do office "housework."[35] Statistics show that women are over-represented (54 percent) in consular work and under-represented (34 percent) in political work, and under-represented (30 percent) in the Senior Foreign Service. State Department projects that this inequity will continue.[36] Palmer also wonders whether anyone at State Department tracks whether the ambassadors who rise up through the Foreign Service ranks (approximately two-thirds of ambassadorships go to career Foreign Service Officers at present while the remainder are political appointments) are representative of the population, and whether women are assigned, even at the most senior level, to career-enhancing posts compared to their male counterparts. She notes the difference in level of responsibility at large posts such as London, UK, compared to small posts like Port Moresby, Papua New Guinea, and asks whether women are assigned to ambassadorships with less responsibility.[37] Sure that these statistics exist within State, Palmer has called for them to be made public. She has yet to receive them. The work of gender equity at State Department, Palmer points out, is far from over.

Notes

1 Presidents since FDR have named powerful or well-connected political women who were not career Foreign Service Officers as ambassadors to particular countries, although this trend was slow to be adopted. Only seven women received political appointments and only four career women served as ambassador before the 1970s. See Calkin (1978) 285–286.
2 For research on women in extra-governmental organizations, see Rupp (1997); Berkovitch (1999); McKenzie (2011); Threlkeld (2014). Research related to Foreign Service wives' roles and non-career diplomats includes Wood (2007).
3 Under Secretary of State Lawrence Eagleburger commissioned the work in 1976. See Calkin (1978), v.
4 The Foreign Service remains an elite group of professional diplomats. There are non-officer positions, too, including a staff corps, with secretaries and clerks, and a specialist corps, with information technology experts and doctors. Over the decades the State Department has referred to the three services interchangeably as the Foreign Service. This chapter addresses only the Foreign Service Officer corps.
5 In 1924 the Rogers Act made the service "more democratic" and efficient by combining the two services into a single service with a single written exam to recruit diplomatic and consular officers.
6 See "November 15, 1950 Comparative Success of Men and Women in the Oral Examinations Since the War," Box 17, Folder 2, Frances Willis Papers, Stanford University. Eleven women and 466 men entered the Foreign Service between 1945 and 1947 from either the Department or the Armed Forces. In September 1947 six women out of 14 passed the exams, a pass rate of 42.86 percent. The same year, 125 out of 170 men passed, a pass rate of 73.5 percent.
7 The number of women FSO's increased dramatically between 1953 and 1956 thanks to the Wriston program: from 16 to 262 (Calkin 1978: 120). This is one reason the number of women actually dropped between 1965 and 1970; women who were recruited during WWII and the early Cold War retired and women still did not pass the exam at high enough rates to replace them.
8 "Opportunities for Women in Consular Work Abroad," RG 59, General Records of the Department of State, Bureau of Security and Consular Affairs, Supplemental Decimal Files, 1945–1953: 18–32. Joseph W. Bosley, Personal File 50/51 to 21–1 General – Implementation Schedules 1952, Box 14, NARA.
9 Harvey won the Presidential Medal of Freedom for acts of bravery in Vichy France; Willis smuggled refugees through Portugal and Spain.
10 In 1951 the Department bragged that the number of women increased nearly tenfold (from a base of two) since before the war. Frances Willis' career was shown to be the exemplar for what women could expect. At the time, Willis, a Stanford University PhD who left Vassar as a professor to enter the service in 1927 was the only woman above the lowest ranks of the service. *New York Times*, April 15, 1953, Box 3, Folder 5 in FW papers, Stanford University.
11 Ivy League universities include Brown, Columbia, Cornell, Dartmouth, Harvard, Pennsylvania, Princeton, and Yale. Yale and Princeton admitted women undergraduate students in 1969 and Cornell in 1970; Brown University became co-educational in 1971; Dartmouth in 1972. Harvard became co-ed in 1977; Columbia University in 1983.

12 Folder 4, pp. 559–658/10, APP/Brown. Author interview with Alison Palmer, February 14, 2017.
13 Even then, Palmer's superior officer in State Department's Personnel Office (PER) tried to postpone her assignment as an officer until she had completed a full two years as his assistant. Alison Palmer interviewed by author, Cape Cod, MA, May 6, 2013.
14 "Scrapbook: Palmer v. Church + State, vol 1 1955–76." APP/Columbia.
15 Letter to AP from Harry D. Brown, American Baptist Convention, October 1, 1971. Letter from Harry D. Brown, World Mission Campaign, American Baptist Convention to AP, October 1, 1971. Box 8, Series 4, APP/Columbia.
16 "Girl is Praised for Bravery in African Post," undated clipping marked in pencil: July 1962. APP/Columbia.
17 Folder 9: Responses to Autobiographical Questions. Palmer asked for pol or econ positions consistently between 1959 and 1964. Was assigned as consular officer. Series 6, Box 2, Folder 9, "Responses to Autobiographical Questions," in APP/Columbia.
18 This chart appears in "FSO Investigation on the Status of Women," p. 11, in Series 4: Litigation, Box 10, folder 13, in APP/Columbia.
19 "Functional Analysis of Foreign Service Officers, June 1962," shows 609 positions in political and economic functions at the FSO-03 and FSO-04 level versus 363 consular and administrative jobs at the same level. See "Personnel for the New Diplomacy: Report of the Committee on Foreign Affairs Personnel, December 1962," 151.
20 In 1965 7 percent of FSO's were women. "FSO Investigation on the Status of Women," p. 2, in Series 4: Litigation, Box 10, folder 13, in APP/Columbia.
21 Introduction to "Women's Action Organization Oral History Project," OH-39, Schlesinger Library, Radcliffe Institute, Harvard University, 1–2.
22 Complaint on Equal Employment, Civil Action No. 2324–71, Alison Palmer, Plaintiff v. William Rogers, Defendant. In APP Papers, Box 1, Folder 16, APP/Brown.
23 August 8, 1969 letter to AP from O/EP. In Grievance hearing against Department of State, RE: Alison Palmer Transcript of Proceedings, Brown University.
24 Testimony of Howard Mace, Deputy Director General and Director of Personnel of the Foreign Service, 58. "Grievance hearing against Department of State RE: Alison Palmer Transcript of Proceedings," Series 1, Box 1, Folder 1, p. 58, in APP/Columbia.
25 Letters from Mrs. Chris Rosenfeld to AP, 10/12/71, and Margaret J. Anstee, UNDP Resident Representative in Rabat, to AP, undated, in "FSO Litigation Correspondence, 1968–70," Series 4, Box 8, Folder 7, APP/Columbia.
26 On sexual harassment as a Women's Lib issue, see Baxandall and Gordon (2000), 274. Alison Palmer identifies as a feminist, but says she was neither a Women's Libber nor radical in the 1970s: Alison Palmer interviewed by author, Cape Cod, MA, May 6, 2013.
27 "Grievance hearing against Department of State RE: Alison Palmer Transcript of Proceedings," in Series 1, Box 1, Folder 2, p. 210, APP/Columbia.
28 Calkin 1978, 157.
29 "Introduction," 1, APP/Brown.
30 Ibid., 7.
31 Ibid., 5.
32 Blodgett (1985).
33 Folder 28, "Gender Studies Paper," APP/Columbia.
34 Women's Action Organization Oral History Project Final Transcripts 1974–1977, OH-39, Schlesinger Library, Radcliffe Institute, Harvard University, pp. 1–2. Marital ban ended January 15, 1971, Calkin (1978), 144.
35 *State Magazine*, June 2015, 2.
36 *State Magazine* projects that the mid-level and Senior Foreign Service together will be 42 percent female in 2024. Note that the projection is not for Senior Foreign Service alone, a number that may have seemed too low to admit. For a recent discussion of possible sexism in the Senior Foreign Service, see Strano (2016).
37 Palmer (2015), 328.

References

Note: There are two main repositories for Alison Palmer's papers, at Brown University and at Columbia University. They are identified as APP/Brown and APP/Columbia. This chapter also draws on records at the United States National Archives Record Administration, identified as NARA.

Baxandall, R., and L. Gordon. 2000. *Dear Sisters: Dispatches from the Women's Liberation Movement* (New York, NY: Basic Books).

Berkovitch, N. 1999. *From Motherhood to Citizenship: Women's Rights and International Organizations* (Baltimore, MD: Johns Hopkins University Press).

Blodgett, N. 1985. "Sexism at State? Foreign Service Bias Alleged," *American Bar Association Journal* 71: 21.

Calkin, H. 1978. *Women in the Department of State: Their Role in American Foreign Affairs* (Washington, DC: Department of State).

Epstein, A. 2009. "International Feminism and Empire-Building between the Wars: the case of Viola Smith," *Women's History Review* (17)5: 699–719.

Foreign Service Journal. 1999. "A Corps is Born: How a State Department Insider and a Young Congressman Joined Forces to Create America's Foreign Service," *American Foreign Service Journal* (May): 24–31.

Freeman, J. 1975. *The Politics of Women's Liberation: A Case Study of an Emerging Social Movement and Its Relation to the Policy Process* (New York, NY: Addison-Wesley Longman).

Freeman, J. 2008. "The Woman's Movement and Democratic and Republican Conventions: In Search of a Radical Flank," *Off Our Backs* 15(2): 11–20.

McKenzie, B. 2011. "The Power of International Positioning: The National Woman's Party, International Law, and Diplomacy, 1928–1934," *Gender & History* (April): 130–146.

McKenzie, B. 2015 "'The Problem of Women in the Department': Sex and Gender Discrimination in the 1960s United States Foreign Diplomatic Service," *European Journal of American Studies* 10(1): 1–14.

Nash, P. 2001. "'A Woman's Touch in Foreign Affairs?': The Career of Ambassador Frances Willis," *Diplomacy & Statecraft* 13(2): 1–20.

Newport Daily News. 1960. "U.S. Car Kills Congo Cyclist: Mob Stabs 2," *Newport* November 21, 4.

Palmer, A. 2015. *Diplomat and Priest: One Woman's Challenge to Church and State* (North Charleston, SC: CreateSpace).

Personnel for the New Diplomacy. 1962. *Report of the Committee on Foreign Affairs Personnel, December 1962*. Carnegie Endowment for International Peace.

President's Interagency Council on Women. 2000. *America's Commitment: Women 2000*. (Washington, DC: President's Interagency Council on Women). Available at http://purl.access.gpo.gov/GPO/LPS15633. Accessed February 23, 2017.

Rupp, L. J. 1997. *Worlds of Women: The Making of an International Women's Movement* (Princeton, NJ: Princeton University Press).

State Magazine. 2015 (June). "In the News: HR Analyzes Women's Advancement," 2.

Strano, Andrea. 2016. "Foreign Service Women Today: The Palmer Case and Beyond," *The Foreign Service Journal* (March), www.afsa.org/foreign-service-women-today-palmer-case-and-beyond. Accessed February 22, 2017.

Threlkeld, T. 2014. *Pan American Women: U.S. Internationalists and Revolutionary Mexico* (Pennsylvania: University of Pennsylvania Press).

Transcript of Proceedings, Department of State Grievance Hearing, RE: Alison Palmer, Washington, D.C., June 8, 1971, Hoover Reporting Company, Inc., Official Reporters

Women's Action Organization Oral History Project Final Transcripts 1974–1977, OH-39, Schlesinger Library, Radcliffe Institute, Harvard University.

Wood, M. 2007. "'Commanding Beauty' and 'Gentle Charm': American Women and Gender in the Early Twentieth Century Foreign Service," *Diplomatic History* 31(3): 505–530.

3 From marriage bar towards gender equality

The experience of women in Ireland's Department of Foreign Affairs 1970–2000

Anne Barrington

Introduction

In 2016, Ireland was ranked in sixth place in the World Economic Forum (WEF) Global Gender Index in terms of its nationwide gender equality. As a country, Ireland came relatively late to the table with tackling gender equality, starting from a lower base than many of its peers in Europe, and although it took some considerable time for the gender equality agenda to take hold, it is now, according to the WEF Index, seen as a leader in the field. However, despite this leadership, Ireland still faces significant challenges in addressing inequalities in political and diplomatic leadership. Thus, despite Ireland's high ranking, there remains much work to be done.

The foreign service of a country should be representative of the country it serves, not just for the sake of it, but because diversity in decision making leads to better outcomes. However, even today, in 2017, there has never been a woman Secretary General in the Department of Foreign Affairs in Ireland. Furthermore, no woman has served as Head of Mission in key cities such as London, Ottawa, Canberra, Moscow, Rome, Berlin, Pretoria, or Brasilia. Only one woman Ambassador has served in the following posts: Washington, the Permanent Missions to the United Nations in New York and the European Union (and the same woman in all of these three posts), Warsaw, Beijing, Cairo, New Delhi, The Hague, and Tokyo.[1] Furthermore, currently, there is only one permanent headquarters-based women members of the Management Board, the managing body of the Department. Therefore, if a foreign service should be representative of the country it represents then it is clear that the Irish Foreign Service has some road to travel.

This book aims to analyse women's roles and impact in diplomacy, historically and in the present day. It is an attempt to rewrite the narrative of diplomacy, which has traditionally focused solely on male actors, by focusing on the women who have been integral to the diplomatic relations, international institutions, and foreign services across the world. As a contribution, this chapter focuses on the experiences of women diplomats who entered the Department (Ministry) of Foreign Affairs in Ireland from 1970 to the year 2000, both at the headquarter level and while serving abroad. It aims to illuminate the different barriers and challenges they faced during this period, identify where progress has been made, and highlight potential routes of further development towards ensuring gender equality in the Irish Foreign Service. The Irish case provides a highly interesting case study for analysis, as there are still women working in the system, or recently retired, who were junior diplomats before the issue of gender inequality in the service was even acknowledged, let alone addressed.

An examination of the experiences of women diplomatic officers who entered and worked in the Department of Foreign Affairs during the period between 1970 and 2000, the content of this chapter is derived from a series of answers to an in-depth questionnaire conducted by the author. It is divided in five distinct, but interlocking, sections. First, the chapter sets out the methodology used at the core of this discussion. The second section addresses the importance of gender equality in the foreign service as whole. The third section reviews the historical and constitutional context in which the Irish diplomatic service has operated, and a number different economic, social, and political influences are discussed. The fourth section, which is placed at the core of the chapter, weaves together the responses of survey participants into a narrative which seeks to illustrate their experiences of recruitment and early careers, sexism, the challenges of, and to, family life, and their perception of progress in the Department. Before concluding, the fifth and final section looks at recent measures taken by the Department of Foreign Affairs to address gender equality issues.

Methodology

With the aim of understanding the experiences of women diplomats over their careers from their recruitment to the year 2000, and to identify the gender issues that affected them and their peers through their working life, the author first identified a pool of women diplomats who were recruited during or before 1985, and who reached Counsellor grade or above, i.e. senior management within the Department of Foreign Affairs. Acknowledging that a number of women recruited during this time did not reach these grades, and their answers could significantly differ from those who were promoted, the responses were limited to those who had received the opportunities for promotion.

Due to the scattered geographical locations of the respondents identified, in four continents and spanning a variety of time zones, a written questionnaire was used. The target group consisted of twenty women. Each were sent written questionnaires of which eight (or 40 per cent) responded. The women who responded were recruited into the Department of Foreign Affairs between 1970 and 1979. By 2015 they had each served between eleven and thirty-two years at head quarter level and between four and twenty-eight years abroad. Four left the Department on secondment or career break, for periods ranging from two to seven years.[2] The earliest retirement was in 2008 and the latest is likely to be in 2021.

A draft of the chapter was circulated to all respondents to ensure that they were content that their views were adequately represented and their anonymity was protected. A small focus group consisting of three officers in headquarters also agreed to act as advisors on the questionnaire and on the text of the draft chapter and offered critical and constructive advice.[3]

Before proceeding, a short introduction to Ireland's civil and diplomatic service may be useful. In the period under review, diplomats were recruited through an open competition for university honours level graduates administered through the independent Civil Service Commission. Career progression was, and is, advanced from the recruitment grade of Third Secretary to First Secretary, Counsellor, Assistant Secretary (or Ambassador) grades and finally to Secretary General. The Third Secretary grade is considered to be junior management; the First Secretary grade is middle management and the Counsellor and Assistant Secretary and above grades are senior management positions. In the period from 1970 after recruitment, the promotion system moved progressively from one of appointment to a higher grade on the basis of seniority to a competitive system based on competencies.

From marriage bar to the eighth amendment: understanding gender equality in Ireland

Understanding the experiences of Irish women diplomatic officers in the period between 1970 and 2000 working in the Department of Foreign Affairs first necessitates addressing the historical and constitutional context in which these women began their careers in the Department.

The women who joined the Department of Foreign Affairs in the years prior to 1985 had grown up in the 1940s, 50s and 60s. Ireland had achieved its independence in 1922, albeit with a border partitioning the two parts of the island with six northern counties remaining in the UK. Dealing with the implications of this partition would have significant implications for the Department of Foreign Affairs from the late 1960s on (Ferriter 2004: 385–386). Nonetheless, in terms of its foreign policy, the fledgling state emerged as an independent voice on the international stage advocating for a rule based international order and the peaceful settlement of disputes (Keown 2016).

The decades following independence were challenging, characterised by an inward-looking and protectionist economic philosophy that clearly did not work as emigration continued apace and levels of poverty remained stubbornly high (Lee 1989). In addition, the conservative influence of the Catholic Church remained strong and its thinking had a profound influence on social and political thought especially in the education and health areas (Foster 1988: 569–582). While economic policy changed radically from the late 1950s, with Ireland joining the EEC in 1973, the dominant influence of Catholic social and moral thinking remained until the 1990s and beyond (Ferriter 2004: 716–742).

An important outcome of this conservative mind set was that even as late as 1970, Irish women had to resign their public service post, on marriage, including from the Department of Foreign Affairs as well as from key private sector employers such as banks and insurance companies. The bar on public sector employment post marriage was introduced in 1932, ten years after independence, and was lifted only in 1973 after Ireland entered the European Economic Community (EEC). At the time a woman did not receive the same pay as a man, could not sit on a jury, buy contraceptives or choose her own official place of residence. Partly due to external pressure from Europe, and partly due to internal groups demanding change, a series of legislative reforms concerning employment was adopted in the 1970s. These legislative measures included the Employment of Married Women Act (1973) which abolished the law requiring women to resign from public service jobs on marriage; the Equal Pay Act (1974) requiring equal pay for equal work and work of equal value; and the Employment Equality Acts (1977). Suffice to say that the women who joined and worked in the Department of Foreign Affairs in the period 1970 to 2000 fared better than their predecessors. Nonetheless, they were working before there was legislation barring sexual harassment, before the move to equality of opportunity and equal treatment, and before there was legislation recognising the need to reconcile work and family life.

As some aspects of Irish society became more liberal, especially in the economic sphere, there was a reactionary response from more conservative elements, which manifested itself in social and moral arenas such as abortion and divorce. As one of the most contested social issues in many countries during the twentieth century, the issue of abortion and the role of the state in providing or regulating services placed Ireland at the centre of the debate. Abortion has been illegal in Ireland since the mid-nineteenth century, and following the successful lobbying of conservative forces in 1983, the Irish Constitution includes an amendment, which prevents future legislators ruling in favour of abortion. This amendment, the eighth amendment to the Irish Constitution, which recognises the right to life of the unborn, was adopted by popular referendum with 67 per cent of the vote in favour, and purported to ban abortion in Ireland forever.

Since its adoption the eighth amendment has been widely debated and many attempts have been made to reframe its legal interpretation. In 1992, the Supreme Court in the X case interpreted the amendment to allow abortion in cases where the mother is deemed at risk of suicide. However, a subsequent referendum held shortly afterwards, on excluding suicide as reason for a legal abortion, was defeated. Other attempts to amend the Irish Constitution on social and moral issues include the 1986 proposal to amend the Constitution to legalise divorce which was defeated by referendum, taking another nine years until the decision was overturned by a second referendum in 1995, access to contraception, and the decriminalisation of homosexuality which brought Ireland before the European Court of Justice.

Despite their personal views on these issues, issues which fundamentally impact the lives and rights of women living in Ireland, diplomats abroad have had to defend the position of the Government and deal with the international fallout. This fallout included adverse international media attention and demonstrations outside of, and petitions to, missions. In this atmosphere, where issues as fundamental as abortion and divorce were being contested on a daily basis, it may not be surprising that the issue of gender equality in the Department of Foreign Affairs, or, indeed in the public service more generally, was not as high on the agenda as it might, or should, have been.

Where were the women?

The exclusion of women when married from public sector employment until 1973 meant that there were, until then, very few women in the diplomatic service. As pointed out by Kennedy (2002) '... the marriage bar had the effect of preventing these women from attaining more than one promotion. The tendency was to remain with the department for three years, rise one grade and then leave'. As a result, by 1970 there were only seven women in the diplomatic stream. The number of women grew in the 1970s due to the expansion of the Department to cope with EEC membership. By 1973 there were sixteen women and by 1974 that number grew to twenty-seven.

In addition, after 1973 and during the period under review there remained a number of incentives for women to leave the civil service in Ireland. One of these was the 'marriage gratuity'. This gratuity entitled women serving in the civil service from 1 February 1974 onwards to one month's pay for each year served (to a maximum of twelve months) if she resigned on, shortly before, or within two years of marriage. The ostensible reason for the gratuity was to compensate for lost pension entitlements but it also acted as a cash incentive for married women to quit their employment. In the period under review the marriage gratuity was not considered to be discrimination based on sex (Equality Tribunal 1999) though the 1986 High Court reasoning in its judgement on this issue was queried (Curtin 1989: 133–135; Bolger and Kimber 2000: 127–128).

Other disincentives for married women staying in the labour force were the married rate of pay and the taxation system. Prior to the enactment of the Employment Equality Act 1977, married men enjoyed a higher rate of pay than that which applied to women and to single men. This was phased out and a common rate of pay applied as from 1 March 1978. In addition, until 1980 a married women's income was taxed with her husband's. From then couples could decide to be taxed individually or jointly but many couples continued to have their incomes taxed jointly, which only served to act as a disincentive for secondary earners (usually the wife) (O'Donoghue 2003). As a result, although the marriage bar was lifted there still remained other disincentives for women to remain in work. It is possible that the pool of women for this survey in the diplomatic grades in the Department of Foreign Affairs could have been somewhat larger if these added disincentives had not existed.

With the exclusion of women through the marriage bar only two women were serving abroad in the diplomatic grades in Department of Foreign Affairs in 1970. One of these women, Mary Tinney, became the first Irish woman career Ambassador in 1973. Previously there had been one woman appointed as Head of Mission, Josephine McNeill, widow of the second last Governor General of the Free State who became a politically appointed Minister to The Hague in

1949. The second one was Carmel Heaney, who was Acting Consul General in Boston. In headquarters the most senior woman was Sheila Murphy who became an Assistant Secretary in 1962 prior to her retirement in 1964 – the first woman ever to reach that rank. Máire MacEntee was a Counsellor at the time of her retirement, on marriage, in 1962. It is the case, therefore, that the recruits from the 1970s on had few role models to follow.

Recent literature has highlighted the lack of role models for women as a key demotivating factor in career advancement (Bohnet 2016: 201–219; Slaughter 2015: 172). In most institutions in Ireland and elsewhere during the period, portraits and images of those working in public service adorning the walls of government buildings, in literature, or in the media inevitably depicted men. The lack of role models and the slow progress of the gender equality agenda in Ireland provides some insight into the barriers, both visible and invisible, which faced the recruits to the Department of Foreign Affairs from the 1970s on. However, things were changing: Mary Robinson was elected in 1990 by popular vote for a seven year term as President – a transformative moment for Ireland. Now, for the first time, the most senior position in the country was held by a woman, a feminist and by someone who believed in the importance of building strong relationships with the international community. As President, Robinson pushed the boundaries of her office to focus the world's attention on the marginalised and the need for the world's institutions to work for peace, freedom from hunger, the rule of law, and gender equality. Moreover, every Irish Embassy around the world had a picture of the President hanging in a prominent place. The first woman President of Ireland became a strong role model for many women in Ireland, including diplomats.

The issues arising from the 1922 partitioning of Ireland remerged in the form of a civil rights movement in Northern Ireland in the 1960s. From the late 1960s, when matters descended into violence, until the late 1990s developments between Britain and Ireland, between North and South on the island of Ireland and within Northern Ireland dominated the political landscape of the country and, to a very significant degree, the Department of Foreign Affairs. Analysing the staff lists for those decades, the Anglo-Irish Division of the Department displayed a remarkably male orientation at diplomatic level. At the same time, working within that division appeared to be the fast-track to promotion and the most high profile and career-enhancing posts were seen to be those dealing with Anglo-Irish matters.

Thus, the women who were recruited into the Irish diplomatic service in the 70s and early 80s were employed in a formative period for gender equality when the legal framework for gender equality was still being put in place. They were facing the reality of dealing with an institution that had been largely populated by men and where all but a very small number of senior posts were held by men.

Discussion and analysis

Five distinct categories of issues and challenges emerged from the survey responses: (1) Recruitment and Career Development; (2) Work Environment;

(3) Networks and Building Relationships; (4) Personal Life and (5) Departmental Progress in ensuring Gender Equality.

Most significantly, respondents identified that they experienced additional issues, challenges, and barriers in the workplace in comparison to their male colleagues including access and opportunity for career development promotion, and experiences of sexism and discriminatory practices in their work environment. The survey responses also indicated that, as women, the respondents felt they were inherently excluded from social and professional networks, which were dominated by their male colleagues. Interestingly, the majority of respondents noted that in response to this exclusion they formed their own female support networks with their female colleagues, especially during their postings overseas. Finally, most respondents found that their careers were to a greater or lesser degree shaped by their personal and family lives, specifically their experience being pregnant or as mothers in a male-dominated work place.

This section weaves together the responses of survey participants to construct a historical narrative of the experiences of women Irish diplomats between 1970 and 2000. It is important to note that not all of the issues highlighted in this chapter affected every respondent surveyed nor every woman working in the Irish Foreign Service. Instead, the discussion below aims to provide a snapshot into the issues and challenges experienced by a small number of Irish female diplomats during the period under scrutiny.

Recruitment and career development

Despite an effort to improve gender parity in the recruitment of diplomatic staff in the Department during the period under analysis, respondents found that they faced a number of different issues in the recruitment process, and that there were a distinct lack of career development opportunities for female diplomats in comparison to male colleagues.

Discussing their experiences being recruited into the Irish Foreign Service and their opportunities for promotion and career development, respondents felt that, although the recruitment process itself was fair and open to men and women, they experienced additional challenges to their male colleagues within the interview and recruitment process. For example, a number of respondents identified that their initial and final interview panels were made up entirely of men, and one respondent noted that she 'had problems with recruitment and HR management', that her 'first meetings with the deputy head of HR was very off-putting and inappropriate comments were made about issues which could affect a female officer'.

On entering the Department respondents commented that there were no institutional mechanisms in place to ensure gender equality and fair treatment, and another said that the structures were archaic and male oriented. There was a general consensus also among respondents in their early years that certain posts were not available to women: the Holy See, Saudi Arabia, Japan, and Africa were mentioned as places that no woman was sent to. One respondent pointed to a tendency to place women officers in human resources and administrative roles, to the fact that no woman has, to this day, been appointed Political Director, and the lack of women in high level posts at HQ and abroad. She noted: 'the Director-Generals in policy divisions are in high visibility posts, therefore making it easier for the holders of these posts to be recognised and appointed to senior Heads of Mission roles particularly at the official/political interface'. However, one respondent did note that she:

> had no reason to believe that women diplomatic officers were treated differently from men in terms of placement or mobility at any stage of my career. I was conscious, in this connection, that the female representation at graduate level in the Department of Foreign Affairs seemed relatively high by comparison with that in other Government Departments.

In reference to their opportunities for career development and promotion, respondents overwhelmingly identified that a number of the issues and challenges they faced were the result of discriminatory practices towards women in the civil service workplace, and specifically the Foreign Service at the time. One respondent recalled her experience of being the first married woman to be offered a posting abroad and how before her departure when she applied for the higher married officer allowance there was consternation. The Department consulted the Department of Finance on whether the regulation referring to 'married officer' covered a woman married officer. The matter was satisfactorily solved, eventually. At the same time her husband, who worked in another government department was the first married man to apply for a career break – which was granted only with the intervention of the Minister for Finance – a reminder that gender discrimination and gender stereotyping affects men too.

Another respondent recalled an incident concerning a post in the US in the early 1980s. Rumours circulated that a member of the Management Advisory Committee (now Management Board) had said that a women would not be appointed to the post. She and a colleague asked for a meeting with the then Secretary (General) of the Department. They expected him to confirm that all posts were available to all officers. He did not do this but expressed the view that Irish Americans would find a male officer more acceptable.

During her experience as desk officer for peacekeeping in Lebanon, a respondent also recalled being given vague excuses as to why she could not go on a troop rotation exercise as all her male predecessors had done. It seemed that the reason eventually given was a lack of sleeping and toilet facilities for women. The outcome was that she did not get to travel and gain first-hand experience as her male colleagues had done. The Department did not stand up for the principle of equal treatment. Another respondent recalled an experience while posted overseas. As a practice, the host government invited Embassies to send observers to a multilateral military manoeuvre. As the responsible officer she expected to be nominated. However, 'the Ambassador decided that it would not be suitable for a woman "to be climbing in and out of tanks" and he nominated the male Third Secretary instead. I protested, but he remained firm.'

Respondents also identified that there was a distinct lack of training and self-development opportunities available to women. Furthermore, one respondent said that all she ever had in nearly forty years in the Department was a few French classes at the weekends and a pre-retirement course. A lack of transparency in the way training was allocated in the early years was also an issue. Whether there was any gender discrimination in the allocation of training opportunities remains an open question, though the blockage to females going on UN Peacekeeping rotation exercises suggests that there was some at the very least.

With reference to whether there were any advantages of being a female diplomat in the Irish foreign service, respondents recalled that at each stage of their career they felt being a female was a disadvantage. One respondent noted that it was more of a disadvantage than advantage, but that being one of the first women Amassadors from Ireland brought a visibility that she would not otherwise have had. This was also reiterated by other respondents. One respondent felt that when there were strong disagreements being a woman 'allows you to come across more balanced and ... men will listen to you perhaps initially out of politeness but as you make your points you may be able to reach a compromise'. Another felt that 'in the early years, in terms of postings abroad and placements at HQ being female limited options', a point also observed earlier in this chapter.

Work environment

Respondents identified that working in a male-dominated work environment often meant they were at the receiving end of sexist behaviour and attitudes. By way of contextualisation, one respondent recalled:

> In the 1970s and 1980s it was not unusual to encounter occasional overt or implied sexist attitudes in Irish society as a whole, as the concept of 'political correctness' had not yet entered, let alone influenced, public consciousness. I remember that my friends and I used to refer occasionally to some men as MCPs (male chauvinist pigs), so we must have had cause. One learned to ignore the occasional sexist remarks from colleagues, or, as appropriate, treat them as a joke. Having said this, I had the impression that these attitudes had largely disappeared by the 1990s.

Another respondent agreed that attitudes had evolved but also mentioned the issue of unconscious bias that is still an issue across government departments, and the sexist treatment of women diplomats in the media.

The inherent nature of this sexism in the Department meant that respondents were often underestimated by their colleagues, superiors, and the public in their ability to do their job as a woman. One respondent spoke of an event in the 1970s where parliamentarians were called to the Embassy for a political briefing and exhibited shock to find that she was the official in charge of this area and that a male colleague was in charge of culture. Another respondent recalled an incident in the early 1980s when a politician at the end of a visit during a party grabbed her and put her on his knee as if this was an acceptable thing to do. She endured it until she managed to escape. At the time, she was junior officer and the more senior male colleagues did nothing to protect her from this inappropriate and sexist behaviour. Another officer recalled that while she worked in a public office she constantly took 'abuse from angry members of the public who wanted to see a "male manager" and not some woman!'. Moreover, a number of Irish-American all-male groups came in for criticism for their prejudiced treatment of women, including diplomats, from the 1970s and even to recent times. One group invited their wives so that an occasion could be adapted to host a woman diplomat. Towards the end of her posting, one respondent learned that men in the community had been so horrified about a woman being sent to represent Ireland, they decided to write to Dublin in protest.

These attitudes also meant that there were sometimes instances where, as women, respondents felt they could not raise an issue or an illness which was affecting them, in fear of being seen as weak and unable to do their job. One respondent said that she did not report or take action on an unspecified issue or an illness because she believed that this would impact on her career prospects. Another recalled being abroad as a delegate at a conference in the 1980s, having a miscarriage and carrying on as if nothing had happened. She said that it was not an environment in which she could excuse herself from work without feeling that she had let herself and the delegation down. One respondent said that she felt vulnerable when pregnant but thinks now that this was internal anxiety because she had previously worked with male colleagues who had negative attitudes to pregnant colleagues. This same respondent also said that she was self-conscious when going through the menopause but was not aware of negative actions or words from colleagues about this.

The sexism of their colleagues and superiors sometimes resulted in every aspect of the female diplomat's life being under scrutiny, including her appearance and her personal life. One respondent relayed an amusing story which was 'doing the rounds' when she entered the Department in the mid-1970s about a female officer, since deceased, who had some time before defied the Department's rule that women should not wear trousers. On entering wearing the offending piece of clothing, one day the officer was accosted by the then, rather retiring, Personnel Officer who reminded her of the rule to which she replied: 'Feel free to take them off me!'.

As a reminder that sexism affects men as well as women, one respondent recalled how on St Patrick's Day 1980, the visiting Minister and the male diplomats were invited to an Irish-American all-male event. The wife of the Head of Mission invited the wives and the woman diplomat to dinner. The husband of the female diplomat was invited to neither event.

Networks and building relationships

As a diplomat, building networks and trust with both internal and external colleagues is integral to developing strong diplomatic relationships. However, respondents found that, as women, they often experienced a number of barriers to forming these relationships and networks that their male colleagues did not face. Furthermore, forming social support networks is also essential in the workplace, but as women working in male-dominated work environments, respondents also found they were often excluded from forming social relationships with their male colleagues, and an issue mentioned frequently by a number of respondents was loneliness and isolation.

Respondents recalled that the Department 'from the 80s until more recent years, operated a cliquey, male-oriented model', where socialising centred around football and after work drinks. One respondent noted: 'the assumption that we all shared a forensic interest in GAA games/soccer/other male dominated sports felt exclusionary'.[4] This sentiment was echoed by another respondent who said: 'A small gripe, I would really prefer if some male colleagues, in a work context, could refrain from so many sports related comments especially regarding their favourite English soccer teams'. Respondents also found that, just by being women, they were excluded from invitations to watch sporting events on the assumption that they were not interested. A number of respondents mentioned the issue of drinks after work and their feelings of exclusion due to home responsibilities, or being the only woman in a male-only group or male-dominated drinking environment. One respondent recalled that, she avoided some social situations as she was being constantly asked why 'a nice girl like you' was not married.

Interestingly, with reference to professional networks, respondents identified that they responded to this exclusion by forming their own formal and/or informal networks with their female colleagues for solidarity and support – a way to make contacts and friends, and a useful place for exchanging views and information. Only one respondent indicated that she did not get involved in any networks, citing time pressure and because organised women's groups in Dublin and elsewhere tended to be business and professionally oriented and her transfers abroad made consistency in membership difficult to sustain. Citing that the creation of formal networks of support women diplomats appears to be relatively recent, respondents also mentioned the creation of the Department's Gender Equality Network as being a recent and welcomed development.

Personal life

Overwhelmingly, most respondents found that, in comparison to their male colleagues, their careers and experiences working in the Irish foreign service were significantly shaped by their personal and family lives, specifically their experiences of pregnancy or as mothers in the workplace. With reference to respondents' experiences of maternity leave, it should be noted that Irish diplomatic units both at HQ and abroad tend to be very small and a three-diplomat mission is considered on the larger side. So, losing an officer for up to six months, as it was then, was considered a significant burden and still is.

At the time, those who took maternity leave were entitled to the statutory minimum of twelve weeks and a maximum of sixteen weeks. After twelve weeks, leave was either unpaid or annual. There was no paternity or parental leave available at that time. In addition, there was a rule to the effect that pregnant women were required to take maternity leave four weeks before their due date, though with a doctor's certificate this could be reduced to two. The four-week rule was, to one respondent, absurd, as pregnancy is not an illness and the time after birth was much more important than the time before. The situation has now improved with women now entitled to twenty-six weeks maternity leave and up to sixteen weeks unpaid leave with only two weeks required to be taken prior to the confinement date. One respondent said that she was the first at Counsellor level to become pregnant so felt somewhat obliged to go back to work probably earlier than she would have wished, and another respondent reported having no option but to take a career break from her Embassy post as her husband was self-employed and she was due to be posted home.

In reference to announcing their pregnancy, respondents recalled that they were anxious and feared how their colleagues and superiors would respond to the news. One respondent recalled that that she was upset as she felt that this would be viewed with concern by male colleagues, and would impact on her career development within the Department 'due to the obvious lack of flexibility in structures and systems in the 80–90s'. She noted also that in her first days in her posting at a formal reception, a senior male colleague enquired critically in front of colleagues and work contacts whether she was pregnant. Summing up the ambiguity and her mixed feelings around pregnancy and maternity leave, one respondent recalled that she was delighted on the one hand but concerned on the other that motherhood would affect her career. Another spoke about her anxiety to perform to a high standard and avoid sick leave, but she felt she was lucky to have had excellent male managers who were very supportive of her pregnancy.

One respondent recalled:

> When pregnant with my second child I strongly considered resigning to become a 'stay at home mum' and was surprised when my family thought that this would not be a great idea. I spoke to my counsellor about my intention; he also thought it not a good idea. I then went to the Head of Personnel (male) who talked me into a career break. As the only basis on which I could formally get a career break was for me to seek study leave, I registered for a doctorate in Irish Foreign Policy 1945–1955 and found the Department very supportive of this project.

Respondents with families also found that they had to negotiate a number of different issues in reconciling their commitments to care for their families with their work commitments. Speaking to institutional issues, one respondent reported a lack of awareness, and no flexibility or working alternatives in the Department. An officer recorded how in the mid-1980s she took a posting as a mid-level diplomat with three children:

In the first week, there was a timetable clash between an EU coordination meeting and a meeting with the Principal of the school my children would be attending. I explained the situation and asked the Ambassador if he thought it [was] essential for me to attend the EU meeting. He said it was and, at considerable inconvenience, I managed to change the time of my meeting at the school.... As I got to know the Ambassador well I realised that he was one of the least sexist people one could meet. However, I also believe that his response that first week was based on the belief that he needed to ensure that this woman with three children and a husband ... must not think that she can drop everything when something arises at home. I have no doubt that a male officer would have been treated differently. Subsequently, I did not seek leave for any family related matter when my children were young. In many ways, as a woman I found that one had to always to prove oneself.

Respondents noted that at times they accepted appointments that did not require travel as this was not an option for them for various reasons, and some took career breaks and job-sharing arrangements for a period during their careers. A respondent who undertook job-sharing to balance family and work life recalled that she had to leave the Department in the late 1990s as she was not allowed to job share there. Subsequently, when the policy changed, she came back to the Department on a job sharing arrangement. Interestingly, a number of respondents indicated they thought it was easier, at times, for women with partners and children to advance in their careers, compared with the experience of single women, who may have lacked such familial and sometimes vital support when posted abroad, or indeed back home. Speaking to her experience balancing her family and work commitments, one respondent recalled that, when she returned from a career break in the early 1980s she was offered a first secretary post in Corporate Services Division, which was not a career enhancing move, but she accepted because she knew she could leave at 5.30 pm every evening and that suited her family circumstances at the time.

One respondent noted that she felt partners and children offer support in a career where there is a lot of change, but found it more difficult to reconcile family commitments and work commitments to maintain the type of posts that help to achieve a promotion: 'A partner and children offer support, stability and personal happiness. But issues surrounding mobility (for partners and children), and tensions surrounding long working hours of diplomatic life, act as constraints on career advancement'.

Department progress in ensuring gender equality

After recalling their own experiences serving in the Department, respondents commented on the ways in which the Department has made progress in terms of ensuring gender equality in the Irish Foreign Service, and the ways in which they think the Department can work towards making further progress.

During her time in the Department one respondent commented that: 'there is no doubt that the Department has become a vastly more comfortable place for women diplomats over the four decades of my career'. Another respondent recalled that the Department was changing with the times, albeit slowly, and another said that changes were supported and promoted mostly since 2012:

> during my time there, more women entered the Department. The end of the marriage bar, the introduction of free secondary education, university grants and eventually free university education, as well as the growth in possibilities for international travel, opened up the career possibilities for women in all walks of life, including in DFA. Equality of opportunity also meant that men and women were working together at all levels, both junior and senior.

However, respondents also noted that even now that many posts are open and filled by women, there are still a number of posts – incidentally posts which are considered the most important – which have never been filled by a woman.

Responding to what the Department could have done differently to ensure better gender equality at the time, one respondent said: 'while the Department could certainly have moved earlier to become a positive champion of gender equality, it was relatively progressive in light of circumstances of the time'. This was reiterated by another respondent who said:

> As regards the Department, I did not always consider that it was making the best use of its potential, but as I grew older I came to appreciate the constraints within which it operated. In particular, I accepted that the Department and we, its officers, were there to serve the country and the Government that the people in its wisdom elected ...

In contrast another respondent answered:

> I think that the Department could have tackled the gender imbalance issue at a much earlier stage. There was plenty of literature on the subject and a number of Irish state and private companies were blazing a trail. But there seemed to be a reluctance to acknowledge that the structures and processes of the Department required changing. This was true of the broader Civil Service generally. The outcomes in terms of gender imbalance in the Department of Foreign Affairs and Trade came to a head in the early 2000s when so few women were advancing to senior management grade. I regret that I was not more vocal at an earlier stage.

Finally, respondents identified the ways in which the Department could seek to ensure and improve gender equality in the Irish Foreign Service. These included: ensuring an open and transparent processes for all posts at home and abroad and adjustments made to ensure no gender imbalance; an improved human resources management to adapt and harness the potential and contribution of a talented and committed work force; and ensuring that there is sufficient staff on hand to cover for women on maternity or men on paternity leave. If supplying and caring for the next generation is a matter of the highest national importance then providing cover for that function should be factored into any personnel policy. In a small outfit, if one person takes nine months or more maternity leave this seriously impacts on the ability of any business unit to function. Maternity/paternity cover can be planned for and management structures need to tackle this as a real equality issue.

Respondents also spoke of the need to recognise the value and achievements of both male and female officers within the system, the need to provide unconscious bias training for all management staff, and the need for an effective and continuous feedback system for junior and mid ranking officers, including training of managers to deliver such guidance. Providing opportunities for group meetings between colleagues, male and female, to discuss issues that affect all officers was seen as another solution.

Recent developments

The issue of gender equality in the Department of Foreign Affairs came to notice in the early years of the new millennium. Despite an equal number of, or more, women being recruited into the Department, positions at the most senior levels remained stubbornly out of reach. The outcomes of promotion competitions for senior managers did not appear to reflect the gender balance of the inputs. At the same time, the Department had been promoting gender equality in theory and practice in its development programmes and in a human rights context, and receiving considerable praise for so doing.

The United Nations Conference on Women in 1975 was the first in the series of Women's Conferences that led the international community to set out the norms and practices on gender equality that ultimately shaped the inclusion of gender equality in the Millennium Development Goals in 2000. Issues addressed included: women in decision making, legal barriers facing women, human rights for women and the need for women's empowerment to address economic development. Transferring what was being done in the developing world into institutions closer to home seemed to make a lot of sense. The Department was also building up considerable expertise on gender equality in its development cooperation division.

As a result of these developments and the commitment of a number of officers, the Department of Foreign Affairs and Trade is now in the process of facing up to the challenge of addressing gender inequality in its diplomatic ranks. In 2011 under the leadership of the then Secretary General David Cooney, a Management Board Gender Equality Sub-Committee was established, co-chaired by two Management Board members, and with a wide participation of staff from all ranks and both genders. The Sub-Committee was tasked with identifying what needed to be done to change outcomes in the Department. Secretary General Niall Burgess, appointed in 2014, has continued to build momentum on the issue.

Steps already taken as a result of the Sub-Committee's work include keeping records of assignments to ensure no gender bias in the allocation of posts. At each posting round, for example, the Management Board has to certify that issues of gender were taken into account in posting assignments. In addition, unconscious bias is being addressed, and the Department has been advocating for gender equality to be attended to more widely in reform processes across the Irish civil service. Examples of the sorts of issues still being addressed by the Sub Committee include: developing a gender equality action plan to address issues such as providing adequate cover for maternity leave, enabling mentoring and coaching, appointing an equality officer, conducting exit interviews and keeping statistics on the gender breakdown of people leaving the Department.

The work that the Gender Equality Sub-Committee continues to do, together with the Gender Equality Network of the Department, has been critical in moving the gender equality agenda forward in the Department of Foreign Affairs, and the Department is now seen within the Irish civil service as a leader in this area.

Conclusion

Through analysing the historical experience of female diplomats working in the Irish Department of Foreign Affairs, this chapter has highlighted that there are additional pressures that women face while working in the foreign service beyond those faced by men, institutionally and socially. Through illuminating the internal culture of the Irish foreign service between 1970–2000, it has demonstrated that ensuring a gender equal foreign service does not only mean ensuring gender parity in appointments. Instead, there needs to be specific adjustments to ensure there is a comfortable, safe, and welcoming working environment for all staff members, regardless of their gender, and there are institutional mechanisms in place to ensure the equal opportunity and full participation and of all staff members in Department. This would include ensuring that posts in high profile and important cities are filled and refilled with women as well as men.

The survey on which this chapter is based was a relatively small one. It would be of interest to know if current diplomats in Ireland and elsewhere identify with the views of the respondents or if the issues have moved on. The ongoing work of the Department of Foreign Affairs and Trade to address the legacy issues of gender inequality would suggest that many of the issues remain the same. Further research could compare and contrast perceptions of gender equality in foreign ministries with a view to setting up a hierarchy of issues to be tackled.

Finally, the experiences of the women surveyed here should serve as a reminder that while diplomacy, like most professions, is gender neutral, the institutions in which diplomacy is practiced within were, and are, not. All public service institutions which espouse equality as a core value have to work hard over time to achieve that equality and then work to sustain it.

Notes

1 Anne Anderson (Washington, PMUN-New York, Permanent Mission to EU), Thelma Doran (Warsaw, Beijing), Isolde Moylan-McNally (Cairo), Margaret Hennessy (New Delhi), Mary Whelan (The Hague), and Anne Barrington (Tokyo).
2 A secondment is the temporary transfer of an official or worker to another position or employment.
3 Dr Michael Kennedy of the Royal Irish Academy and Carol Baxter and Deirdre Ní Néill of the Department of Justice and Equality were also most helpful during this process.
4 The Gaelic Athletic Association (GAA) is Ireland's largest sporting organisation and a world leader in amateur sports with over 500,000 members worldwide.

References

Bohnet, Iris. 2016. *What Works: Gender Equality by Design* (Cambridge, MA: The Belknap Press of Harvard).
Bolger, Marguerite and Kimber, Clíona. 2000. *Sex Discrimination Law* (Dublin: Round Hall).
Curtin, Deirdre. 1989. *Irish Employment Equality Law* (Dublin: Round Hall).
Equality Tribunal (Ireland). 1999. www.workplacerelations.ie/en/equality_tribunal_import/database-of-decisions/1999/ee-1999-26.pdf. Accessed 6 February 2017.
Ferriter, Diarmuid. 2004. *The Transformation of Ireland 1900–2000* (London: Profile Books Ltd).
Foster, Robert. 1988. *Modern Ireland 1600–1972* (London: Penguin Press).
Kennedy, Michael. 2002. '"It is a Disadvantage to be Represented by a Woman": The Experiences of Women in the Irish Diplomatic Service'. *Irish Studies in International Affairs* 13: 215–235.
Keown, Gerard. 2016. *First of the Small Nations* (Oxford: Oxford University Press).
Lee, Joseph. 1989. *Ireland 1912–1985* (Cambridge: Cambridge University Press).
O'Donoghue, Cathal. 2003. *Redistributive Forces of the Irish Tax-Benefit System* (Working Paper No. 0072) Department of Economics, National University of Ireland, Galway. https://aran.library.nuigalway.ie/xmlui/bitstream/handle/10379/1084/paper_0072.pdf?sequence=1. Accessed 20 November 2016.
Slaughter, Anne-Marie. 2015. *Unfinished Business* (London: Oneworld).
World Economic Forum Gender Equality Index 2016.

4 Women of the South

Engaging with the UN as a diplomatic manoeuvre

Devaki Jain[1]

Introduction

In recounting the history of the United Nations (UN) as a diplomatic entity, it is important to register the times, and purpose, which led to its inception. The two World Wars, 1914–1918 and 1939–1945, which dominated the international political stage of the twentieth century, had their epicentre firmly placed within the Northern hemisphere, and were waged between two powerful blocs of nations which aligned themselves decisively with the North. Both wars were the direct cause of catastrophic destruction and death to these regions and beyond, and led to the belief that all global actors now required, without delay, an institution, which would enable wars to be fought with words, not guns, and conflicts to be concluded within halls, not battlefields. Hence, the powers who reigned on the post-World War II stage, developed many initiatives, one of which was to build an international, democratic institution, which would allow people to negotiate rather than destruct.

However, the major players in these dialogues and reconstruction activities overlooked the fact that the belligerents of these wars not only were comprised almost entirely of Northern Hemisphere nations, but were actually colonisers themselves, who had enslaved countless countries in the Southern continent. In fact, the belligerents who had fought these wars did so using the labour and resources of the colonies in which they had ruled. It could be then argued that while the UN was created to be a democratic space, a space in which to resolve conflict and build a level playing field for all actors within, it did not quite carry the voice, backing, or legitimacy, to deal with the injustice and violence caused and perpetuated by the years of colonisation and destruction towards the nations of the South. Nations, which were also to enter this newly democratised, international space.

Recounting the history of the birth of the UN from a Southern lens, I argue in my book, *Women, Development and the UN: A Sixty-Year Quest for Equality and Justice*, that:

> writing history from a South perspective is a rewarding yet challenging task. The knowledge base – the identification of sources, the narration of history, especially as underpinned by ideas – is visibly Eurocentric. Global breezes,

defining moments in history, descriptions of the evolution of thought, intellectual paradigms, critical thinkers are attributed to the world, but that world's boundaries are West derived. Thus, the periodization of history is Eurocentric. For example, World War II and its aftermath – the defining events of the Northern Hemisphere that were, in fact, the impetus for the founding of the United Nations – were not the most important externalities for nations in the South. Slavery, including the use of indentured labor; economic plundering; the effacing of cultural and intellectual identities by the imperial powers were the strong forces that shaped the history of those nations. Mahatma Gandhi was more relevant to Indian recovery from colonization than Keynes. To the black people of South Africa, historical periods are defined in apartheid-regime terms, and Nelson Mandela's twenty-seven years in Robben Island on and off between 1952 to 1990 were the definitions of historical time. As such driving forces as Keynesian economics, the Marshall Plan, and new strands of development thought plotted a trajectory for the North to follow, the South heard a different rhythm of liberation, socialism, and exciting experiments with government. My efforts to redress the balance of history, however unsatisfactory and incomplete, have often meant the muting of conventional images of resounding 'success'.

(Jain 2005: 3)

Set firmly within this overarching framework, the central argument put forth in this chapter, is that while the UN and its early diplomatic manoeuvres set forth an agenda which enabled not only the resolution of international conflict and worked towards the crafting of human rights and international development goals for all, Northern countries continued to intellectually and physically lead much of the founding and decades which followed. This skewed distribution of power between the North and South[2] resulted in many Southern countries' initiatives in the post-World War II world being overlooked or dismissed. The dominant historical narrative concerning the beginning of the UN has also marginalised the role of these initiatives, not only in the respect to the women's movement, but also in relation to their position within the United Nations institution at large.

Starting with an exploration of the idea of Non-Aligned Movement (NAM) in the context in which it was born, this chapter recalls its basic, rather radical tenets – tenets that find resonance with the women's movement. The following section seeks to understand NAM as a space for women by recalling some of the historical NAM women's conferences and their contribution to the international agenda on women. Drawing on the work of the NAM, this chapter then progresses to a discussion of women's diplomatic manoeuvres within the United Nations as a whole, and how women of the South in particular sought to advocate for and advance an inclusive growth paradigm, which would take into account the historical and strategic potential of the women within Southern nations. The chapter concludes by sketching out some of the challenges and possible ways forward for the women's movements of the South and North, as they develop their tools and ideas for negotiating with new power clubs nationally, regionally, and internationally, and the continued generation of powerful unity-based ideas in pursuit of gender equality in every sphere.

Non-aligned movement (NAM)

NAM was a bold and somewhat impertinent formation, which challenged notions of expected behaviour by a 'motley' group of newly independent and 'young' nations. US writer Richard Wright, who was present at the 1955 Bandung Conference (attended by African and Asian states, and hosted by President Sukarno of Indonesia), when NAM aspirations were unfurled, had this to say about the meeting: 'The scorned, insulted, offended, dispossessed, in short, the destitute people of the human race were meeting.... That meeting of the rejected was in itself like bringing the western world to trial!' (cited in Quest n.d.). In 1955, as the USA and the USSR were busy carving up the world and creating blocs and puppet regimes, a group of intrepid leaders decided to refuse to align themselves with either superpower. The Cold War was not the sole or only critical issue on the agenda of the Non-Aligned Movement, however. Many Western countries were so preoccupied with the Cold War that they gave scant attention to other North–South issues that underlay much of the debate that concerned NAM (Grovogui 2003). A cursory glance at the history of NAM reveals that the basic elements that informed its approach to international issues included the right of its member countries to independent judgement, the struggle against imperialism and neo-colonialism, and moderation in relations with all major powers. Rather than a passive neutrality or isolationist policy of non-involvement in all conflicts, it was an assertion of agency on the part of Third World nations that was considered the hallmark of being 'sovereign' and 'independent'.

This attempt to forge a community of this sort was markedly different from the idea of a clan, a tribe, or even a nation – all of which were considered more 'natural'. Nor was it a regional entity marked by geographical boundaries, as is the European Union; or an open non-discriminating space that admitted practically all nations, like the more powerful United Nations. The grouping was formulated on clear political and ideological lines, and in this respect NAM was a pioneer. The demands of newly liberated countries for agency and voice in dealing with the mainstream are similar to those that women around the world have made at various times – that is, not to be treated as passive patients but to have their agency and its persistence recognised, even under circumstances of oppression, together with the roles that it plays in facilitating resistance. The idea of self-determination of those considered less capable and often incapable of making such decisions has informed feminist discourse and practice, as it has the NAM conferences and declarations. When India's Prime Minister Manmohan Singh said at the NAM conference in Havana, 'We account for over half of humanity ... yet we do not have commensurate voice in the international institutions of the world' (cited in Abraham 2005), he could very well have been speaking of the women of the world.[3]

The basic values on which NAM was premised were solidarity, justice, equality, and peace. A song that became popular in the late 1980s in Belgrade (where the first non-aligned summit was held in 1961, while Yugoslavia continued to play a key role in NAM) was an attempt to capture and popularise its spirit. One verse states:

> When they [the leaders of NAM] built the movement of the Non-Aligned
> In making us believe in the right things
> They gave us a song which the world sings
> Wisdom listens, violence is blind.
> The only promise is that of the Non-Aligned.
>
> (Gupta 1992: 64)

This Third World solidarity that NAM underlined appeared as early as 1964: 'at UNCTAD I, which was the biggest, the longest, and the most frustrating international conference, the developed countries were caught unawares by the unprecedented unity shown by the Group of 77' (Kumar 1983: 447–448). The conference passed unanimous resolutions by what some referred to as the '"sheer moral shock power" exercised by the developing countries' (Mehta 1981: 174–175). Even before this, in 1952, the US Secretary of State Dean Acheson had declared that the outstanding fact of the General Assembly was its dominance by the Arab–Asian bloc (Luck 1999: 107). By 1964, the non-aligned countries had succeeded in placing their economic problems forcefully on the international agenda. The women's movement too has time and again banded together across the usual divides to flag up one issue and move its agenda forward – right from the inception of the UN, when the small group of women who were present met together, although they came from different countries, were of varied backgrounds, and held a range of positions within and outside the official government delegations (Jain 2005).

Besides being a platform on which to hammer out a common cause, NAM has been a source of new ideas, of varied scope and intent. For example, the New International Economic Order (NIEO) challenged the economic arrangements that privileged the already privileged. The NAM-sponsored 'non-aligned news agency pool' (Ivacic 1986) aimed to counter the fact that Western media ignored large tracts of the world, or covered them only when some disaster struck or when Western interests were in some way affected. These ideas sprung from the needs, experiences, and politics of the South; and were attempts to correct some of the world's gross imbalances.

Similarly, women's knowledge has challenged mainstream assumptions, supposed facts, and most classificatory systems in every discipline – from questioning notions of what constitutes 'productive' and 'unproductive', to seemingly natural dichotomies of private and public, secure or insecure, and so on.

A space for women: tracing the journey of women and NAM

The establishment of NAM as a political entity held out much hope for many social movements. For example, it was the spirit of the Bandung Conference that was evoked by the Indonesian feminist Sukina Kusima when she visited Egypt in 1959 to promote a stronger bond between the women in Africa and Asia (Bier 2002). Pearl S. Buck, the Nobel laureate, publicly expressed her wish for the triumph of the 1955 Bandung Conference of non-aligned nations, arguing that it was valuable for the world and for women (Shaffer 1999: 164).

Non-alignment provides the ideological foundation for developing a paradigm of international interaction, which allows nations to work towards peace and prosperity in co-operation, while maintaining their national identity, spirit, and character – and it is these same values of equality, non-discrimination, and social justice that are the bedrock of the women's movement.

NAM affirmed that it clearly saw women's role in development as an international and political issue. In contrast to the conceptualisation of issues relating to women's status as social or cultural phenomena that predominated in other bodies in the early 1960s, its analysis of women in development was sharper and reflected a more complex understanding of the interconnection between trends in women's roles and status in their societies and the nature and pattern of development processes, including the latter's dependence on international, economic, and political relations.

The Non-Aligned Movement's idea of the path to women's equality departed from UN strategies. The UN system in the 1980s saw 'women's status' largely as a social development issue and did not strongly connect it to the larger context of international development. Within the UN, women were still viewed as resources whose potential could be tapped. But NAM gatherings offered a space where the women from former colonies could reassert the standpoint that they were active agents in their nations, contributors to their country's progress, and not mere consumers of social services.

NAM also brought early news about the impact of global economic trends on women. The 1981 Ministerial Conference in New Delhi reported the impact of harmful practices of multinational corporations on women in both developing and developed countries: 'By exploiting the cheap labour force multinational companies find new sources of extra profits in developing countries. At the same time, they fire workers and lower the wage of female workers in the developing countries' (Pravlic and Hamelink 1985). Modern technology was not serving women workers well, in the NAM's analysis. It saw the self-reliance model as the antidote: 'What is particularly important to understand is that [the] self-reliant development pattern has the welfare of the people and not growth of GDP as its principal objective' (Ibid.). The NAM's model of development was to draw policy from the reality on the ground and change policies when those realities changed. The ideal that it represented was a co-operative sharing of resources between men and women, community members, and states.

The President of the 38th General Assembly in July 1984, Jorge Illueca of Panama, told the meeting that the Movement and the policy of non-alignment was 'the most dynamic and constructive force to promote the objectives of the Charter of the United Nations, as the only valid formula for achieving a new world order based on equality, justice and peace' (UN Chronicle 1984). The contribution made by NAM to the UN therefore was to strengthen it and to explore it as a space that could reflect the concerns of the Third World, rather than one entirely dominated by the powerful nations. The manner in which NAM members grouped together to use the UN space underlines their ability to strategise and band together, as well as their faith in the UN as an organisation. This resonates with what the women's movement has done. Similarly, the self-identity as a 'third bloc' constituted an important unifying strategy for these nations and enabled them to resist to some degree the UN's idea of all nations being equal – in that this was a way of going beyond formal equality to a more substantive type of equality. The achievement of women's equality is an elusive goal, since too often the ideal of realising women's rights is tied to formal and legalistic declarations about treating men and women alike.

NAM also proved to be an exciting learning ground. The NAM and Afro-Asian People's Society Movement had promoted numerous related conferences, such as the Afro-Asian Youth Movement and the Afro-Asian Writers' Movement and educational exchanges, and the July 1962 Cairo Economic Conference (Bier 2002). The resulting exchanges and networks were part of what made possible the sorts of imagining that overflowed the boundaries of the nation-state. Women participated in these conferences and meetings and thus deepened their knowledge of international relations and honed their negotiating skills and abilities. Similarly, NAM provides experience for new states and states that are not very strong and also offers a protective umbrella for dealing with other multilateral bodies such as the UN. NAM became a space for expressing an 'imagined community of third world oppositional struggles.... [that] women with divergent histories and social locations have woven together by the political threads of opposition to forms of domination that are not only pervasive but systematic' (Bier 2002). Therefore, what bound the Women of the South together was not merely a common suffering but also a struggle for similar political ends.

The women's movement of the South and North: a united cause

As illustrated with the construction and work of NAM, the women's movement of the post WWII period and the United Nations' early discussions which centred around the rights and struggles of women did not quite resonate with these 'divisions'. Women and the laws related to their struggles were to some extent politically neutral and went on as a separate movement towards justice. In order to influence public policy in favour of equal opportunities, a network of relationships, referred to as the 'Velvet Triangle', was initiated between the interest groups. Here, 'Velvet' refers to the fact that all the players are women in a predominantly male environment. The 'Triangle' refers to the actors who come respectively from the organisations of the state, of civil societies and the universities and consultancies (Woodward 2003).[4] 'Femocrats', that is, women who were UN officials, women who came to the UN as representative of Women's movements from the Northern countries and women who came as representatives from the Southern countries worked together towards gender justice.

However, many of the women who emerged from their freedom movements in the former colonies became prominent leaders of social and economic struggles and also established national women's organisations.[5] This phenomenon, women's emergence as leaders, as part of the process and outcome of the freedom struggles, was a characteristic of many nations in continents of the South in the post-colonial era, and there did not exist many counterparts in the Northern countries. Thus, from 1975–1985, it is clear that it was women from Southern countries – who in some sense were already politicised (i.e. experienced in negotiating with the formal political processes) – who generated some of the radical covenants and proposals for justice and equality for women.

These Southern female leaders contributed ideas on agendas and language at crucial moments.[6] For example, at the birth of the UN, during the Conference to draft the UN Charter (1945), it was a woman from the Dominican Republic, Minerva Bernardino, one of the signatories, who, with her feminist sisters, ensured that the document read 'equal rights among men and women' instead of 'equal rights among men'. Similarly, Hansa Mehta, an Indian woman, a member of the UN Commission on the Status of Women involved in drafting the Universal Declaration of Human Rights in 1948, protested at the use of gender-opaque language. 'That would never do,' she said. '"All men" might be interpreted to exclude women' (Jain 2005: 20). Mehta argued with Eleanor Roosevelt at the unthinking exclusion of women in the original draft. Eleanor Roosevelt disagreed. She came from a long tradition of women's activism in the United States that based its actions on women's special needs as workers. She supported gender inclusive language, but she tried to bridge the gap between 'difference' feminism and 'equality' feminism with the statement that she 'wished to make it clear that equality did not mean identical treatment of men and women in all matters; there were certain cases, as for example the case of maternity benefits, where different treatment was essential' (Jain 2005: 20).[7] She argued that the women of the United States had never felt they were left out of the Declaration of Independence because it said 'all men'. However, she eventually agreed with the other women who felt strongly on this point – notably, most came from developing countries. In total, thirty-two countries voted in favour of the change; only two voted against it and three abstained. The language was changed from 'all men' to 'all human beings' (Jain 2005: 20).

With that said, as women began to participate in the increasing activities of the UN, both at the centre and through its specialised agencies, the difference in context and aspirations between South and North began to show itself. For instance, in the preparations for the UN Second World Conference on Women held in Copenhagen in 1980, women from the South began to see the 'differences' in perspectives between feminists from the North and South. There was a sense of discomfort, about how we – women from the former colonies and the developing nations – were profiled, and what we were hearing as the approach to our countries' needs. There was also an invisible claim of political superiority and we were viewed as poor and illiterate, trapped in archaic cultures and conventions, in desperate need of rescue from the modern system. Additionally, there was a certain inequality in the descriptions, since from the perspective of women from the South, Northern women seemed to be economically marginalised and socially trivialised in their own societies.

As a collective response, a group of women of the South formed a Third World network called Development Alternatives with Women in the New Era (DAWN) in 1984.[8] It destabilised the Northern moorings of the feminist movement and gave voice to Southern feminist perspectives. DAWN was able to carry out negotiations with the UN as their emphasis on women's equality and justice had a tone of universality that struck a chord with all women across the barriers of race and location. However, liberation from the economic exploitation and domination by the North still seemed a distant dream for the former colonies of the South.

In order to mould a separate economic identity of the South, Julius Nyerere set up a commission called the South Commission (1985) and invited three women to join as members, of whom two were founders of DAWN. Unlike DAWN, the South Commission worked independently from the UN as their views on economic and political development strongly differed from the Anglo-Saxon countries that dominated the UN ideology (South Commission 1990). At the diplomatic level it can be argued that the three women members were not able to make a substantive impact on the analysis, ideas, and recommendations of the South Commission. This was in part because most of the establishment members were conventional bureaucrats or retired politicians who had no exposure to the Women's Movement in that country. The purpose of the South Commission, however, was not to influence the UN, but to transform the economic policies of the Southern countries which it represented and to create a club of solidarity amongst its members.

The diplomatic manoeuvres of women in the United Nations

One of the volumes (Emmerji, Jolly, and Weiss 2001) on the intellectual history of the United Nations suggests that the UN is 'a marketplace for ideas' (Emmerji, Jolly, and Weiss 2001: 10). This description captures the role it played for the women's movements too. Activities of the entire UN family – from the central structure, through the specialised agencies, to its country and regional offices – offered spaces for women from diverse parts of the world to share their experiences, as well as learn from each other. The excitement of finding extraordinary similarities of gendered living, the forging of bonds that never broke, arguing, negotiating, merging identities, flowed into that crucial term, *power*. A new constituency called 'women' was created, as was the entry of a powerfully endowed idea called 'women' in UN thought (Jain and Chacko

2008). Women's participation in the politics of development influenced both the politics of the UN and the understanding of development within that body.

In its initial decades – the 50s and 60s, the United Nations not only set the stage for international covenants to protect nations from the wars and injustices that had preceded it, but, as mentioned earlier, also became a marketplace for the exchange of knowledge and the building up of transformatory ideas.[9] Women leaders from various countries formed themselves into groups and not only generated new covenants but also new agencies to carry forward the UN's commitment to equality, justice, and peace. The institutional architecture for women's advancement at the UN has also been continuously changing. Its components initially included the Commission on the Status of Women, 1946 (CSW),[10] United Nations Development Fund for Women, 1976 (UNIFEM),[11] International Research and Training Institute for the Advancement of Women, 1979 (INSTRAW),[12] the Convention on the Elimination of All Forms of Discrimination Against Women, 1982 (CEDAW),[13] and the Division for Advancement of Women (DAW).[14] Some of these structures have changed and many new components have been added in the last 70 plus years. These were the institutions and laws enabling women, as they sought to bring their intellectual contributions about women and development into the mainstream of the world body. Over time, women emphasised or de-emphasised various components of this architecture, as needs and circumstances demanded.

The UN Decade for Women, 1975–1985

It is difficult to find words to describe the experience of the UN Decade for Women, 1975–1985, for women around the world. The Decade was life-changing for many, and a watermark in public policies and programs that would transform gender relations everywhere – despite the fact that most people may not be aware of the context in which these changes took place: from laws against discrimination against women to changes in men's role in domestic life and increasing responsibility for housework and childcare, from the introduction of Women's Studies and other programs at universities to the increase in women's access to a range of academic and professional fields previously closed to them. The Decade linked academics and researchers, bureaucrats and activists in processes of policy-making that would change women's lives in countries across continents of the South and the industrialised North. In the academy, it produced new understandings, knowledge, and theories that challenged conventional wisdom.

The Decade was framed by the convening of three UN World Conferences on Women: the first in Mexico City (1975),[15] the second (mid-decade) in Copenhagen (1980), and the third in Nairobi (1985). The impact of the Decade on Women in the South may be traced through the emergence of Southern women's voices as a powerful force, reflected in the exponential increase in the numbers of Southern participants representing governments and women's organisations. At the Mexico City conference, Southern governments first challenged US hegemony by including on the agenda calls for a New International Economic Order,

1970 (NIEO)[16] and by presenting a political Declaration linking racism and Zionism.[17] At the Copenhagen conference, the Secretary-General, Ambassador Lucille Mair of Jamaica, permitted the inclusion of the NIEO and the plight of Palestinian women on the agenda. The culmination of this growth in strength was most apparent at the NGO Forum and Conference in Nairobi in 1985. Nita Barrow of Barbados, a well-known leader in international circles,[18] headed the NGO Forum, while Gertrude Mongella of Tanzania, the Secretary-General, presided over the governmental Conference. Ms Mongella was the assistant Secretary-General for the Division of Advancement of Women during the Fourth UN World Conference in Beijing 1995. The overwhelming majority of participants at both events were women from the Southern continents. Thousands of Kenyan women walked for miles from towns and villages across the country to Nairobi to participate in the NGO Forum.

UN efforts in collaboration with the women's movement led to the emergence of various regional and subjective identities in the form of women's networks.[19] These networks acted as voices outside the UN, providing knowledge and collective power to transact with their states and other power clubs for change. The Velvet Triangle also conducted these strategic operations and could be deemed to be a sub sect of diplomatic engagement.

Knowledge as a tool of diplomacy

Feminist scholarship, especially that of socialist feminists on political economy, history, and anthropology played an important role in heightening awareness of the situation of women around the world. Ester Boserup's (Boserup 1970) pathbreaking book *Woman's Role in Economic Development*, drew attention to the vital role of women in agriculture. There was also the significant work of Marxist and socialist feminists on political economy, history, sociology, and anthropology, whose research and writings sought to bring a gender perspective to various fields, and laid the basis for ground-breaking work on reproduction and the care economy.[20] Women Studies centres within and outside universities in both the North and South were bringing women together to reflect on their particular views on various issues. For example, the Indian Association of Women Studies, (Founded 1982, IAWS)[21] and the International Association for Feminist Economics, (Founded 1992, IAFFE)[22] have regular gatherings annually and bring to light facts and analysis as well as new ideas. Civil society organisations, such as Women in Informal Employment: Globalizing and Organizing, (Founded 1997, WEIGO), also bring out knowledge through the field.[23] Scholars in universities challenge old theories including religion, as was done at the Harvard Divinity school (Eck and Jain 1986), giving opportunity for women from different religions to challenge stereotyping of women including religion (Jain 1986), unpacking theories (Jain 2012), challenging given knowledge and rewriting histories (Jain and Rajput 2003).

UN agencies such as the International Labour Organization (ILO)[24] and Food and Agriculture Organization (FAO)[25] were also collecting and analysing data on women's role in economic development. A regional conference on 'Women in the Labour Force in Latin America', was held at the Instituto Universitario de Pesquisas do Rio de Janeiro (IUPERJ),[26] Brazil in 1980 which brought together feminist demographers and other scholars. Its purpose was to improve the understanding, and collection and analysis of data on women's role in the labour force, but it was located within the broader political economy of patriarchy and the sexual division of labour. It was a turning point in building intercontinental connections. The New York-based donor agency encouraged the Latin Americans to invite one representative each from Africa and Asia – they were Marie Angelique Savane (Senegal), President of the Association of African Women for Research and Development (AAWORD, 1977), the first pan-African association of women, and Devaki Jain (India), Director of the Institute of Social Studies Trust (ISST),[27] a women's research centre based in Bangalore. This led to the convening of similar ILO-funded meetings in Asia and Africa. Thus women joined hands in grasping every opportunity for collective effort to negotiate *every* space – governments, international agencies, knowledge areas, laws changes for justice. This was a brilliant display on their part.

The UN Second World Conference on Women held in Copenhagen in 1980 is, in particular, noted to be a moment of significance, where women began to see and publicly highlight the 'differences' in perspectives between feminists from the North and South. In the non-official spaces, the 'differences' were expressed in other ways. Women from the South were uncomfortable with some of the assumptions of their Northern sisters, expressed in the latter's research, analyses and conclusions regarding the 'South'. In preparation for the Third World Conference on Women (Nairobi, 1985), the UN and other multilateral agencies were looking for ideas to incorporate into the conference documents that reflected Third World women's experience-based critique of UN development cooperation. The Women in Development (WID) group of the Organisation for Economic Cooperation and Development (OECD)[28]/Development Assistance Committee (DAC)[29] invited me to review over 48 UN and donor agency evaluations of development projects, as well as another 63 which had focused on the poor and women in the South. I prepared a paper and a lecture, which I called 'Development as if Women Mattered' (Jain 1983). The review was discussed at the OECD/DAC/WID pre-Nairobi meeting held in Paris in 1983. It revealed, as other national studies had done,[30] that in addition to not relieving the burdens of hunger and poverty, development cooperation projects in developing nations were often worsening the economic, social, and political situation of women, especially poor women. The presentation of this topic led to support from the donor agencies to a conclave to suggest a program for the forthcoming Nairobi conference. Towards that purpose, I convened a first brainstorming meeting of informed women[31] – one from each continent of the South – in Bangalore with the support of the Ford Foundation, and it was this very meeting which led to the birth of the DAWN network.

DAWN gave Southern women a powerful voice internationally in UN fora, in academic circles, and in advocacy in general. Before the emergence of DAWN as a developing nations network, women's advocacy tended to be Eurocentric and narrowly defined. For example, advocacy on economic issues focused on affirmative action and 'equal pay for work of equal value', a demand based on the assumption that women who worked operated in the formal labour force, and, indeed, that there were jobs to be had. Little attention was paid to the fact that many women worked in the informal sector, or to the factors other than patriarchy that made it difficult for women to find work outside the home.[32] There was little appreciation of the inter-connections between women's lived realities and the larger political, economic, and social relations of class, race/ethnicity and gender embedded in the power structures and policy frameworks that determined women's access to resources and opportunities necessary for their well-being and advancement. DAWN's identification and analysis of the 'reproductive crisis' which arose from economic policies that separated economic production/ growth from social reproduction/human development was ground-breaking in the WID discourse. The analysis of gender and colonialism also highlighted the significance of unequal gender relations to processes of colonial exploitation. Indeed, DAWN's book[33] and panels had a massive impact on the Third UN World Conference on Women held in Nairobi in 1985, not least because it served to challenge Northern definitions of feminism and the notion that feminism was irrelevant to poor women. DAWN's analysis and advocacy at the Nairobi conference destabilised the Northern moorings of the feminist movement and gave voice to Southern feminist perspectives. This impact reinforced, if not determined, the decision of DAWN's founding members to continue the work of the network.

With the analysis, skills, and confidence developed in the previous decade, women who had worked with each other in a variety of projects, programs, consultations, and negotiations since the mid-1970s came together through alliances and coalitions to participate in the international, regional, and other fora of the 1990s. Methodologically grounded in the lived experiences of women in South, sensitive to regional differences, and holistic in its consideration of political, economic, social, and cultural factors, DAWN contributed to the formulation and negotiation of common and global positions articulated by women engaged in these conferences.

Moving forward

Since the 1950s, the UN has attempted to play the roles of a development activist, a champion of human rights, and a negotiator of peace and security. In that process, the UN converted itself into an inter-governmental agency, developing frameworks and goals for member countries to adhere to and monitoring implementation. An intergovernmental negotiating body by its very nature must incorporate all the differences into preparing a coherent platform, thus muting any possible change. In my view, building up coherence out of these differences has had a negative impact on the goals of peace and justice that women have striven for, and muted the potential of the UN to engage in radical change.

As globalisation took hold and the private sector, along with corporate and international capital, became the thrust of international politics, governments and intergovernmental organisations like the UN no longer stood firm against these policies and practices of inequality, and took a backseat in the negotiation of justice. In fact, since the 1990s, we can say that the UN's mandates, on which it was built, have not been working. It has not been able to resolve internal conflict and wars, nor has to been able to wholly promote the use of negotiation over destruction. As a result, women are now choosing to form their own networks and engage in the public space at a rate never before seen, negotiating within their own or regional agencies. It is common in any evolutionary process that the maturing of these groups has brought forward the need for separate tables. Furthermore, with the increased emergence of economic powers in the Southern continents and their affirmation in clubs like BRICS, IBSA etc., the theatre of negotiations has moved away from the UN and towards regional and sub-regional economic formations, away from the North and towards the South.

The UN's role as a designer and monitor of development has receded. It might be more effective as a marketplace for ideas, offering a space for feminist reasoning and collective power to engage. However, it needs to dismantle its bureaucracy engaged in development and allow ideas coming from regions and networks to make it a knowledge bank, which will help women develop their tools and ideas for negotiating with new power clubs nationally, regionally, and internationally, and generate powerful unity-based ideas. Therefore, the time has come for the international feminist movement to reconsider its desire to be involved in the post-2015 UN agenda.[34] In my view, it would be more useful if the same energy could be used to lobby for the UN to revert to its previous role as the marketplace for ideas – a structure which truly promotes the exchange of knowledge, the formation of a collective voice, and involvement with the new political and geographical spaces. Therefore, the time has come for women to rise as opinion builders, drawing from their lived experience as economic political and social agents, as social scientists and politicians. Using their skills in networking and building opinion, they must seek to influence not only the UN, but the global intellectual spaces and the economic structures which shape the international fora.

Notes

1 Assisted by Neha Choudhary and Smit Gadhia.
2 Many Southern nations were gradually freed of colonial domination through their own struggles. India gained freedom from British in 1947; countries of the African continent gained it in around the 1960s, such as Ghana in 1960, Tanzania in 1961. It is ironical that, when the UN had was registered in 1945, many of these countries were under colonial domination. Interestingly, the Latin American countries gained freedom from the Spanish and Portuguese domination much earlier, the late eighteenth and early nineteenth century.
3 Today, NAM continues to provide an important forum for interaction with partner countries across continents, including from Africa, CARICOM, Small Island Developing States (SIDS) and LDCs. At the United Nations, it is an influential grouping on

a range of issues such as UN peacekeeping and disarmament, and continues to represent space for action in pursuance of the collective interests of the developing world, along with the G-77, especially on international issues such as the reform of the global economic system and demilitarisation.

4 The concept of the 'Velvet Triangle' was coined by the political scientist Alison Woodward (2003) in connection to her analysis of gender in informal governance structures of the European Union. The idea of 'Velvet Triangle' is theoretically based on literature on patronage, clientelism, and informal governance, although Woodward also points out that informal and personalised networks are just a variety of the more comprehensive concept of policy networks at large (77–84). Within the framework of clientelism, several aspects are of concern. Policy-making and women's position in European Union policy-making came to the fore to shape the concept of the velvet triangle. In her chosen framework, Woodward emphasised personal ties, common biographies, and career mobility between both individuals and representatives of movements and institutions in the area of European gender policy.

5 Such as the National Federation of Indian Women (NFIW) founded in 1954 by Aruna Asaf Ali, All India Women's Conference (AIWC) founded in 1927 by Kamaladevi Chattopadhyay, the Textile Labour Association, India's oldest and largest union of textile workers founded in 1920 by Anasuya Sarabhai, the Central Social Welfare Board founded in 1953 by Durgabai Deshmukh. Sarojini Naidu went on to preside over the Asian Relations Conference in March 1947. Post-independence in the 1940s Kamladevi Chattopadhyay struggled for the township of Faridabad in the outskirts of Delhi. Sucheta Kripalani became the first woman to be elected as the Chief Minister of a state (Uttar Pradesh) in 1963.

6 A fact of somewhat extraordinary significance, providing many leads to the rest of this story, is that there were just four women among the 160 signatories to its Charter at the UN Charter Conference at San Francisco in 1945. Three of them were from 'developing countries' or the Third World: Minerva Bernardino (Dominican Republic), Bertha Lutz (Brazil), and Wu Yi-Fang (China). The fourth was Virginia Gildersleeve (United States).

(Jain 2005: 12)

7 For Eleanor Roosevelt's objections to a separate commission, see Mathiason (2001) 13–14.
8 www.dawnnet.org/feminist-resources/about/history.
9 As has been conceptualised by the authors of the fourteen volumes on UN History, Richard Jolly, Louis Emmerij and Thomas Weiss (For more details visit www.un history.org).
10 www.unwomen.org/en/csw.
11 http://orgs.tigweb.org/united-nations-development-fund-for-women-unifem.
12 www.unfoundation.org/how-to-help/donate/instraw.html?referrer=www.google.co.in/.
13 www.un.org/womenwatch/daw/cedaw/committee.htm.
14 www.un.org/womenwatch/daw/cedaw/cedaw25years/content/english/about_daw.html.
15 UN (1976).
16 www.africaportal.org/dspace/articles/new-international-economic-order-nieo-review.
17 The Declaration failed to get US support and has been largely forgotten.
18 Nita Barrow, a nurse by profession, had been President of the World YWCA and a member of WHO's Commission on Public Health.
19 Such as the Association of African Women for Research and Development, 1977 (AAWORD), Development Alternatives with Women for a New Era, 1984 (DAWN), the Casablanca Dreamers and transcontinental associations of waste pickers and home-based workers such as Women in Informal Employment: Globalizing and Organizing, 1997 (WEIGO) and Self Employed Women's Association, 1972 (SEWA).

20 They included Eleanor Leacock, Rayna Reiter, Michelle Rosaldo, and Gayle Rubin, to name a few.
21 http://iaws.org/.
22 www.iaffe.org/.
23 http://wiego.org/.
24 www.ilo.org/global/about-the-ilo/lang-en/index.htm.
25 www.fao.org/home/en/.
26 www.iuperj.br/.
27 www.isstindia.org/.
28 www.oecd.org/.
29 www.oecd.org/dac/developmentassistancecommitteedac.htm.
30 For example, Devaki Jain (1984), 'Integrating Women into a State Five-Year Plan', Report to the Planning Board of the State of Karnataka, Institute of Social Studies Trust, Bangalore, India.
31 They were: Africa: Fatima Mernissi (Morocco), Marie-Angelique Savane (Senegal); Asia: Hameeda Hossain (Bangladesh), Noeleen Heyzer (Malaysia), Gita Sen and Devaki Jain (India); Latin America and the Caribbean: Neuma Aguiar (Brazil), Peggy Antrobus (Caribbean), Lourdes Arizpe and Carmen Barroso (Mexico); Pacific: Claire Slatter (Fiji Islands).
32 See Antrobus (2015).
33 The original DAWN platform document, *Development, Crises and Alternative Visions: Third World Women's Perspectives*, was published for the Nairobi Conference by Kali for Women, India, with funding from NORAD in 1985. The book, authored by Gita Sen and Caren Grown, was subsequently published by Monthly Review Press in 1987.
34 UNDP (2014). *Post-2015 Development Agenda.* (available at www.undp.org/content/undp/en/home/mdgoverview/mdg_goals/post-2015-development-agenda/).

References

Abraham, T. 2005. 'Reviving an Old Dream of Afro-Asian Cooperation'. *Yale Global Online*, 24 May. http://yaleglobal.yale.edu/display.article?id=5752 (retrieved 15 December 2008).

Antrobus, P. 2015. 'DAWN, The Third World Feminist Network: Upturning Heierachies' in R. Baksh and W. Harcourt (eds) *The Oxford Handbook of Transnational Feminist Movements*. Oxford University Press, 159–187.

Bier, L. 2002. 'Our Sisters in Struggle: Non-Alignment, Afro-Asian Solidarity and National Identity in the Egyptian Women's Press: 1952–1967'. New York University. Working Paper No. 4.

Boserup, E. 1970. *Woman's Role in Economic Development*. George Allen & Unwin.

Eck, D. L., and D. Jain. (1986). *Speaking of Faith*. Kali for Women.

Emmerji, L., R. Jolly, and T. G. Weiss. 2001. *Ahead of the Curve? UN Ideas and Global Challenges*. Indiana University Press.

Galey, M. 1995. 'Women find a Place' in A. Winslow (ed.) *Women, Politics, and the United Nations*. Greenwood Press, 11–27.

Grovogui, S. N. 2003. 'Postcoloniality in Global South Foreign Policy' in J. A. Braveboy-Wagner (ed.) *The Foreign Policies of the Global South: Rethinking Conceptual Frameworks*. Lynne Rienner, 31–48.

Gupta, A. 1992. 'The Song of the Nonaligned World: Transnational Identities and the Reinscription of Space in Late Capitalism'. *Cultural Anthropology* 7(1): 63–79.

Ivacic, P. 1986. 'The Non-Aligned Countries Pool their News'. *UNESCO Courier*, May–June. http://findarticles.com/p/articles/mi_m1310/is_1986_May-June/ai_4375051 (retrieved 28 April 2009).

Jain, D. 1983. *Development as if Women Mattered, or, Can Women Build a New Paradigm*. Institute of Social Studies Trust.

Jain, D. 1984. 'Integrating Women into a State Five-Year Plan'. Report to the Planning Board of the State of Karnataka, Institute of Social Studies Trust, Bangalore, India.

Jain, D. 1986. 'Power Through the Looking Glass of Feminism'. Paper presented at the symposium on 'Gender and Power', University of Leiden, the Netherlands.

Jain, D. 2005. *Women, Development and the UN: A Sixty-Year Quest for Equality and Justice*. United Nations Intellectual History Project Series, Indiana University Press.

Jain, D. 2012. *Women's Participation in the History of Ideas and Reconstructing of Knowledge*. National Institute of Advanced Studies, Bangalore, India.

Jain, D. and Chacko, S. 2008. 'Unfolding Women's Engagement with Development and the UN: Pointers for the Future'. *Forum for Development Studies* 35(1): 5–36.

Jain, D. and Rajput, P. (eds.) (2003) *Narratives from the Women Studies Family: Recreating Knowledge*. Sage Publications.

Kumar, S. 1983. 'Nonalignment: International Goals and National Interests'. *Asian Survey* 23(4): 445–462.

Luck, E. C. 1999. *Mixed Messages: American Politics and International Organization, 1919–1999*. Washington, DC: Brookings.

Mathiason, J. 2001. *The Long March to Beijing: the United Nations and the Women's Revolution, Vol. 1, The Vienna Years*. AIMS, Inc.

Mehta, S. S. 1981. 'Non-Alignment and the New International Economic Order' in K. P. Misra and K. R. Narayanan (eds) *Non-Alignment in Contemporary International Relations*. Vikas Publishing House, 137–147.

Pavlic, B. and C., Hamelink. 1985. *The New International Economic Order: Links Between Economics and Communications*. UNESCO.

Quest, M. n.d. 'The Lessons of the Bandung Conference: Reviewing Richard Wright's *The Color Curtain* 40 Years Later'. www.spunk.org/texts/pubs/lr/sp001716/bandung.html (retrieved 30 January 2017).

Shaffer, R. 1999. 'Women and International Relations: Pearl S. Buck's critique of the Cold War'. *Journal of Women's History* 11(3): 151–175.

UN. 1976. 'Report of the World Conference of the International Women's Year: Mexico City, 19 June – 2 July 1975'. www.un.org/womenwatch/daw/beijing/otherconferences/Mexico/Mexico%20conference%20report%20optimized.pdf (retrieved 3 February 2017).

UN Chronicle. 1984. 'Anniversary of Non-aligned Movement'. www.questia.com/magazine/1G1-3332143/anniversary-of-non-aligned-movement (retrieved 3 February 2017).

UNDP. 2014. 'Post-2015 Development Agenda'. www.undp.org/content/brussels/en/home/mdgoverview/mdg_goals/post-2015-development-agenda.html (retrieved 3 February 2017).

Woodward, A. 2003. 'Building Velvet Triangles: Gender and Informal Governance' in T. Christiansen and S. Piattoni (eds) *Informal Governance in the European Union*. Edward Elgar Publishing Limited, 76–93.

Part II
At the table
Broken boundaries and persisting institutional challenges

5 Towards a feminist US foreign policy?
Secretary of State Hillary Clinton's metaphorical diplomacy[1]

Eric M. Blanchard

Introduction

Despite her stunning loss in the United States presidential election of 2016, Hillary Clinton's legacy as Secretary of State remains significant and worthy of serious attention. Clinton shaped the future diplomatic environment through her diplomatic and institutional accomplishments as well as her rhetorical commitment to the rights and betterment of women and girls worldwide. Clinton's redefinition of both American and global security may face serious challenges in the coming years, but her feminist leadership and efforts to integrate gender into American diplomacy offer important lessons for future policymakers and scholars. Despite Cynthia Enloe's (2014) influential exploration of the significance of diplomatic wives, there are surprisingly few examinations of the role of gender in international diplomacy (but see Svedberg 2002; Blanchard 2011). Following recent scholarship that understands diplomacy as a practice that constitutes world politics through the process by which diplomats construct, not merely represent, national interests (Adler-Nissen 2015, 290), this chapter traces how Clinton's re-envisioning of US diplomacy along gender-sensitive lines amounts to the first steps in a renegotiation of America's relationship with the world.

To do this, this chapter analyzes Clinton's rhetoric and policy during her tenure as America's first diplomat using the insights of gender scholarship and discourse analysis to address the broad question of the difference gender makes in US diplomacy and foreign policy. While the feminist literature in International Relations (IR) rightly focuses on the systematic effects of gender in IR, and the consequences of femininities and masculinities performed and asserted across time, space, and culture, it can leave the impact of individual (feminist) leaders and the workings of significant femininities oddly understudied. This chapter addresses these oversights first by focusing on the discursive strategies of Clinton herself (rather than the proliferating representations of her as a national political figure over her three decades in public service) and the particular manifestations of gender found in Clinton's official rhetoric as it relates to the question of how Clinton links gender to diplomacy and international security. Second, the chapter examines Clinton's identity construction as a mother (and more recently a grandmother) and her metaphorical promotion of the "investing in women" strategy in order to trace relationships among different conceptions of what it means to be a woman within Clinton's discourse. The investigation in this chapter is based on a discourse analysis of Clinton's memoir of her time as Secretary of State, as well as records of her public speeches, events, statements, and interviews from 2009–2013 culled from the US State Department website. Though curated by the State Department, the records collected on www.state.gov capture Clinton's formal speeches, question and answer sessions and interviews with members of the global news media, thus providing a relatively comprehensive sample of Clinton's prepared and unscripted remarks.

The political career of Hillary Rodham Clinton: gendered anxiety

Hillary Rodham Clinton's long public life has attracted a truly astounding level of attention and controversy. After serving as Arkansas' First Lady, Clinton arrived on the national scene during her husband Bill Clinton's campaign for the presidency in the 1992 election. Although this path was well worn by John and Abigail Adams, James and Dolly Madison, Abraham and Mary Lincoln, etc., Hillary Clinton and Bill "received steady criticism for presenting themselves in a way some believe to be unprecedented for a president and his spouse: as political as well as marital partners" (Sheeler and Anderson 2013: 6). Portrayals of Hillary Clinton, "remarkably self-contained" from childhood and possessing "glacial self control" as an adult (Marton 2002: 310, 326) must be seen in light of both the way Clinton disturbs traditional gender roles in the US and of several major image overhauls (of varying success) undertaken as Clinton attempted to navigate American gender expectations. The gendered anxiety surrounding Clinton was such that minor events, such as her efforts to be taken seriously through an announcement that she wanted to be known as Hillary Rodham Clinton, have often distracted from Clinton's transformative impact, for instance her influence on the number of female senior political appointments during the Clinton transition (Marton 2002: 319). The perceived failures of Hillary Clinton in her public role as a policy maker and lead health care reform advocate led to a period of retrenchment where Clinton refocused her attentions on the international sphere, particularly the rights of women and children. After the Monica Lewinski and impeachment scandals, Clinton's career entered a fraught, "stand by her man" phase, and the resulting quixotically high levels of support among the American public helped enable Clinton's Senate campaign run in New York State. After serving as New York's junior Senator from 2001, and an unsuccessful run for President in 2007, Clinton served as Barack Obama's Secretary of State from 2009 to 2013 before seeking the US presidency as the Democratic Party's nominee in 2016.

Because Clinton has served, in the words of Betty Friedan, as a "Rorschach test of the evolution of women" in American society (cited in Mandziuk 2008: 312), academic and scholarly attention to Clinton has been voluminous to the extent that a satisfying comprehensive overview is impossible. Research on Clinton ranges from critical analysis of the public attention to Clinton's pantsuits (Mandziuk 2008) to studies of Clinton's laughter during media interviews (O'Connell and Kowal 2004). The literature treating Clinton's rhetoric throughout her career is also substantial (e.g., Kelly 2001; Anderson 2002; Sheldon 2015). However, in this chapter, I focus on aspects of Clinton's discursive performance of gender and leadership during her tenure as US Secretary of State, and specifically her construction of female leadership and women's role in national security.

Clinton's turn as America's top diplomat will be remembered for its response to growing global anti-Americanism and loss of stature after the foreign policy activism of the George W. Bush administration, as well as its reaction to the challenges of the Arab Spring and several notable diplomatic successes, such as the release of Chinese dissident Chen Guangcheng and the 2009 environmental pact with the Chinese at Copenhagen. As Secretary of State, Clinton's rhetoric emphasized public diplomacy, image rebuilding, values promotion, bringing American diplomacy into the Internet age, and the nurturing of people-to-people contacts. Clinton's State Department also promoted the use of private sector partnerships with corporations such as Goldman Sachs and Exxon Mobil and foundations such as the Rockefeller Foundation, to facilitate diplomatic and development initiatives. For example, Clinton worked with Avon in a partnership aimed at confronting global domestic violence (Clinton 2010a). One observer argued in 2013 that Clinton's tenure was "highly competent" and successful in its attempt to "undo the damage the habitual unilateralism of the George W. Bush administration had done to the global image of the United States" (Hirsh 2013: 82).

By the late summer of 2016, however, Clinton's record at the State Department—including initiatives in Myanmar, an agreement with Russia to reduce strategic nuclear weapons, and the expulsion of Libyan dictator Muammar Gaddafi in 2011—looked less solid as events such as the Arab Spring and authoritarian adventurism of Russia's Putin developed in a more negative direction than expected (Wilkinson 2016). Clinton's campaign for the presidency was dogged by unfavorable media attention given to the 2012 Benghazi attacks in Libya and her use of a private email server during her tenure, which the campaign of her opponent Donald Trump emphasized and distorted to apparently great effect.

Even though the Trump campaign came to represent the resurgence of a normalized misogyny, the precise role gender played in Clinton's defeat in the 2016 presidential election will be debated for years and may never be known with any certainty. Political analysts and pollsters note that Clinton's perceived ambition and nonconformity to traditional gender roles seem to work against her with the voting public. Clinton has

> generally been most popular when conforming to traditional gender roles (working on women's issues as first lady, sticking by her husband during the Monica Lewinsky scandal, loyally serving Barack Obama as secretary

of state) and least popular when violating them (heading the health-care task force, serving in the Senate, running for president).

(Beinart 2016)

This chapter takes up the argument that Clinton's most long-lasting and significant accomplishment at the State Department is the one most overlooked in mainstream accounts: her gender related agenda. Valerie M. Hudson and Patricia Leidl (2015: xiv) have argued that the idea first presented by Clinton at a December 2010 TED talk, the "Hillary Doctrine," that women's global subjugation constitutes a threat to the national security of the United States represents a rhetorical centering of women's rights and female empowerment at the heart of US foreign policy. Inaugurated in 2010 by Clinton, the Quadrennial Diplomatic and Development Review (QDDR) (US State Department and USAID 2010), laid out a strategy for integrating gender, framed as "investing" in women and girls, into US development efforts in economic, food, health, environmental, political, and human security, mentioning women and girls 133 times over 242 pages (Hudson and Leidl 2015: 53). Hudson and Leidl argue that in addition to integrating women in the State Department's strategic planning, Clinton can be credited with promoting programming emphasizing women and girls, support of the newly created UN Women organization and UN Security Council resolutions 1325, 1820, 1888, 1889, and 1960, instituting significant changes in internal State policy regarding gender awareness, improving women's access to annual diplomatic meetings, and even a "larger Hillary effect," inspiring and paving the way for women in other countries to join political and economic life (54–59). Under Clinton, the State Department established the Ambassador-at-large for the Office on Global Women's Issues charged with ensuring women's issues are considered in the formation and implementation of US foreign policy, a position that President Obama later made permanent.

A feminist Secretary of State

Clinton reimagined American diplomacy as "21st century statecraft," diplomacy based on personal engagement, technologically enabled interpersonal connections, and a concern for women's progress. As she explained at a 2009 commencement ceremony:

> When I graduated from college, diplomacy was mainly conducted by experts behind closed doors. They were primarily men. And very little of what they did was really visible to the rest of us. Today, diplomacy is no longer confined to the State Department or to diplomats in pin-striped suits. In this global age, we are engaging in 21st century statecraft, and it is carried out beyond the halls of government – in barrios and rural villages, in corporate boardrooms and halls of government as well, but also church basements, hospitals, union halls, civic and cultural centers, and even in the dorms and classrooms of colleges like this.

(Clinton 2009a)

As Secretary of State, Clinton's approach was marked by its melding of "soft power" and "hard power" into a hybrid Clinton called "smart power," which she viewed as combining traditional diplomatic and military tools with energy diplomacy and cultural influence through social media and the use of technology (Clinton 2014: 31). At an awards gala in Houston, Clinton linked her vision of smart power to a liberal feminist agenda, arguing that "women's rights and empowerment is an indispensible ingredient of smart power" (Clinton 2009b).

In March 2010, at a speech at the UN Commission on the Status of Women in New York City, Clinton laid out a thoroughly feminist vision of contemporary global challenges to complement her vision of twenty-first century diplomacy powered by the use of smart power. Sounding feminist themes, she noted that while women comprise the majority of the world's farmers and caregivers and are rarely seen to cause armed conflicts, they suffer from lack of access to credit and land ownership, inadequate healthcare, the risk of death during childbirth, the consequences of military conflict, and exclusion from peace negotiations. In response to this gendered reality, Clinton argued for gender equality, which would result in more responsive and efficient government, economic growth, prosperous communities and "more stable, peaceful, and secure" nations, and for the recognition of the importance of women's informal labor (Clinton 2010b).

In this speech and the media interviews that followed, Clinton articulated her position that women's rights are both a US national security issue and a global security challenge. According to Clinton:

> President Obama and I believe that the subjugation of women is a threat to the national security of the United States. It is also a threat to the common security of our world, because the suffering and denial of the rights of women and the instability of nations go hand in hand.
>
> (Clinton 2010b)

At the global level, Clinton linked US foreign policy to the empowerment of women and promotion of gender equality found in the UN Millennium Development Goals. During an interview with CNN the day of the speech, Clinton linked women's security to so-called Democratic Peace theory (democracies do not fight other democracies though they are often antagonistic to non-democracies), arguing that:

> by definition, the denial of women their rights means that you don't have a democracy. One of the things we've learned is that democracy doesn't guarantee peace, but it's a pretty good criteria for determining whether you're going to have a peaceful, stable relationship.
>
> (Clinton 2010c)

In an interview later that month, Clinton also linked gender to global counterterrorism efforts, arguing there is "a direct correlation between societies like that

that deny women their opportunities and societies that are breeding grounds for extremism and, unfortunately, terrorism" (Clinton 2010d).

The feminism of Clinton's approach can also be seen in its acknowledgment of structural violence, outreach to grassroots and civil society groups, and recognition of women's agency. Clinton's development strategy focused on women's empowerment through education, health care, employment, and access to credit and reflected a recognition of the effects of the structural violence of malnutrition, the absence of safe drinking water, and limits to girls' education. Analysis of Clinton's speeches, interviews and Q&A sessions indicates a serious level of diplomatic outreach on issues of security and development in relation to improving the lives of women and girls. This outreach is on view in Clinton's meetings with civil society groups and in town hall style events in countries as diverse as Georgia, Armenia, Pakistan, and Kosovo. Finally, Clinton's diplomatic rhetoric aimed at restoring women's agency; she argued US foreign policy was "putting women front and center, not merely as beneficiaries of our efforts but as agents of peace, reconciliation, economic growth, and stability" (Clinton 2010e). For example, Clinton argued that women could be effective peacemakers and deserved a seat at the negotiating tables in post-conflict situations.

Clinton's successes as a female Secretary of State promoting gender sensitive policies were achieved despite a gendered set of assumptions about leadership in general and the powerful constraints on women's leadership that these assumptions entail. Sjoberg (2009) notes the ways in which concepts of good leadership are gendered such that masculine behaviors and characteristics are viewed as constituting leadership and women are presumed incapable until they prove their masculine bona fides. Because of this, success in politics often means emphasizing values coded as male, such as instrumentality, over those associated with women such as warmth, caution, and expressiveness (Sjoberg 2009: 157). Lim (2009) points to the "double bind" of femininity and leadership identified by many gender scholars that pressures women actors to simultaneously perform in masculine and feminine ways. To be taken seriously in masculinized public domains such as diplomacy or foreign affairs, women leaders must downplay "feminine" characteristics and emphasize strength, toughness, rationality, and other characteristics associated with (masculine) leadership. A female leader thus risks both being coded domineering, demanding, and arrogant if she adapts masculine role characteristics, or being seen as weak, vulnerable, and underqualified if she does not (Lim 2009: 255). A female leader like Clinton, then, must be able to navigate the "double bind" of femininities and masculinities (prevailing ways of performing like "real" men and women). But she must also have a discursive strategy to present herself in relation to prevailing codes and practices of masculinity.

Rhetoric, metaphor, and gender

This chapter focuses on a particular aspect of public rhetoric, the use of metaphor. I argue that metaphors offer female leaders a rhetorical basis for establishing their legitimacy and mitigating some of the obstacles inherent in male dominated fields of discourse such as diplomacy and international relations. Metaphor theory argues that humans use metaphors to understand one abstract or new experience in terms of another. In other words, we understand and reason by *mapping* (finding systematic correspondences) between two *conceptual domains* (any coherent organization of experience, such as knowledge about journeys), one a *source* domain and the other a *target* domain (Kovecses 2002; Lakoff and Johnson 1980). Metaphors can be potent tools for political discourse in part because of the *entailment*, the potentially applicable source knowledge latent in any particular metaphorical transfer of knowledge from source to target. Metaphorical entailments are underspecified (in the sense that all possible elements of the source conceptual schema are not developed in the target domain) and thus only contextually realized. The fact that, in any given projection, the full complement of entailments is not exploited means that political actors can count on various interpretations, using ambiguity to appeal to multiple audiences.

This chapter takes a social constructivist (Mutimer 1997; Drulák 2006; Hülsse 2006) as distinct from a cognitivist (Lakoff and Johnson 1999; Slingerland *et al.* 2007), approach to metaphor analysis (see Blanchard 2013 on this distinction) to focus on developing the insight that "by seeing something as a certain kind of thing, some arguments and actions become available to us whereas other arguments and actions become unavailable" (Ringmar 2008: 58). In other words, metaphors matter because they hide some features of reality and foreground others.

Such analysis allows us to recognize both metaphors that underwrite taken-for-granted constructions of social reality and those used instrumentally by elites to politically justify certain policies. Critical metaphor analysis holds that text producers (political actors in this case) have the ability to strategically deploy metaphors that draw on certain source domains and underplay others (Hart 2010). As Christopher Hart argues:

> when conventional metaphors occur in discourse, text-consumers are not necessarily aware that they are processing metaphor" and thus "text consumers may therefore assume that certain representations are neutral, natural and accurately reflect reality when they are, in fact, metaphorical and so motivated, constructed and skewed towards certain construals.
>
> (Hart 2010: 127)

Further, as Jonathan Charteris-Black (2005) argues, metaphors are persuasive because they trigger both conscious and unconscious responses; they directly persuade us by their descriptions and the attendant, entailed analysis while indirectly influencing us by evoking emotions (30). Charteris-Black argues that metaphorical political discourse allow users (such as politicians) "to legitimate policies by accessing the underlying social and cultural value system" (14). From an analytic perspective, the recognition of these insights opens a space for critique; some scholars even argue that investigating metaphors is a "precondition for political criticism and for transformative social change" (Ringmar 2008:

67). Metaphor analysis can thus offer a powerful critique of contemporary international security practices (Chilton 1996).

One understudied aspect of political metaphor is the use of gender in political rhetorical strategies. Hillary Clinton's rhetorical strategies should be of particular interest to scholars because of the wide attention her career has received, the centrality of gender to representations of that career and her persona, and the significant power and agency she has amassed and exercised in the process. We can view Hillary Clinton's discursive strategies as *metaphorical* when they depend on the transfer of meaning and ideational structure from one, fairly well understood realm of previous or concrete experience to another less-well understood or abstract realm (target). In this case, knowledge and experience about women found in societal discourses is called upon to map, structure, and make sense of the realm of political femininities. We can generally accept that, in the case of Hillary Clinton as Lim explains, the relevant target domain is the "relatively unknown phenomenon of women in power" while the source domain is "our understanding and lived experience of the role of women in society" (Lim 2009: 258). The partial transfer of knowledge from a source contributes in significant ways to the social construction of particular realities. These realities can be understood to include the worlds created by diplomatic practice.

Hillary Clinton's rhetoric

According to Karlyn Kohrs Campbell (1998: 5), the rhetorical performance of femininity "has meant adopting a personal or self-disclosing tone (signifying nurturance, intimacy, and domesticity)," taking on a feminine position such as mother, "preferring anecdotal evidence (reflecting women's experiential learning in contrast to men's expertise), developing ideas inductively (so the audience thinks that it, not this presumptuous woman, drew the conclusions." Rhetorical femininity has also normally entailed "appropriating strategies associated with women—such as domestic metaphors, emotional appeals to motherhood" while avoiding "tough language, confrontation or direct refutation, and any appearance of debating one's opponents" (5). By these criteria, Clinton's rhetorical style early in her career as a national political figure was bereft of "virtually all of the discursive markers by which women publically enact their femininity" as Clinton opted instead for a deductive, lawyerly approach, and impersonal tone, using few if any personal examples (Campbell 1998: 6). This early rhetorical style, "a clearer, more explicit violation of gender roles than [had] been the case with any other presidential spouse" (Campbell 1998: 14), gave way to a chastened style through which Secretary of State Clinton deployed strategically rhetorical femininity.

An analysis of Clinton's use of metaphors shows both the use of a conventional political repertoire and the reliance on particular gendered metaphors. For example, Clinton's (2011a) landmark December 6, 2011 speech in Geneva, Switzerland on the human rights of the LGBT community ("gay rights are human rights, and human rights are gay rights") delivers themes like progress through metaphorical means. In this dramatic if belated defense of gay rights, Clinton uses several metaphors typically found in political rhetoric, like path or journey, to express both the necessity of continued political struggle and the centrality of empathy. In this construction, progress is a journey or "march" and the goal of gender/sexuality justice is a long and difficult road while "progress comes from being willing to walk a mile in someone else's shoes" (Clinton 2011a). Here, Clinton's rhetoric defines leadership as "getting out in front" of historical processes and "standing up" for human dignity.

But Clinton also used metaphors that seemed to draw upon her roots in second wave feminism. One common metaphor in Clinton's political discourse, which sees politics as a conversation, is distinctly gendered, and in the Geneva speech is deployed to finesse a call for dialogue in order to bring about progress (including Clinton's own evolution on gay rights). As Sheeler and Anderson (2013) argue in their analysis of candidate oratory in the 2008 presidential campaign, Clinton's video message announcing the formation of her presidential exploratory committee ("I'm not just starting a campaign ... I'm beginning a conversation—with you, with America" (94)) embodied the feminist value of collaboration, focused on developing political consensus, and was meant to stand in contrast to the approaches of the outgoing Bush Administration and Clinton's opponent in the Democratic primary, Barack Obama. Conversational metaphors entail a two-way dynamic in which the candidate hears the voice of the electorate, thus signaling responsiveness.

Clinton's rhetoric traditionally deployed various metaphors of domesticity and family to create connections and imagine a public sphere where Clinton had the political advantage. For example, Clinton imagined, in her 1996 Democratic Convention speech, the "kitchen table" as an inclusive and intimate political space where "we ... just us, [could sit around] talking about our hopes and fears, about our children's futures" (Sheeler and Anderson 2013: 96). Closely related is the "kitchen sink" metaphor ("I'll tell you what, I feel really comfortable in the kitchen") used by both Clinton's 2007 presidential campaign and media accounts to describe the all-out campaign tactics it used against Obama (Lim 2009: 261–262). In Lim's interpretation, the use of this particular metaphor backfired "reinforcing the very stereotypes that their candidate's metaphorical inventiveness was intended to destroy" supporting characterizations of Clinton's campaign as unconventional and ruthless (262).

In her rhetoric as Secretary of State, Clinton has blended conventional metaphors and more gendered metaphors. For example, in Clinton's memoir of her time as Secretary of State, *Hard Choices*, she relates American leadership to a relay race, whereby a "Secretary, a President, a generation are all handed the baton and asked to run a leg of the race as well as we can, and then hand off the baton to our successors" (Clinton 2014: 21). This imagining of leadership and politics as SPORTS is masculine (physical contests) while at the same time cooperative (envisioning politics as competition among players, but with rules and a horizon of the future unseen in WAR metaphors of politics). At the end of her memoir, Clinton explicitly links this relay race metaphor to the family, attempting to create a seamless link between international politics and the domestic realm where the goal is to give generations of children "opportunities to thrive" (Clinton 2014: 485).

Maternal leadership

In *Hard Choices*, Clinton frames her political identity and the lessons she has learned as a result of her status as a grandmother (Clinton 2014: 491). Clinton's recent grandmotherhood, in her account, underscores a career long belief that "every child should have the chance to live up to his or her God-given potential" (493) and highlights "the responsibility we all share as stewards of the world we inherit and will one day pass on" (494). These bromides may seem to be aimed at creating a non-threatening identity, perhaps ready-made for a coming presidential run. However, seen metaphorically, this discursive strategy uses experiences of family and the roles of elders to map to the less familiar terrain of women in power, specifically the relatively less common realm of female Secretary of States and the unknown realm of women in the role of American president. The strategy carries dangers, as Clinton nemesis Maureen Dowd of the *New York Times* demonstrated when the columnist used the grandmother strategy as confirmation of Clinton's inauthenticity and clumsy campaigning: "presenting herself as a sweet, docile granny in a Scooby van, so self-effacing she made only a cameo in her own gauzy, demographically pandering presidential campaign announcement video" (Dowd 2015). Generally speaking, however, such positioning allows Clinton to appropriate the cultural and moral authority of a matriarch, assume a position from which political attacks can more easily be deflected, and set her behavior in a reassuringly family-oriented frame.

As feminists have shown, maternalism can serve as a politically enabling resource and as an identity used to organize against war and political violence, despite its depoliticizing effects. Cohn and Jacobson (2013) show how groups like the Committee of Soldiers' Mothers of Russia (CSMR) in the 1980s and the Madres of Plaza de Mayo of Argentina that organized in the late 1970s on the basis of motherhood are able to exploit both their moral authority derived from cultural understandings of the mother/child bond, and their political irrelevance (a result of the dismissive attitude towards mothers in patriarchal societies) in order to effectively press their cases and even delegitimize state terrorist regimes.

Maternal imagery can also combine with stereotypes in domestic and international spheres that equate women and peace, thereby relegating women to certain political possibilities. Sjoberg and Gentry's (2007) study of the stereotypes that represent women, such as Lynndie England and Sabrina Harman, engaged in violence surrounding the Abu Ghraib case often frames these women as mother figures whose need to nurture and loyalty to men inspires their violence. This discourse functions to obscure the reality of violent women and preserve the idea that "real" women are incapable of violence.

Clinton has used the mother/grandmother framing as a resource throughout her career. Anderson's (2002) study of Hillary Clinton's tactical use of metaphor from 1995 to 1999 points to the way that Clinton employed maternal metaphors (and thus a certain female identity) to rebuild her political image and reputation after being framed as a "bitch" in the wake of the health care debacle and the political pressures created by "her choice to test the boundaries of the role of First Lady and violate conventions of femininity" (5). According to Kelly (2001: 239), Clinton's

> chief rhetorical strategy for managing the scandals in Bill Clinton's administrations was to take advantage of the press by joining with them in creating good stories about herself and her role as First Lady, wife, mother and woman that were more interesting to ... the press, and therefore the public, than were the narratives about her husband.

This strategy of "emphasized femininity" was evident when, after 1996, Clinton began to refer to Bill Clinton in spousal terms, calling the president "my husband" rather than "the President" (Kelly 2001: 239).

What Anderson calls the "Madonna" metaphor has deep roots in American political culture and for this reason supplied Clinton with ample rhetorical resources during her "turn towards femininity" (2002: 3) in the mid 1990s and at other points in her career. Framing her 1990s comeback in maternal terms meant altering her appearance, traveling abroad to promote the rights of women and children advocacy, and being photographed with daughter Chelsea (Anderson 2002: 6). Clinton also published a book, *It Takes a Village* where she "portrayed herself as mother and protector of the nation's children" (Lim 2009: 259).

Investing in women

While the (grand) mother metaphorical framing uses the knowledge and experience of families to portray female leadership in a reassuring but potentially depoliticized, docile, and subordinate frame, Clinton's laudable relationship with global women has in a large part been framed in metaphorical terms of a vision of female empowerment that takes women as investments, a formulation that caries both advantages and risks. According to many reports, Clinton's interest in advancing the global cause of women's and children's rights is a sincere and longstanding commitment, possibly stemming from a "deep belief" that "the world would never be a better place until half the population was no longer neglected" (Ghattas 2013: 24). In Clinton's Secretary of State nomination speech in 2009, she expressed concern with the situation of women and girls, arguing, "If half of the world's population remains vulnerable to economic, political, legal, and social marginalization, our hope of advancing democracy and prosperity will remain in serious jeopardy" (Clinton 2009c).

In 2009 in an address to the Council on Foreign Relations, Clinton announced that the US "development agenda will also focus on women as drivers of economic growth and social stability" (Clinton 2009d). In Paris, early in 2010, Clinton stated her thesis boldly: "Women and girls, who are one of the world's greatest untapped resources, deserve our investment in their potential" (Clinton 2010f). Clinton argued later in 2010 that "when we invest in women, we're not just investing in individuals. We are investing in families, and we are investing in the next generation, and we are investing in communities and countries" (Clinton 2010g). In 2011, Clinton claimed the benefits of women's economic empowerment justified "putting women and girls at the center of our global efforts on food security, health, and entrepreneurship" arguing that giving women "the opportunity to own their land, start their businesses, access markets, steps that will ultimately lift up not only their families but entire economies and societies" (2011b). Clinton repeatedly conveyed this understanding in her public diplomacy as well. On a trip to the patriarchal, traditional American ally Egypt, Clinton told a town hall meeting at a women's college that:

> I, of course, believe that educating young women is not only morally right, but it is also the most important investment any society can make in order to further and advance the values and interests of the people. The Egyptian poet Hafez Ibrahim said, "A mother is a school. Empower her and you empower a great nation."
>
> (Ghattas 2013: 135)

In her defense of women and girls as smart investments, and portrayal of women as drivers of growth and stability, as untapped resources, as investment opportunities, and as saviors of entire societies, Clinton's aims to persuade her audience that placing women at the center of US diplomatic efforts is the proper approach. As a framing tool for a political argument, investments, like journeys, persuade in part because they promise a reward or payoff in exchange for some small contribution and patience. There are two main things to note about this metaphorical framing. First, Clinton's framing privileges solutions that address economic marginalization, an approach that may downplay the other political, legal, and social forms of the marginalization of women.

Second, in this metaphor, the source domain of market-based interactions is often mapped onto the target domain of subordinated women of the Global South. Clinton's embrace of the investment metaphor resonates with other metaphors, such as those that see women as drivers or engines (of growth) or (latent) resources, metaphors championed by international development agencies and pundits. The investment metaphor echoes the liberal "making women productive" strategy, which, feminist critic Rahel Kunz argues, ignores the gendered expectations and responsibilities of (in this case poor) women who, once granted microloans or otherwise integrated into the global market, must still perform household and community duties, legitimating policies that lead to "triple burdens" (responsibility for productive, reproductive and community work) (Kunz 2011: 169).

Runyan and Peterson (2014: 11) also critique the kind of "very narrow and capitalist-centered vision of women's empowerment" of the type promoted in

Clinton's discursive use of metaphor. Runyan and Peterson see its instrumentalist evocation of gender as part of an effort to deploy Western charity-based and capitalist market-based solutions to solve the problems created and exacerbated by Western governments, corporations, and international organizations and the historical and on-going Western accumulation of wealth. They conclude that "the empowerment of women has become only a means to an end, not an end in itself—just the latest mechanism to manage global problems as opposed to representing an actual commitment to gender equality and social justice" (Runyan and Peterson 2014: 10).

Understanding women through the metaphor of investment not only places global women (implicitly women of the less developed Global South) in a default "non-productive" frame, but situates Clinton and other Western authorities as rescuers and empowerers as it elides both the gendered burdens entailed in market participation and Western complicity in the very conditions investments in women's empowerment are intended to relieve. In the process, Clinton's at least partial acceptance of the metaphorical framing draws a relationship between the kind of dominant, if concerned, capitalist Western femininities represented by Clinton, and the subjugated femininities of the Global South.

Conclusion

A cursory inventory of Clinton's positions demonstrates the abundance of typically "masculine" positions—those associated with authority and power—one might expect a woman to have to take in a masculinized policy space. Examples include Clinton's hawkishness and willingness to use military force seen in her vote to support the Iraq War Resolution in 2002, her slow "evolution" on the rights of subordinated femininities and masculinities (LGBT and same sex marriage) around the world, and her faith-based opposition to divorce and allowing unmarried couples to stay overnight at the White House at home (Marton 2002: 316, 333). Her promotion of women's human rights as the "smart thing to do" and women's empowerment as solution to human rights of women and girls displays rationalist and instrumental qualities, both hallmarks of masculinism. Yet the positioning of Clinton's presentation of femininity and any masculinist mimicry underwriting her claims to leadership have to be seen in their symbolic context of a strong woman, dedicated to women's rights, representing American policy and constituting the United States through diplomatic practices around the globe.

Hilary Clinton's tenure at the State Department left a legacy of gender sensitive policies, institutions, and discursive strategies. While these institutions may be eroded or even eliminated by subsequent administrations, the rhetorical resources Clinton developed remain for future generations to utilize. These rhetorical resources, however, are not without dangers. As this chapter's brief review of two of the guiding metaphors in Clinton's rhetoric—leaders are mothers, women are investments—shows, despite her recognition of women's agency, formulations such as Clinton's may leave little space for alternatives such as non-maternal identities or non-market based empowerment. The metaphorical view of women as investments implicitly holds capitalism (and by extension, the masculinized sphere of neoliberal economy) as the only alternative without problematizing the relative dominance of wealthy, white Western femininities. This can have the effect of trapping non-hegemonic femininities in positions of subservience. Of course, even if relatively hegemonic, Clinton's construction of femininity does not show the contempt scholars have argued that hegemonic, heterosexual masculine ideologies have for femininities and subordinated masculinities. With any luck, Clinton's contributions to the causes of women's human rights, gender progress, and gender security will be recognized and built upon by future American diplomats.

Note

1 The author gratefully acknowledges the support of a SUNY Oswego Undergraduate Research Assistantship grant and the assistance of Susannah St. Clair.

References

Books and articles

Adler-Nissen, R. 2015. "Conclusion: Relationalism or Why Diplomats Find International Relations Theory Strange," in *Diplomacy and the Making of World Politics*, edited by O. J. Sending, V. Pouliot, and I. B. Neumann, 284–308. Cambridge: Cambridge University Press.

Anderson, K. V. 2002. "Hillary Rodham Clinton as 'Madonna': The Role of Metaphor and Oxymoron in Image Restoration," *Women's Studies in Communication* 25(1): 1–24.

Beinart, P. 2016. "Fear of a Female President," *The Atlantic* (October). Available at www.theatlantic.com/magazine/archive/2016/10/fear-of-a-female-president/497564/. Accessed February 6, 2017.

Blanchard, E. M. 2011. "Why is There No Gender in the English School?" *Review of International Studies* 37(2): 855–879.

Blanchard, E. M. 2013. "Constituting China: The Role of Metaphor in the Discourses of Early Sino-American Relations," *Journal of International Relations and Development* 16(2): 177–205.

Campbell, K. K. 1998. "The Discursive Performance of Femininity: Hating Hillary," *Rhetoric and Public Affairs* 1(1): 1–19.

Charteris-Black, J. 2005. *Politicians and Rhetoric: The Persuasive Power of Metaphor*. Basingstoke: Palgrave Macmillan.

Chilton, Paul A. 1996. *Security Metaphors: Cold War Discourse from Containment to Common House*. New York, NY: Peter Lang.

Clinton, H. R. 2014. *Hard Choices*. New York, NY: Simon and Schuster.

Cohn, C., and Jacobson, R. 2013. "Women and Political Activism in the Face of War and Militarization," in *Women and Wars*, edited by C. Cohn, 102–123. Cambridge: Polity.

Dowd, M. 2015. "Granny Get Your Gun," *New York Times*, April 18. Available at www.nytimes.com/2015/04/19/opinion/sunday/maureen-dowd-granny-get-your-gun.html?smid=tw-NYTimesDowd&seid=auto. Accessed February 6, 2017.

Drulák, P. 2006. "Motion, Container and Equilibrium: Metaphors in the Discourse about European Integration," *European Journal of International Relations* 12(4): 499–531.

Enloe, C. 2014. *Bananas, Beaches and Bases* (Second Edition). Berkeley, CA: University of California Press.

Ghattas, K. 2013. *The Secretary: A Journey with Hillary Clinton from Beirut to the Heart of American Power.* New York, NY: Picador.

Hart, C. 2010. *Critical Discourse Analysis and Cognitive Science.* Basingstoke: Palgrave Macmillan.

Hirsh, M. 2013. "The Clinton Legacy: How Will History Judge the Softpower Secretary of State?" *Foreign Affairs* 92(3): 82–91.

Hudson, V. M., and Leidl, P. 2015. *The Hillary Doctrine: Sex and American Foreign Policy.* New York, NY: Columbia University Press.

Hülsse, Rainer. 2006. "Imagine the EU: The Metaphorical Construction of a Supra-Nationalist Identity," *Journal of International Relations and Development* 9: 396–421.

Kelly, C. E. 2001. *The Rhetoric of First Lady Hillary Rodham Clinton: Crisis Management Discourse.* Westport, CT: Praeger.

Kovecses, Z. 2002. *Metaphor: A Practical Introduction.* Oxford: Oxford University Press.

Kunz, R. 2011. "The 'Making Women Productive' Strategy," in *Gender and Global Restructuring: Sightings, Sites, and Resistances*, edited (Second Edition) by H. Marianne and A. S. Runyan, 163–180. New York, NY: Routledge.

Lakoff, G., and Johnson, M. 1980. *Metaphors We Live By.* Chicago, IL: University of Chicago Press.

Lakoff, G., and Johnson, M. 1999. *Philosophy in the Flesh: The Embodied Mind and Its Challenge to Western Thought.* New York, NY: Basic Books.

Lim, E. T. 2009. "Gendered Metaphors of Women in Power: The Case of Hillary Clinton as Madonna, Unruly Woman, Bitch and Witch," in *Politics, Gender and Conceptual Metaphors*, edited by Kathleen Ahrens, 254–269. New York, NY: Palgrave Macmillan.

Mandziuk, R. M. 2008. "Dressing Down Hillary," *Communication and Critical/Cultural Studies* 5(3): 312–316.

Marton, K. 2002. *Hidden Power: Presidential Marriages that Shaped Our History.* New York, NY: Anchor Books.

Mutimer, D. 1997. "Reimagining Security: The Metaphors of Proliferation," in *Critical Security Studies*, edited by K. Krause and M. C. Williams, 187–221. Minneapolis, MN: University of Minnesota.

O'Connell, D., and Kowal, S. 2004. "Hillary Clinton's Laughter in Media Interviews," *Pragmatics* 14(4): 463–478.

Ringmar, E. 2008. "Metaphors of Social Order," in *Political Language and Metaphor: Interpreting and Changing the World*, edited by T. Carver and J. Pikalo, 57–68. New York, NY: Routledge.

Runyan, A. and Peterson, V. 2014. *Global Gender Issues in the New Millennium* (Fourth Edition). Boulder, CO: Westview.

Sheeler, K. H. and Anderson, K. V. 2013. *Woman President: Confronting Postfeminist Political Culture.* College Station, TX: Texas A&M University Press.

Sheldon, A. 2015. "'Thank You for Heckling Me' Hillary Rodham Clinton's Discursive Management of Her Public Persona, Her Political Message and the 'Iron My Shirt!' Hecklers in the 2008 Presidential Election Campaign," in *Discourse, Politics and Women as Global Leaders*, edited by J. Wilson and D. Boxer, 195–216. Philadelphia, PA: John Benjamins.

Sjoberg, L. 2009. "Feminist Approaches to the Study of Political Leadership," in *The Ashgate Research Companion to Political Leadership*, edited by J. Masciulli, A. Molchanov, and W. Andy Knight, 149–173. Farnham: Ashgate.

Sjoberg, L., and Gentry, C. 2007. *Mothers, Monsters, Whores: Women's Violence in Global Politics*. New York, NY: Zed Books.

Slingerland, E., Blanchard, E., and Boyd-Judson L. 2007. "Collision with China: Conceptual Metaphor Analysis, Somatic Marking, and the EP-3 Incident," *International Studies Quarterly* 51: 53–77.

Svedberg, E. 2002 "Academics, Practitioners, and Diplomacy: An ISP Symposium on the Theory and Practice of Diplomacy—Feminist Theory and International Negotiations," *International Studies Perspectives* 3: 139–175.

US State Department and USAID. 2010. *Leading through Civilian Power: The First Quadrennial Diplomacy and Development Review*. Available at: www.state.gov/documents/organization/153108.pdf.

Wilkinson, T. 2016. "Hillary Clinton Won Praise as America's Top Diplomat, But Time Has Tarnished Her Record," *Los Angeles Times* (August 18). Available at: www.latimes.com/politics/la-na-pol-clinton-foreign-policy-20160816-snap-story.html.

Speeches

All speeches accessed January 25, 2016.

Clinton, H. R. 2009a. "Remarks at Barnard College Commencement Ceremony," New York, NY. May 18. Available at www.state.gov/secretary/20092013clinton/rm/2009a/05/123599.htm.

Clinton, H. R. 2009b. "Remarks at Planned Parenthood Federation of America Awards Gala," Speech delivered in Houston, TX, March 27. Available at www.state.gov/secretary/20092013clinton/rm/2009a/03/120968.htm.

Clinton, H. R. 2009c. "Nomination Hearing to be Secretary of State," Statement before the Senate Foreign Relations Committee in Washington, DC, January 13. Available at www.state.gov/secretary/20092013clinton/rm/2009a/01/115196.htm.

Clinton, H. R. 2009d. "Foreign Policy Address at the Council on Foreign Relations," Speech delivered in Washington, DC, July 15. Available at www.state.gov/secretary/20092013clinton/rm/2009a/july/126071.htm.

Clinton, H. R. 2010a. "Remarks at the International Women of Courage Award Ceremony," Speech delivered in Washington, DC, March 10. Available at: www.state.gov/secretary/20092013clinton/rm/2010/03/138217.htm.

Clinton, H. R. 2010b. "Remarks at the UN Commission on the Status of Women," Speech delivered in UN Headquarters in New York City, NY. March 12. Available at: www.state.gov/secretary/20092013clinton/rm/2010/03/138320.htm.

Clinton, H. R. 2010c. "Interview with CNN's Jill Dougherty," New York City, NY. March 12. Available at: www.state.gov/secretary/20092013clinton/rm/2010/03/138322.htm.

Clinton, H. R. 2010d. "Interview on CBC's The Hour with George Stroumboulopoulos," Interview in Ottawa, Canada, March 29. Available at: www.state.gov/secretary/20092013clinton/rm/2010/03/139289.htm.

Clinton, H. R. 2010e. "Remarks at the 10th Anniversary of UN Security Council Resolution 1325 on Women, Peace and Security," Speech delivered at United Nations Headquarters in New York City, October 26. Available at: www.state.gov/secretary/20092013clinton/rm/2010/10/150010.htm.

Clinton, H. R. 2010f. "Remarks on the Future of European Security," Speech delivered at L'Ecole Militaire, Paris, France, January 29. Available at: www.state.gov/secretary/20092013clinton/rm/2010/01/136273.htm.

Clinton, H. R. 2010g. "Women's Empowerment Event," Remarks delivered in Port Moresby, Papua New Guinea, November 3. Available at: www.state.gov/secretary/20092013clinton/rm/2010/11/150343.htm.

Clinton, H. R. 2011a. "Remarks in Recognition of International Human Rights Day," Speech delivered at Palais des Nations, Geneva, Switzerland, December 6. Available at www.state.gov/secretary/20092013clinton/rm/2011/12/178368.htm.

Clinton, H. R. 2011b. "Remarks on Women, Peace and Security," Speech delivered in Washington, DC, December 19. Available at: www.state.gov/secretary/20092013clinton/rm/2011/12/179173.htm.

6 Gender, status, and ambassador appointments to militarized and violent countries

Birgitta Niklasson and Ann Towns

Introduction

A few decades ago, exceptionally few women served as ambassadors. Although men are still dramatically overrepresented in this role, women now constitute 16 percent of ambassadors world-wide (Towns and Niklasson 2015). Women have come to make up a large minority of the ambassador appointments made by some states, such as Finland (44 percent), the Philippines (41 percent), Sweden (40 percent), the United States (30 percent), Canada (29 percent), Colombia (28 percent) and more (Ibid). One aim of this chapter is to provide a basic mapping of the ambassador appointments made world-wide in 2014, to show the variations among countries and regions in terms of sending and receiving male and female ambassadors.

A second aim of the chapter is to show that female ambassadors are more likely to be posted in states of lower military and economic standing whereas men are overrepresented in states of greater military and economic clout. This corresponds with the findings of prior scholarship on other kinds of office, which has also concluded that men tend to end up in positions of higher status and women in those of lower status (e.g., Putnam 1976; Bashevkin 1993). We will draw on our previous study of almost 7,000 ambassador appointments made in 2014 to show that women were not as likely to be posted as ambassadors in countries of high economic and military status as their male counterparts (Towns and Niklasson 2015).

A third aim of this chapter is to dig deeper into the military aspect of ambassador appointments. We will show that the gender pattern in ambassador appointments that we have pointed to previously is not just related to the status of certain positions, but also to what degree receiving countries are perceived as militarized and violent. As militarism and violence are both gendered phenomena associated with masculinity rather than femininity (Sjoberg and Via 2010b), men are also more likely to be posted in countries where theses phenomena are palpable. Ambassador appointments thus follow the same pattern that has been observed in so many other kinds of organizations, namely that women and men are assigned different positions in accordance with traditional gender roles. And just as in so many other cases, we believe that this division of labor contributes to male ambassadors reaching higher status positions. One reason for this is that postings in countries that experience a high degree of militarization and violence can, at least in some cases, be considered to be hardship postings. And hardship postings have proven to serve as stepping-stones in diplomatic careers, since they generate valuable experiences (Brösamle 2012). If women are less likely to be posted to these kinds of positions, this particular potential career path is less available for them than for their male colleagues, something that may contribute to limiting women's diplomatic career possibilities.

Our chapter speaks to the increasing interest in gender in the burgeoning and dynamic literature on diplomacy. As we will show below, most of the gender-related diplomacy studies, while rich and insightful, are limited to individual Ministries of Foreign Affairs (MFAs) and thus say little about diplomacy as an aggregate set of practices. The few studies that have moved beyond individual MFAs ask different kinds of questions of diplomacy, such as those concerning the role of women as diplomatic wives and as negotiators. Some of the fundamental questions of where the women and men are positioned in diplomacy thus still remain to be asked. How many female ambassadors are there in the world? Which states send a higher share of female ambassadors than others? Where are male and female ambassadors posted, especially with respect to status and potential stepping-stone and career positions? In answering these basic questions, we seek to broaden the knowledge base about men, women, and diplomacy.

The rest of this chapter proceeds in five sections. We begin by briefly situating our contribution in the literature on gender and diplomacy as well as that on diplomatic careers. The following section discusses the theoretical foundations of the study, including the reasons one may expect men and women to end up in different positions in diplomacy. The third section then presents our design, unique data, and methods, followed by the fourth section on results and analyses. The fifth and final section provides a concluding discussion of the implications of the relationship between gender, militarism, and violence for diplomatic careers.

The scholarship on gender in diplomacy and diplomat careers

Diplomacy, in which ambassadors play a pivotal part, has now become the object of study of a large and fast-moving academic field, involving some of the cutting-edge scholars of international relations (e.g., Neumann 2012; Adler-Nissen 2013). A number of prior studies have mapped out the gender patterns and gender norms within individual MFAs, such as the US Department of State and the Norwegian Ministry for Foreign Affairs (e.g., Crapol 1987; Jeffreys-Jones 1995; McGlen and Sarkees 2001; Neumann 2012). Moving beyond the single case study, Niskanen and Nyberg (2010) provide a comparison of gender patterns within the MFAs of Norway, Denmark, Finland, Sweden, and Iceland. However, very little prior work has addressed the "big picture" of gender and diplomacy. A widely read chapter by Cynthia Enloe (1990) remains one of very few academic treatments of diplomacy in the aggregate, as an international institution and set of practices. Writing in the late 1980s, she presented diplomatic work as a male world, guided by norms of masculinity and inhabited by men. While important and insightful, Enloe's analysis does not include an empirical mapping of numbers and postings. We thus know very little about where the women who actually do enter diplomacy and reach the ambassador level end up or even how many female ambassadors there are. Our focus on charting the basic number and kinds of postings of male and female ambassadors is, to our knowledge, the first attempt of its kind (Towns and Niklasson 2015).

Nor is there a lot of previous research on diplomatic careers. There are biographies of individual ambassadors as well as case studies and comparative studies of what kinds of people enter diplomacy with regards to e.g., social background, education, and gender (Nightingale 1930; Galtung and Holmboe Ruge 1965; Niskanen 2010; Kopp and Gillespie 2011). However, there are not many systematic studies of what paths diplomatic careers tend to follow, or what factors drive diplomatic careers forward. This chapter is thus an important contribution to our understanding of the career paths of diplomats.

One exception is the work of Klaus J. Brösamle (2012). Brösamle carries out a cohort study of all diplomats who entered the British Foreign and Commonwealth Office (FCO) between 1966 and 1974 and he observes that diplomats who have been posted in countries that experience some kind of unexpected crisis (natural disaster or armed conflict) advance faster through the ranks due to the valuable experiences that this kind of challenging position entails. These results are in line with research on other kinds of organizations that also stresses the importance of experiences for career advancement (Gibbons and Waldman 2006).

Brösamle (2012) focuses on *unexpected* crisis in order to be able to isolate the effect that the crisis has had on the diplomats' careers. Had the crisis situation been known before the post was assigned, the FCO could have responded by sending one of their most promising diplomats whom they trusted to handle the situation well. Without this design, the post-crisis career development of crisis-exposed diplomats might as well have been a consequence of prior expectations rather than an effect of the additional competence that the crisis position might have provided.

The question we want to answer is not whether a hardship position promotes career development—we assume that this is indeed the case based on Brösamle's results. Instead, we are interested in precisely the selection process that Brösamle wants to avoid capturing, namely if certain groups of diplomats are more likely to be assigned to certain kinds of challenging positions. More specifically, we ask if male ambassadors are more often sent to countries that are perceived as militarized and violent. Before attending to that question (and others) empirically, we explore why, theoretically, that might be the case.

Theories of gender, militarization, and violence

Following Scott's (1986: 1067) classic formulation, we use the concept of gender as "a constitutive element of social relationships based on perceived differences between the sexes." Gender can furthermore be institutionalized in social and political institutions, such as those of diplomacy. Indeed, prior scholarship has shown that men tend to cluster in more prestigious institutional assignments and work roles, whereas women tend to cluster in the less prestigious ones (e.g., Putnam 1976; Bashevkin 1993; Studlar and Moncrief 1999; Connell 2006). Gender thus centrally involves the distribution of social power and prestige among actors. In a classic statement on political elites, Robert Putnam's (1976: 33) proposed "law of increasing disproportion" claims that the ratio of women will decrease with each step toward the apex of power. There are several reasons why such hierarchical patterns may emerge, which we have discussed elsewhere (Towns and Niklasson 2015). For the purposes of this chapter, it is sufficient to point out that prior scholarship has shown a relationship between gender and positional status, and that we will show men to be overrepresented also in the ambassador appointments of higher status.

A new hypothesis that we will explore is the expectation that male ambassadors will be overrepresented (and women underrepresented) in postings in militarized and violent states. There is a wealth of scholarship exposing the distinctive understandings about femininity/women and masculinity/men as well as the implications of these distinctive understandings for male and female behavior, options, and life chances. This scholarship has underscored that traditional understandings of femininity emphasize vulnerability, subordination, care, and being conquered. War histories are thus often about pure, innocent, and naïve women who are defended and rescued by male warriors (e.g., Elshtain 1987). Masculinity, on the other hand, is associated with heroism, strength/violence, protection, aggression, and domination (Elshtain 1987; Cohn 1987; Campbell 1992; Ruddick 1993; Kinsella 2005; Sjoberg and Via 2010b; Sjoberg 2011, 2012). Military, defense, and security activities have therefore been associated with the male gender and with masculinity (e.g., Kronsell 2012). Masculine qualities remain essential to military life even as the people making up these institutions become more heterogeneous (Peterson 2010).

Apart from being a bastion of hyper-masculinity, military organizations also constitute a part of a norm system that considers warfare a legitimate measure to resolve problems and conflicts, a norm system that Annica Kronsell (2012) defines as militarism. Militarism can also be described as "a set of attitudes and social practices which regards war and the preparation for war as a normal and desirable social activity" (Mann 1987: 35). Militarism is thus a concept that moves beyond war and military institutions. It is rather "the extension of military practices into civilian life" (Sjoberg and Via 2010a: 7), an extension that may blur or even erase the distinctions between war and peace, military and civilians.

One reason why many feminists are critical of militarism is because militarism is also closely associated with war and organized violence (Kronsell

2012), two other thoroughly gendered phenomena that tend to affect women to a disproportionately great extent (Sjoberg and Via 2010a), e.g., as victims of rape (Hale 2010). Together, these concepts form "the war system" (Reardon 1996: 13), which Laura Sjoberg and Sandra Via (2010a: 6) describe as "a cycle of violence that at once relies on and perpetuates the oppression of women." Cynthia Cockburn (2004) describes the relationship between gender and violence in a similar way by comparing hierarchical gender systems to a kind of conductor through which violence is channeled.

A starting point of our study is therefore that militarism and violence are not gender neutral phenomena.[1] On the contrary, gender, militarism, and violence are three interdependent, inseparable, and mutually constitutive concepts (Sjoberg and Via 2010a, 2010b). Militarism and violence generate gender roles and ideologies, just as gender roles and ideologies constitute the basis of militarism and violence. The question is what this means for the appointment of ambassadors.

Our idea is that gendered beliefs about female ambassadors as particularly vulnerable, and thus less effective in their capacity as ambassadors, in capitals and diplomatic milieus that are militarized and violent may contribute to a male dominance at these kinds of diplomatic postings. Women should be protected from war, not sent straight into it. Such a gender pattern in ambassador appointments may, however, give male ambassadors a career advantage since working in these kinds of challenging environments make them acquire valuable experiences that are likely to accelerate their future careers.

Design and data

The analyses in this chapter are based on a unique data set containing all ambassador appointments made by the 50 highest ranked countries in terms of GDP in 2014.[2] These 50 countries are selected primarily because they have the financial means to send out a substantial number of ambassadors, which allows for enough variation in the variables under study. The average number of appointments made by these states is 96, varying between 33 (Singapore) and 165 (China). As a comparison, five of the lowest ranked GDP countries in the world—Comoros, Marshall Islands, Micronesia, Palau, and Tuvalu—only appoint on an average four ambassadors each and information about these appointments is hard to come by. Lower ranked countries are therefore excluded from this study, something that of course limits its generalizing scope. We are nonetheless convinced that an analysis of the ambassador appointments made by the top 50 countries is still highly relevant for improving our understanding of the role gender plays in the international game of which these appointments are an important part. After all, the great majority of the ambassador appointments in the world are made by these 50 countries.

In total, 6,990 ambassador appointments have been coded. A maximum of 4,740 of these will be used in the analyses, for several reasons. First, several positions were vacant at the time of the data collection. Second, ambassadors posted in the home MFA have been excluded, primarily because it has not been possible to find information about all ambassadors posted in the sending states' home MFAs. Third, not all ambassador appointments are unique, as some ambassadors act as envoys to several countries simultaneously. In these cases, we have only considered the position where the ambassador is actually stationed, since we assume that this is their most important position.

Measures

The focus of this study is threefold (1) the variations among states in terms of the overrepresentation of men in ambassador postings; (2) the overrepresentation of men in postings of power and prestige; and (3) whether men are overrepresented as ambassadors posted to militarized and violent countries. This focus requires a discussion of how we operationalize our most central theoretical concepts: gender, status, militarization, and violence. Table 6.1 below offers descriptive statistics of all the variables included in the analyses.

We apply two categories of gender: women and men. All contemporary ambassadors seem to present themselves as either male or female (regardless of what sex they may have been assigned at birth), with no ambassadors presenting themselves openly as transgender or queer. There is no missing data on this variable, which means that we have been able to identify all ambassadors in the data set as women or men. The coding has been based on their names, pictures, and presentations of the ambassadors available on the embassies' websites.

The measures of economic and military status of receiving countries will be the same as in our previous work (Towns and Niklasson 2015). Economic status will therefore be based on GDP rank (World Bank 2015) and G20 membership (OECD 2015). High military status will be operationalized as being a permanent member of the UN Security Council (UN 2015) and being a nuclear power (SIPRI 2015).

The degree of militarism in a receiving state is operationalized in two ways. First, we look at the military expenditure in US dollars and as a percent of GDP. We also rank countries in relation to each other with regard to how much money they spend on the military. The state that spends the most is ranked number 1, the state that spends the second most is ranked number 2, etc. The information about military expenditure is retrieved from SIPRI (2014) Military Expenditure Database and the Quality of Government (QoG) standard dataset (Teorell *et al.* 2015).

Militarization is also operationalized as the number of people who work in the military and how great a share of the total labor force these people constitute. These figures do also come from the QoG standard dataset (Teorell *et al.* 2015). This operationalization says nothing about how prevalent military values and ideals are in the receiving cultures in general, but these figures capture at least how much resources the receiving states spend on the military, from which how highly this sector is valued can be assumed.[3]

Whether a receiving state is violent is measured through the extent to which the state is involved in intra- or inter-state armed conflicts. We thus focus on

Table 6.1 Descriptive statistics of included variables

Variable	Comment	Mean	Median	Std. div.	Min.	Max.	N
Gender	1 = woman, 2 = man	1.85	2.00	0.359	1	2	4,730
Economic status							
Top 10 GDP rank	1 = Brazil, China, France, Germany, India, Italy, Japan, Russia, UK, and USA	0.10	0	0.297	0	1	4,740
Top 50 GDP rank	1 = the receiver is one of the 50 highest ranked GDP countries	0.43	0	0.496	0	1	4,740
G20 member	1 = member	0.19	0	0.396	0	1	4,740
Military status							
UN Security Council	1 = member (USA, Russia, UK, France, and China)	0.05	0	0.215	0	1	4,740
Nuclear power	1 = yes (USA, Russia, UK, France, China, India, Pakistan, Israel, and North Korea)	0.08	0	0.276	0	1	4,371
Militarization							
Military expenditure	In million USD	20,072	3,472	73,901	0	640,221	3,762
Military rank	Based on military expenditure. 1 = the country that spends the most, 2 = the country the spends the second most, etc.	52	47	35	1	134	3,762
Military expenditure	Percent of Gross Domestic Product	2.1	1.5	1.7	0	11.6	3,801
Military staff	Number of people	247,407	79,100	481,043	0	2,945,000	4,258
Military staff	Percent of the total labor force	1.4	0.9	1.5	0	10.5	4,250
Violence							
Armed conflict (interval)	Number of intra- and interstate armed conflicts	0.3	0	0.7	0	4	3,026
Armed conflict (ordinal)	0 = no conflict, 1 = one conflict, 2 = two or more conflicts	0.3	0	0.6	0	2	3,026
GPI							
GPI score	Global Peace Index score	2.00	1.96	0.49	1.16	3.44	4,194
GPI rank	Global Peace Index rank	75	69	49	1	162	4,194

Gender, status, and ambassador appointments 107

state organized violence. The information about these armed conflicts is taken from the UCDP/PRIO Armed Conflict Dataset (Themnér and Wallensteen 2015) and the QoG standard dataset (Teorell *et al.* 2015).

Finally, we also look at the receiving country's score and rank according to the Global Peace Index (GPI). The GPI is an appreciation of a state's peacefulness that relies on qualitative as well as quantitative indicators. These indicators are focused on three broad themes: the level of safety and security in the society (e.g., criminality, share of refugees and displaced people, terrorist activity, violent crime, likelihood of violent demonstrations, and the number of internal security and police officers compared to the rest of the population), the degree of domestic or international conflict (e.g., number of internal and external armed conflicts, number of deaths from organized conflict, and relations with neighboring countries), and the degree of militarization (e.g., military expenditure, size of military staff, involvement in arms traffic, possession of nuclear and other weapons). Hence, the GPI includes both our measures of militarization and war, as well as a whole range of other indicators related to how violent the recipient country is in a broad sense. We will therefore use this index as a way of summarizing and checking the robustness of our results. The information about the GPI is provided by the Institute for Economics and Peace (IEP 2013).

Something that complicates the possibility of drawing conclusions based on this data is that we do not have any information about how long the ambassadors have held their present positions, which means that we do not know what the values on the included variables were for the receiving countries at the time of their appointments. We have only tried to find the most recent data. The credibility of our results thus relies partially on how quickly the values of the variables in Table 6.1 are likely to change. According to the IEP (2013), the increase in the overall GPI score was only 0.1 between 2008 and 2013, which indicates that there is not a lot of change in this measure globally. Lotta Themnér's and Peter Wallensteen's (2014) report on armed conflicts also shows that the situation on a global scale has been relatively stable since 2002, with slight increases in conflicts around 2006 and 2010. However, as in the case of the GPI, the variation may be much greater for individual countries. A conflict may therefore arise in a country after a female ambassador has already been assigned to it. If this is the case, we risk concluding, contrary to our argument, that females are not less frequently sent to militarized and violent countries. In case of the opposite situation (a male ambassador is sent to a country just before it experiences an outbreak of an armed conflict), we may wrongly conclude, in line with our argument, that female ambassadors are indeed less likely to be sent to these kinds of challenging positions. The question is if one of these situations is more likely to occur than the other. If not, this "noise" in the data will not bias our results in either direction. We are inclined to think that the risk of such a bias is small.

Variations in underrepresentation of female ambassadors

The first aim of this chapter is to offer a general overview of the share of female and male ambassadors both in terms of sending country and in terms of where they are sent. Table 6.2 shows the extent to which different geographic regions send out female and male ambassadors (as a percentage of the total number of appointments).

From this first analysis, we can conclude that women are clearly underrepresented in ambassador appointments made anywhere in the world. Indeed, women only make up 15 percent of this top level of the diplomatic corps. There are regional differences, however. The Nordic countries stand out as those who appoint the most women as ambassadors (35 percent), a share that stands in sharp contrast to the female ambassadors of the Middle East (6 percent) and Asia (10 percent). Several countries in the two latter regions (Saudi Arabia, Qatar, Kazakhstan, Iran, and South Korea) actually appoint no women at all. Nonetheless, it is important to note that there are exceptions to this general regional pattern; 17 percent of Israel's ambassadors are women, for example, as are 41 percent of those from the Philippines. The Philippines thus appoints almost as many female ambassadors as Finland (44 percent) and nearly twice as many as Denmark (22 percent), whereas Russia, which is included as a part of Europe, appoints almost no women (1 percent). Other exceptions worth mentioning are South Africa, which sends out 27 percent female ambassadors, and Colombia with 28 percent female ambassadors.

If we turn to look at where the ambassadors are sent, the general picture remains. The figures in Table 6.3 follow a similar, if weaker pattern, with regard to which regions receive the highest and lowest proportion of female ambassadors.

The Nordic countries turn out not just to belong to the region that sends out the most women; they also receive them to a greater degree than the other regions. Twenty-two percent of the ambassadors placed in the Nordic countries are women, compared to 15 percent of the ambassadors overall. Similarly, fewer

Table 6.2 Share of women and men (percent) of different regions' ambassador appointments[4]

	Women	Men	Total	Gender difference
Nordic countries	35	65	100 (347)	−30
North America	29	71	100 (238)	−42
Oceania	25	75	100 (81)	−50
Africa	17	83	100 (247)	−66
South America	17	83	100 (536)	−66
Europe	14	86	100 (1,696)	−72
Asia	10	90	100 (1,020)	−80
Middle East	6	94	100 (565)	−88
Total	15 (719)	85 (4,011)	100 (4,730)	−70

Table 6.3 Share of women and men (percent) of the ambassadors received by different regions[5]

	Women	Men	Total	Gender difference
Nordic countries	22	78	100 (172)	−56
Europe	18	82	100 (1,233)	−64
South America	18	82	100 (312)	−64
Oceania	17	83	100 (111)	−66
North America	16	84	100 (368)	−68
Africa	14	86	100 (879)	−70
Asia	11	89	100 (839)	−78
Middle East	10	90	100 (446)	−80
Total	15 (652)	85 (3,708)	100 (4,360)	−75

women are sent to Middle Eastern (10 percent) and Asian (11 percent) countries, these also being the two regions that appoint the lowest share of female ambassadors. This implies that there is some degree of reciprocity in the ambassador exchanges; countries may be more willing to send female ambassadors to postings whence they are also more likely to receive women. None of the 42 foreign ambassadors posted in Saudi Arabia are women, for example, and, as noted above, Saudi Arabia sends none. At the same time, 15 percent of the ambassadors posted in Qatar are women, even though Qatar also is one of the countries without any female ambassadors of its own. Curiously, the Philippines, which is one of the countries that appoints the most women, only receives 5 percent female ambassadors.

It is interesting to note that the variation in the share of female ambassadors received is lower than that of the share sent. Even though there seems to be an aspect of reciprocity in the distribution of female ambassadors, there is also an element of leveling. The difference in percentage points between the regions that send the most (Nordic countries: 35 percent) and the least (Middle East: 6 percent) female ambassadors is 29. The corresponding number when it comes to receiving female ambassadors is 12 (Nordic countries: 22 percent and Middle East: 10 percent). It thus appears that the extreme gender inequality that prevails in the diplomatic corps in some countries is mitigated on an international level so that the gender composition of the diplomatic communities becomes fairly similar in most regions of the world.

After this quick review of the geographic distribution of ambassador appointments, we now move on to a deeper analysis of where ambassadors are sent. Our first finding – that there are relatively few female ambassadors overall – is hardly surprising. The question we will turn to next is where male and female ambassadors end up in terms of the status of the posting. Are women posted to positions of lesser status than men?

Gender differences in the status of ambassador postings

The second aim of this chapter is to show that women are less likely than men to reach the ambassador positions of the highest economic and military status. Since this is an argument that we have already elaborated in a previous paper (Towns and Niklasson 2015), we will only review some of the main results here.

Table 6.4 summarizes the differences in economic status of the postings of female and male ambassadors. Two of the measures in this table are based on GDP rank. In the left column, we look at the share of ambassadors who are sent to one of the 10 highest ranked GDP countries. This is the case for 7 percent of the female ambassadors and for 10 percent of the males. Thus, it appears that male ambassadors are significantly more likely[7] to be posted in one of these economically prestigious places. This is also the case if we expand the group of prestigious countries to the top 50 GDP countries (the right column). Forty-four percent of the male ambassadors are sent to one of these countries compared to 40 percent of their female colleagues.

In the middle column, we use a different indicator of economic status, namely G20 membership. According to the OECD (website), G20 members represent economies "whose size or strategic importance gives them a particularly crucial role in the global economy." Sixteen percent of the female ambassadors are sent to one of these strategically important economies, whereas the same is true for 20 per cent of the male ambassadors. Thus, based on the GDP rank and the G20 membership status of the receiving countries, we can conclude that female ambassadors are in general placed in countries of lower economic status than their male colleagues.

This gender pattern reoccurs when we look at the military status of the receiving countries. Table 6.5 shows that only 5 per cent of the female ambassadors are sent to a state that controls nuclear weapons, for example, whereas this is the case for 9 per cent of the males. A lower share of women is also stationed in one of the permanent member states of the UN Security Council (4 percent compared to 5 percent). The difference is not great in percentage points, but it is statistically significant[9] and it leans in the expected direction.

The similarities in outcomes between our two military status measures might not be so surprising, considering the fact that all five permanent members of the UN Security Council also are nuclear powers. We have therefore run the analysis

Table 6.4 The extent (percent) to which female and male ambassadors are sent to countries of high economic status[6]

Receiving country is ...	... of top 10 GDP rank			... a G20 member			... of top 50 GDP rank		
	Yes	No	All	Yes	No	All	Yes	No	All
Female	7	93	100	16	84	100	40	60	100
Male	10	90	100	20	80	100	44	56	100
Gender difference	−3***	+3***		−4***	+4***		−4***	+4***	

Table 6.5 The extent (percent) to which female and male ambassadors are sent to countries of high military status[8]

Receiving country is ...	... a nuclear power			... a permanent member of the UN Security Council		
	Yes	No	All	Yes	No	All
Female	5	95	100 (652)	4	96	100 (719)
Male	9	91	100 (3,709)	5	95	100 (4,011)
Gender difference	−4***	+4***		−1*	+1*	

based solely on the nuclear powers that are not permanent UN Security Council member states, which leaves us with Israel, North Korea, India, and Pakistan. This does not change the main result, however; 1 percent of the female ambassadors are posted in one of these four nuclear powers, compared to 4 percent of the males. The gender pattern thus remains and it is still significant.[10] Just as in the case of economic status, we thus conclude that female ambassadors stand a lower chance of being appointed to positions of high military status.

The main interest of this chapter, however, is whether the interdependent relationship that feminist theories have identified between gender, militarism, and violence also is discernable in ambassador appointments. We will answer this question by testing whether female ambassadors are less likely than their male counterparts to be appointed to countries that are closely associated with militarism and armed conflict.

Militarism, armed conflict, and ambassador postings

The third aim of this chapter is to dig deeper into the military aspect of ambassador appointments. Below, we will demonstrate that women are underrepresented in militarized and violent countries. The section will first analyze the postings of male and female ambassadors by degree of militarism of the receiving state, then look at postings in terms of the degree to which the receiving state is characterized by armed conflict, ending with postings in light of the Global Peace Index.

Militarism

Are female ambassadors less likely than their male counterparts to be posted in militarized states? To answer this question, we start out by looking at the degree of militarism in the receiving states. This is measured in two ways: by their military expenditure and by the size of their armed forces. The results are shown in Table 6.6.

We use three different indicators of military expenditure: how much money the receiving state spends on its military compared to other countries in the world (military rank), military expenditure in million US$, and military expenditure as

Table 6.6 Degree of militarism of the receiving countries to which female and male ambassadors are sent[11]

	Females	Males	All	Gender diff.
Military rank	56	51	51 (3,756)	+5***
Military expenditure (in million US dollars)	11,934	21,607	20,103 (3,756)	−9,673***
Military expenditure (% of GDP)	1.85	2.11	2.07 (3,791)	−0.26***
Armed forces personnel (number)	165,418	262,808	247,863 (4,248)	−97,390***
Armed forces personnel (% of total labor force)	1.32	1.44	1.43 (4,241)	−0.12**

a percent of GDP. All three measures point in the same direction; countries to which female ambassadors are appointed are generally less militarized than those of the male ambassadors. For example, the average military rank of the countries that male ambassadors are sent to is 51. For female ambassadors it is 56, indicating that countries that female ambassadors are posted in spend less money on their military forces.

This is also true if we look at the absolute figures of how much the countries spend. The average military expenditure of the countries to which male ambassadors are sent is almost twice as high (US$21,607 million compared to US$11,934 million for the female ambassadors). Since average military expenditure can be somewhat misleading as a few leading countries may spend enormous amounts and thus have a disproportional effect on the means, we have also compared the median values for women and men. The difference here is not as striking, but it is still convincing. The median military expenditure of the female ambassadors' postings is US$3,230 million compared to US$4,064 million for the males.

Seen in relative terms, the countries in which male ambassadors are posted also spend a greater share of their economic resources on their military. On average, 2.1 percent of their GDP is spent this way. The corresponding figure for the countries that the female ambassadors work in is only 1.9 percent.[12]

Furthermore, the countries that male ambassadors are posted in do not just pour significantly more economic recourses into their military; they also invest more of their human capital into this sector. On an average, they employ 262,808 people, which is almost 100,000 more than the countries in which female ambassadors are posted.[13] This also corresponds to a greater share of the total population. 1.4 percent of the people living in the countries in which the male ambassadors work are employed by the military, which this is slightly more than in the countries where the female ambassadors are posted (1.3 percent).[14]

Table 6.7 Share of female and male ambassadors (percent) that are sent to countries with different levels of armed conflict[15]

	Females	Males	All	Gender diff.
Receiving countries with two conflicts or more	4	6	5	−2
Receiving countries with one conflict	16	22	21	−6
Receiving countries with no conflict	80	73	74	+7
All countries	100.0	101.0	100.0	

Armed conflict

In the next step, we look at the degree to which receiving countries are involved in intra- or interstate-armed conflicts. Seventy-eight out of the 106 countries (73 percent) included in the analysis are not involved in either of these kinds of conflicts. Twenty-two percent are involved in one conflict and only five countries (Ethiopia, India, Mali, Myanmar, and the Philippines), which equals 5 per cent of all counties included, are involved in two conflicts or more. These five countries receive in total 161 ambassadors from the top 50 ranked GDP countries. Fifteen of these are assigned to Mali, whereas India, which is the only country that is involved in as many as four conflicts, receives ambassadors from 47 out of the 50 highest ranked GDP countries. Very few of these ambassadors are women, however. Only 4 percent of the ambassadors sent to India are women, which is much lower than the global average of 15 percent. This is a pattern that seems to reoccur in general among the countries that are involved in some kind of armed conflict.

In line with our argument, Table 6.7 shows that female ambassadors are less likely to be assigned to a country that is involved in some kind of armed conflict. Only 4 percent of the female ambassadors are posted in a receiving country with two armed conflicts or more, compared to 6 percent of the males. This is not a great difference in percentage points, but it is significant. Similarly, 16 percent of the female ambassadors work in countries that are involved in at least one armed conflict, compared to 22 percent of the male ambassadors. In peaceful countries, however, where there is no ongoing armed conflict at all, the gender pattern is the opposite; 80 percent of the female ambassadors are assigned a post in one of these countries, but only 73 percent of the men. A comparison of the average number of ongoing armed conflicts in the countries in which female and male ambassadors are posted shows the same pattern; the number of armed conflicts is significantly lower in the countries of the female ambassadors (0.24 compared to 0.36 conflicts).[16]

Global Peace Index (GPI)

We will end this empirical analysis by looking into what the GPI tells us about the postings of female and male ambassadors. As mentioned in the "Design and data" section, GPI is composed of three themes: the level of safety and security in society, the involvement in armed conflicts, and the degree of militarization. It can thus serve as a summarizing measure of our previous indicators of status, militarism, and armed conflict, but it also allows us to test to our argument on a variable that captures the degree of organized violence in the receiving country in a broader sense and not just violence organized and planned by the state.

The three most peaceful countries in 2013 were, according to the GPI, Iceland, Denmark, and New Zealand. These countries receive in total 79 foreign ambassadors of whom 24 percent are women. On the opposite end of the GPI scale, we find Afghanistan, Somalia, and Syria. Together, these countries receive 46 foreign ambassadors. Only 7 percent of them are women. At this quick glance, the GPI thus seems to confirm our previous results; female ambassadors are less likely to be posted in militarized countries that are involved in armed conflicts. This gender pattern remains even if we expand the groups to the ten most and the ten least peaceful countries (see Table 6.8).

The gender differences presented in Table 6.8 are not great, but they are significant and they go in the expected direction. A greater share of the female ambassadors (12 percent) is assigned to one of the ten most peaceful countries, compared to their male colleagues (9 percent) and the pattern to the least peaceful countries is the opposite. There, 6 percent of the male ambassadors are posted, but only 2 percent of the females. An analysis of the average GPI score and rank shows the same gender pattern (see Table 6.9).

The assigned GPI scores range between 1.162 for the most peaceful country (Iceland) and 3.440 for the least peaceful country (Afghanistan). The average GPI score of the countries that female ambassadors are sent to is 1.887, which corresponds exactly to the score of Tanzania (rank 55), a country that is defined to enjoy a high state of peace (IEP 2013). Male ambassadors, however, score on average 2.014, which is a value that lies somewhere in between the country scores of Tunisia (2.005) and Kazakhstan (2.031): the latter of these two countries is only considered to enjoy a medium state of peace (IEP 2013). Tunisia

Table 6.8 Share of female and male ambassadors (percent) in receiving countries of different GPI rank[17]

	Females	Males	All	Gender diff.
Top 10 GPI countries[a]	12	9	9	+3**
Bottom 10 GPI countries[b]	2	6	5	−4***

Table 6.9 Average GPI score and rank of the receiving countries to which female and male ambassadors are sent (means)[18]

	Females	Males	All	Gender diff.
GPI score	1.887	2.014	1.996	−0.127***
GPI rank	65	77	75	−12***

may be a better estimate of the average male ambassador posting, however, since the GPI rank of this country (77) also corresponds to the average GPI rank of the male ambassadors.

A comparison of the average GPI ranks brings the female and male ambassadors closer together, but the gender difference still points in the same direction and it is significant. The average GPI rank of the female ambassadors is 65, which equals Cuba (GPI score 1.922). As mentioned above, the rank of Tanzania, which corresponds to the female ambassadors' average GPI score is only 55, so when looking at the GPI rank, the distance between the female and male ambassadors' ranks shrinks from 22 (55–77/78) to 12 (65–77).

The overall impression of the empirical analyses carried out here is, however, that there does indeed seem to be a gender pattern in ambassador appointments with regard to status and how militarized and violent the receiving country is. Female ambassadors appear less likely than male ambassadors to be posted in high status countries that are highly militarized and that are engaged in intra- or inter-state armed conflicts.

Conclusions

We started out this chapter by making the observation that the number of women in the diplomatic corps around the world has increased substantially during the last decades, even at the most prestigious ambassador level. The overall proportion of female ambassadors is only 15 percent, but as our chapter shows, there are considerable variations among states. The Nordic countries, the Philippines, the US, Colombia, and others appoint nearly 30 percent or more female ambassadors. One pressing question then concerns the extent to which this means that women and men employed by the MFAs also face the same working and career conditions. Experiences from other professional fields show that women's and men's work tasks tend to be segregated as well as hierarchically related to one another such that men end up with tasks and in positions of higher status. In this chapter, we set out to study whether a similar pattern can also be discerned in the diplomatic field.

With respect to the economic and military status of the receiving countries, this seems indeed to be the case. The GDP of the countries that female ambassadors are sent to is, for example, lower and they are less often G20 members. Similarly, female ambassadors are less likely to be stationed in military powers that control nuclear weapons, or which are permanent members of the UN Security Council.

Taking our starting point in feminist theories on gender, militarism, and violence, we then proceeded to explore whether women are less likely to be assigned to countries that are highly militarized and that are engaged in some kind of armed conflict. The reason for this is that traditional gender roles associate women with vulnerability, weakness, and peace, characteristics that are not valued in war. Concerns that women may not function as very effective representatives in violent contexts, together with beliefs that women should be protected from war, not exposed to it, may therefore result in male ambassadors mainly being the ones who are sent to postings in militarized and violent countries.

Such a gender pattern could be seen as an advantage to female ambassadors. After all, they do not need to serve in these potentially dangerous contexts. On the other hand, previous research has indicated that postings in countries that experience armed conflicts work as stepping-stones in diplomatic careers. The experience of serving in these kinds of challenging environments develops competences that speed up people's career advancement. Hence, if women are systematically overlooked when it comes to assigning positions in militarized and violent countries, they also are shut out from a potential career path. There may be other career paths open to them, of course, but not this particular one.

The empirical analyses carried out here confirm that this may indeed be the case. All measures used for the degree of militarization, as well as for organized violence in the receiving country indicate that female ambassadors are sent to countries that score highly on these two factors to a lower extent. It is important to remember that the observed gender pattern in ambassador appointments is not entirely the doing of the people who make these appointments. On the contrary, it is likely to be the cumulative effect of a long row of variables, e.g., individuals' career choices (as preferences are also shaped by gender), the existence of discrimination in the diplomatic corps, male homosocial networks, etc. The observed correlation between gender and the degree of militarization and violence in the receiving country thus needs to be re-run under control for other explanatory variables,[19] but this first exploratory study points to the relevance of delving deeper into the work and career conditions of female and male ambassadors. The data presented here shows that it is far too early to count out the role that gender plays in the diplomatic corps, particularly in ambassador appointments.

Notes

1 When we speak of violence in this chapter, we refer to state organized violence, unless otherwise stated.
2 This means that the lowest ranked sender country has the rank of 51, since Hong Kong, which is ranked 39, is not an independent country with foreign representation of its own.
3 Theoretically, it is possible to distinguish between military status and militarism; a state can be impregnated by a military culture without being one of the most important military actors internationally, but this distinction is harder to uphold empirically. Our indicators of military status could, for example, arguably also be used as measures of militarization; without a considerable military force, a state is unlikely to enjoy a high military status. Thus, in the data collected for this study, the two concepts of military status and militarism tend to overlap. This fact does not constitute a major problem to our main argument, however, since we also look at how violent a state is.
4 Number of cases in parenthesis. Gender difference in percentage points. The Nordic countries include Finland, Sweden, Norway, and Denmark. Russia and Turkey are included in Europe, as well as the following sending countries: Austria, Belgium, France, Germany, Greece, Ireland, Italy, the Netherlands, Poland, Portugal, Spain,

Switzerland, and the UK. The following sending countries are included in the Middle East: Saudi Arabia, United Arab Emirates, Qatar, Israel, Egypt, Iran, and Iraq.
5 The number of cases in parenthesis. Gender difference in percentage points. The Nordic countries include Finland, Sweden, Norway, Denmark, and Iceland. Russia and Turkey are included in Europe as well as the following receiving countries: Albania, Andorra, Austria, Belarus, Belgium, Bosnia and Herzegovina, Bulgaria, Croatia, Cyprus, Czech Republic, Estonia, France, Germany, Greece, Hungary, Ireland, Italy, Kosovo, Latvia, Lithuania, Luxemburg, Macedonia, Malta, Moldova, Monaco, Montenegro, the Netherlands, Poland, Portugal, San Marino, Serbia, Slovenia, South Ossetia, Spain, Switzerland, Ukraine, and UK. The following receiving countries are included in the Middle East: Bahrain, Jordan, Kuwait, Lebanon, Saudi Arabia, United Arab Emirates, Qatar, Israel, Palestine, Egypt, Iran, Yemen, and Iraq.
6 Number of cases is 4,730. ***$p<0.01$ (Pearson's R). Gender difference in percentage points.
7 $p=0.009$ (Pearson's R).
8 Number of cases in parenthesis. *$p<0.1$, ***$p<0.01$ (Pearson's R). Gender difference in percentage points.
9 $p=0.092$ (Pearson's R).
10 $p=0.000$ (Pearson's R).
11 ***$p\leq0.01$, **$p\leq0.05$ (two-tailed t-test). Number of cases in parenthesis.
12 The median value for the postings of male ambassadors is 1.5 percent compared to 1.4 percent for the female ambassadors.
13 The corresponding median values are 80,500 for the postings of male ambassadors and 56,856 for the postings of female ambassadors.
14 The corresponding median values are 0.92 percent for the postings of male ambassadors and 0.88 percent for the postings of female ambassadors.
15 Note: $p=0.00$ (Pearson's R). Number of cases is 3,020. Gender difference in percentage points. The reason why the percentage for the male ambassadors does not add up to 100, but to 101, is because the figures have been rounded off.
16 $p\leq0.01$, two-tailed t-test.
17 Note: **$p=0.05$, ***$p=0.00$ (Pearson's R). Number of cases is 4,185. Gender difference in percentage points.

   a Iceland, Denmark, New Zealand, Austria, Switzerland, Japan, Finland, Canada, Sweden, and Belgium.
   b Afghanistan, Somalia, Syria, Iraq, Sudan, Pakistan, the Democratic Republic of Congo, Russia, North Korea, and the Central African Republic.

18 Note: ***$p=0.00$ (two-tailed t-test). Number of cases is 4,185.
19 Preliminary logistic regression analyses have been made in which the receiving countries' GDPs, Gender Inequality Index ranks, and Gender Development Index ranks have been included. The results indicate that the effect of the level of peacefulness of the receiving country still remains.

References

Adler-Nissen, Rebecca (2013) "European Diplomats: State Nobility and the Invention of a New Social Group" in Niilo Kauppi and Mikael Rask Madsen (eds.): *Transnational Power Elites*. London: Routledge, 65–80.
Bashevkin, Sylvia (1993) *Toeing the Lines: Women and Party Politics in English Canada*. 2nd edn. Toronto: University of Toronto Press.
Brösamle, Klaus J. (2012) "Misery as a Stepping Stone: Whether and Why Natural Disasters Accelerate Diplomats' Careers." Working paper. Berlin: Hertie School of Governance.

Campbell, David (1992) *Writing Security: United States Foreign Policy and the Politics of Identity*. Minneapolis, MN: University of Minnesota Press.

Cockburn, Cynthia (2004) "The Continuum of Violence. A Gendered Perspective on War and Peace" in Wenona Mary Giles and Jennifer Hyndman (eds.): *Sites of Violence: Gender and Conflict Zones*. Berkeley, CA: University of California Press, 24–44.

Cohn, Carol (1987) "Sex and Death in the Rational World of Defense Intellectuals." *Signs* 12(4): 687–718.

Connell, Raewyn (2006) "Glass Ceilings or Gendered Institutions? Mapping the Gender Regimes of Public Sector Worksites." *Public Administration Review* 66(6): 837–849.

Crapol, Edward ed. (1987) *Women and American Foreign Policy: Lobbyists, Critics, and Insiders*. Santa Barbara, CA: Greenwood Press.

Elshtain, Jean Bethke (1987) *Women and War*. Chicago, IL: University of Chicago Press.

Enloe, Cynthia (1990) "Diplomatic Wives" in Cynthia Enloe: *Bananas, Beaches, and Bases: Making Feminist Sense of International Politics*. Berkeley, CA: University of California Press, 93–123.

Galtung, Johan and Mari Holboe Ruge (1965) "Patterns of Diplomacy. A Study of Recruitment and Career Patterns in Norwegian Diplomacy." *Journal of Peace Research* 2(2): 101–135.

Gibbons, Robert and Michael Waldman (2006) "Careers in Organizations: Theory and Evidence" in Orley C. Ashenfelter and David Card (eds.): *Handbook of Labor Economics, vol. 3B*. Amsterdam: Elsevier, 2373–2437.

Hale, Sondra (2010) "Rape as a Maker and Eraser of Difference: Darfur and the Nuba Mountains (Sudan)" in Laura Sjoberg and Sandra Via (eds.): *Gender, War, and Militarism: Feminist Perspectives*. Santa Barbara, CA: ABC-CLIO, 105–113.

Institute for Economics and Peace (IEP) (2013) *Global Peace Index 2014. Measuring Peace and Assessing Country Risk*. Sydney: IEP.

Jeffreys-Jones, Rhodri (1995) *Changing Differences: Women and the Shaping of American Foreign Policy, 1917–1994*. New Brunswick, NJ: Rutgers University Press.

Kinsella, Helen (2005) "Discourses of Difference: Civilians, Combatants, and Compliance with the Laws of War." *Review of International Studies* 31(S1): 163–185.

Kopp, Harry W. and Charles A. Gillespie (2011) *Career Diplomacy. Life and Work in the US Foreign Service*. Washington, DC: Georgetown University Press.

Kronsell, Annica (2012) *Gender, Sex, and the Postnational Defense: Militarism and Peacekeeping*. Oxford: Oxford Scholarship Online, DOI:10.1093/acprof:oso/97801998 46061.001.000.

Mann, Michael (1987) "The Roots and Contradictions of Modern Militarism." *New Left Review* 162: 35–50.

McGlen, Nancy E. and Meredith Reid Sarkees (2001) "Foreign Policy Decision Makers: The Impact of Gender" in Susan J. Carroll (ed.): *The Impact of Women in Public Office*. Bloomington, IN: Indiana University Press, 117–148.

Neumann, Iver (2012) *At Home with the Diplomats*. Ithaca, NY: Cornell University Press.

Nightingale, Robert T. (1930) "The Personnel of the British Foreign Office and Diplomatic Service 1851–1929." *The American Political Science Review* 24(2): 310–331.

Niskanen, Kirsti (2010) "Kön och makt i Norden – ett jämförande perspektiv" in Kirsti Niskanen and Anita Nyberg (eds.): *Kön och makt i Norden. Del II Sammanfattande diskussion och analys*. Tema Nord 2010: 525, 19–52.

Niskanen, Kirsti and Anita Nyberg eds. (2010) *Kön och makt i Norden. Del I och Del II*. Tema Nord 2010:525.

OECD (2015) www.oecd.org/g20/about.htm. Accessed February 4, 2015.
Peterson, V. Spike (2010) "Gendered Identities, Ideologies, and Practices in the Context of War and Militarism" in Laura Sjoberg and Sandra Via (eds.): *Gender, War, and Militarism: Feminist Perspectives*. Santa Barbara, CA: ABC-CLIO, 17–29.
Putnam, Robert D. (1976) *The Comparative Study of Political Elites*. Englewood Cliffs, NJ: Prentice-Hall.
Reardon, Betty A. (1996) *Sexism and the War System*. Syracuse, NY: Syracuse University Press.
Ruddick, Sara (1993) "Notes Toward a Feminist Peace Politics" in Miriam Cooke and Angela Woollacott (eds.): *Gendering War Talk*. Princeton, NJ: Princeton University Press, 109–127.
Scott, Joan (1986) "Gender: A Useful Category of Historical Analysis." *The American Historical Review* 91(5): 1053–1075.
SIPRI (Stockholm International Peace Research Institute) (2014) Milex data 1988–2013 plus.
SIPRI (Stockholm International Peace Research Institute) (2015) www.sipri.org/research/armaments/nuclear-forces. Accessed June 25, 2015.
Sjoberg, Laura (2011) "Gender, the State, and War Redux: Feminist International Relations across the 'Levels of Analysis'." *International Relations* 25(1): 108–134.
Sjoberg, Laura (2012) "Gender, Structure, and War: What Waltz Couldn't See." *International Theory* 4(1): 1–38.
Sjoberg, Laura and Sandra Via (2010a) "Introduction" in Laura Sjoberg and Sandra Via (eds.): *Gender, War, and Militarism: Feminist Perspectives*. Santa Barbara, CA: ABC-CLIO, 1–13.
Sjoberg, Laura and Sandra Via (2010b) "Conclusion: The Interrelationship between Gender, War, and Militarism" in Laura Sjoberg and Sandra Via (eds.): *Gender, War, and Militarism: Feminist Perspectives*. Santa Barbara, CA: ABC-CLIO, 231–239.
Studlar, Donley and Gary Moncrief (1999) "Women's Work? The Distribution and Prestige of Portfolios in the Canadian Provinces." *Governance: An International Journal of Policy and Administration*, 12(4): 379–395.
Teorell, Jan, Stefan Dahlberg, Sören Holmberg, Bo Rothstein, Anna Khomenko and Richard Svensson (2015) "The Quality of Government Standard Dataset, Version Jan 15." Gothenburg: University of Gothenburg, the Quality of Government Institute, www.qog.pol.gu.se. Accessed June 1, 2015.
Themnér, Lotta and Peter Wallensteen (2014) "Armed conflicts, 1946–2013." *Journal of Peace Research* 51(4): 541–554.
Towns, Ann and Birgitta Niklasson (2015) "International Glass Ceilings? International Hierarchy, Gender and Ambassador Appointments." Paper presented at the ISA conference in New Orleans, February 18, 2015.
UN (2015) www.un.org/en/sc/members/. Accessed June 25, 2015.
World Bank (2015) (GDP rank): http://data.worldbank.org/data-catalog/GDP-ranking-table. Accessed February 2, 2015.

7 Women in foreign lands

Women diplomats and host-country cultures

Jane Marriott OBE

Introduction

Whilst posted overseas, diplomats, male and female alike, are expected to conform as much as possible to the country where they reside; 'one is expected to respect the host's culture' (Leki 2011). However, in countries where the political and legal status, and cultural understandings of women in society differ significantly from one's own, this is often a complex, and sometimes challenging, process. The host country will be cognisant of how it should react to Her Majesty's Representatives, but some countries adjust better than others in reconciling the potential juxtaposition of hosting and working directly with female diplomats with their own cultural, political, and legal understandings regarding the roles they expect their own women to play in society and public life.

The roles and lives of male diplomats and their relations overseas have been extensively documented in memoirs, history books, and in the media.[1] Insights into the relationship between the Foreign Service and host-country culture have been provided by ambassadorial and diplomatic wives regaling tales of spousal support.[2] However, existing academic literature focusing on navigating host-country culture for male and female diplomats is sparse.

Moreover, there is a distinct lack of academic literature focusing on the role of a female diplomat and how she has been received by the country to which she has been posted. Where attention is paid to the roles and lives of female diplomats, it is usually through the prism of uniqueness implying their rarity, or a historical analysis of prominent female pioneers in the world of diplomacy, such as Gertrude Bell, Nancy Lambton, or Freya Stark.[3] Furthermore, even in 2017, when a female diplomat is given academic or media attention, the emphasis is usually on her uniqueness as woman in diplomacy, with perceived interest in her lifestyle and clothing choices. McCarthy (2015) aims to bridge this gap by tracing the multitude of roles that women have played in British diplomacy from the nineteenth century onwards, providing a historical analysis of the issues and prejudices faced by female ambassadors and diplomats at the time and their remarkable attempts to overcome the barriers they faced. Focusing on the challenges that female diplomats face whilst working overseas, Linse (2004) also provides insight into the experience of eleven female diplomats working in

Minsk. However, there is still a fundamental lack of literature focusing on the role of female diplomats and their roles and lives in the host countries to which they are posted.

The aim of this book is to remedy the absence of women in the academic literature on diplomacy. As a contribution, this chapter conducts a preliminary investigation into the experiences of British female diplomats working in sometimes difficult host-country contexts. This chapter aims to provide a unique contribution to the existing literature by identifying the type and range of issues faced by female representatives of Her Britannic Majesty's Government when they operate in an overseas environment in the present day, specifically in host countries where the political and legal status, and cultural understandings of women in society differ significantly from their own.

This chapter does not cover the challenges of navigating the internal culture of one's own organisation. Interestingly, the respondents repeatedly asserted that they found dealing with foreign governments and cultures, including those whose value of women was partial, easier than their own foreign ministry. However, there are other chapters in this volume which extend a focus to internal gender diversity and equality within Ministries of Foreign Affairs (MFAs); notably Anne Barrington's chapter 'From marriage bar to gender equality' and Birgitta Niklassson and Ann Towns' chapter, entitled 'Gender, status, and ambassador appointments to militarized and violent countries'.

Methodology

As a relatively new field of study, the methodology used in this chapter is a necessarily qualitative one. Through conducting a written questionnaire, the author surveyed thirty-six members of the UK's Foreign and Commonwealth Office (FCO), all but one of whom were active members of the diplomatic service at the time of the survey; one had retired. All respondents had worked overseas for the FCO with experience varying from those on their first posting to those who had had multiple postings. Two members of staff were serving their third posting as an Ambassador or Head of Mission. The age, relationship and child status, and length of time in the FCO was broadly representative of serving female diplomats. The women had been posted across the continents and served in a range of posts from junior administrative grades to Heads of Mission. Some respondents included information from postings in the 1990s and beyond and all but one (retired) included contemporaneous (within the last decade) examples.

Contributions were also received from one serving US State Department Officer and a former Canadian officer, both of whom had served in Afghanistan. The author also drew on her own experience from postings to Al Amara and Baghdad in Iraq; Kabul, Afghanistan; Washington DC, USA; Tehran, Iran as Chargée[4]; and Sana'a, Yemen as Ambassador. All respondents named in this chapter have provided consent for their responses to be attributed to them.

Findings

Four distinct categories of issues and challenges emerged from the survey responses: (1) navigating cultural norms; (2) building trust and relationships; (3) working in male-dominated environments; (4) personal life.

A number of respondents, including the author, also discussed their experiences with verbal and physical harassment during their postings abroad, and others discussed the role race or sexual orientation played in the issues and challenges they faced, all of which have been incorporated into the analysis.

The majority of respondents identified that female diplomats face additional pressure when working in difficult host-country cultures – the pressure to counter being underestimated as being female by 'getting it right' and proving to be an effective diplomat and interlocutor in the different environments to which they were posted. However, when discussing the issues and challenges they faced, the majority of respondents also reported the ways in which they transformed many of these challenges into opportunities, working to ensure their gender was either not relevant nor a disadvantage in their diplomatic roles.

Most significantly, respondents identified that their adjustment to some host-country cultures and their work was shaped by the categorisation of their gender as 'different kind of woman' to the local women. Several respondents used the term 'Third Gender'[5] to describe how they were viewed by host-country cultures, where they did not fit into the societal-assigned roles for either men or women: for example, in a named Asian country, a Western woman could drink with the elite of the host-country men, but those same men would not accept their own women imbibing alcohol. In host countries where the role and status of women is traditionally domestic-focused and their power is influenced primarily 'behind the scenes', categorising female diplomats as different to local women, thus not subject to the same cultural and societal norms, was an enabling factor for building relationships and trust and insulated respondents from certain local prejudices. As the discussion below will illustrate, embracing this newly assigned gender role enabled respondents to not only strengthen their relationships with male colleagues and interlocutors but also resulted in better engagement with local women who were often seen as an irrelevant or less accessible population for male ambassadors and diplomats.

It is important to highlight that not all of the issues covered affected every respondent surveyed nor every woman working in the British Foreign Service, nor all female diplomats working in similar contexts.

Discussion

Navigating cultural norms

Expectations and perceptions played an important role in how diplomats interacted with host cultures. Respondents reported that they were realistic and open-minded about how they would relate to the culture of the host country, and many had more positive experiences during their posting than they expected. Previous knowledge of the country in question or a similar culture and full use of pre-posting preparation time to understand a country and culture played a role in managing a respondent's expectations prior to departure to a difficult host-country culture. Sharing experiences was also vital; staff initiatives in the FCO to share knowledge and understanding for working in countries in conflict or women in the Middle East has allowed the dispelling of many myths and enabled identifying key issues and challenges prior to a diplomat's posting.

First impressions

Arriving in a host country where physical contact or direct communication between unrelated men and women is not usually culturally acceptable provided the first of many challenges for the respondents. Respondents agreed that navigating whether to shake hands or not with their interlocutors could be initially challenging, although an easy adjustment once the norm had been set. Working in other contexts, however, where men refused to even look at the female diplomat when reporting their duties was a more complicated obstacle to overcome. One diplomat recalled conducting allegiance ceremonies in Mumbai where, on occasion, she would administer the service to men from a certain religious sect who would position themselves so they did not have to look at either her or the portrait of Her Majesty The Queen. Anticipating the rise of the Houthi movement in Yemen, the author intensified her meetings with them, establishing new contacts. One such interlocutor could not look at her and directed all his comments, including direct answers to the author's – the Ambassador's – questions, to the Defence Attaché, who was taking the notes of the meeting.[6]

Persistent and patience are regular diplomatic values, but female respondents noted that working in these environments necessitated increased persistence and patience on a regular basis. Pride, respondents noted, was not an option. It would have been possible to take personal offence at the Houthi interlocutor's behaviour, but the job was to represent the United Kingdom. With that persistence and patience, the same Houthi, after a few meetings, started to look in the author's direction and then make eye contact, as he grew more comfortable with female presence. Not long afterwards, he uttered the flirtation: 'Oh Ambassador, if only your policies were as attractive as you'. Respondents consistently noted how they used patience to wear interlocutors down and encourage mutual adjustment, although the majority found that the emotional toll of having to be more persistent and patient than their male counterparts could be demanding and sometimes draining.

Dress codes

An additional issue highlighted by respondents was thinking about culturally appropriate female attire and the impact that their wardrobe could make on interlocutors, especially at the first meeting. The author reported that during an evening meeting at a Middle Eastern intelligence agency, she had enquired and been told that a trouser suit and no headscarf would be culturally appropriate. She was pleasantly surprised and, indeed, once in the meeting, the senior officials appeared entirely comfortable in her presence and were clear that they were interested in what she had to say. Prior to the meeting, however, all the other participants – all men – had been served coffee as part of the greeting ritual, but the respondent was assiduously ignored. Gender was the only variable factor and perhaps reflected the discomfort of the male coffee servers. Solidarity being crucial, she saw that the absence of coffee had made one of her male colleagues uncomfortable, which in turn made her feel less isolated and able to focus on the meeting.

Adapting to the female-specific dress code in some host-country cultures was not an easy process either. In Tehran, Iran the author was shouted at on the street for wearing light-coloured versions of the required clothing style.[7] In the religious city of Qom, in a four-hour visit, she was stopped on three occasions by the religious police for accidentally revealing a small triangle of hairline beneath the hood of her chador.

Travel

Another adjustment in navigating the cultural norms of the host country was the ways in which female diplomats were allowed to travel, or the issues they faced when travelling alone, or with a male-only security team. The author once got on at the front of a Tehran bus to pay, only to discover that after she had paid, she had to get off, walk halfway down the bus and get on at the 'exit' door, which led to the bus's female section. Whilst today's female diplomats in the Kingdom of Saudi Arabia have to rely on male drivers to enable them to conduct their business,[8] Susan Brodribb Pughe, in Jeddah in the late 1960s and early 1970s, 'opted for a camel, which she rode to work side-saddle and "parked" outside the Embassy compound' (FCO Historians 1994: 4). The author discovered that travelling in Yemen with an all-male close protection team had its own challenges because they went wherever the author went – including an advance deployment to check out the women's toilets. 'I learned to cross my legs and plan in advance to avoid the understandable upset [to Yemeni women] that occurred if polite but armed Yemeni men opened the door to the women's toilets'. This experience was reiterated by a number of respondents on conflict postings who relayed accounts of desperately holding in the need to go to the toilet (or using multiple tampons) because there was nowhere to squat with dignity in the open desert and one was keen not to be seen as a 'problem'.

Same woman: different perspective

Despite these issues, a number of respondents highlighted that whilst working overseas, they were first and foremost seen as a British diplomat, with the accompanying prestige, power, and history of the nation which that brought.

In most countries, respondents identified that after finding ways to navigate the cultural norms of the host country, gender was treated as a secondary characteristic to their nationality. That, and the fact that one was not a local woman who was expected to comply with local social norms, insulated female diplomats to some extent from many of the prejudices that local women may face.

Respondents identified that once being subconsciously assigned this 'Third Gender' role, being a female diplomat began to open doors in the first place as interlocutors would often be curious as to who the new arrival was, a curiosity exacerbated by the relative uniqueness of her gender. Female diplomats, particularly in Middle Eastern countries, were aware that their novelty value could often secure meetings that male colleagues may have had difficulty procuring. In 2015, when visiting a Gulf state where there had never been a female ambassador, the author was guest of honour at a dinner of twenty (all male) Ambassadors to brief them on events in Yemen. One Ambassador initiated a conversation as to whether the host nation would ever accept a female ambassador. The male US Chargé d'Affairs (Acting Ambassador) proffered his view that a female Ambassador would get much better access than most of them: 'most of the senior Arabs don't get to talk to that many women here: any female Ambassador worth her salt could easily punch above her weight. The hardline Islamists might not see a woman', he continued, 'but then they don't like seeing us either'. The author agreed, nuancing the 'hardline' point as well: she had taken tea with hardline Salafists in the Pearl Continental hotel in Peshawar, Pakistan, a few weeks before it was blown up in 2009. In Yemen, she found that the Salafists were enthusiastic about being invited to a Western Embassy for the first time and apologised profusely for not being able to shake her hand.

Building trust and relationships

Novelty aside, respondents identified that building the trust and understanding essential for strong diplomatic relationships with interlocutors was more complex and challenging, in comparison to their male colleagues. The adjustment process for both the host government and for the diplomat herself was often a steep, but ultimately rewarding, one.

First impressions

When new ambassadors arrive at post, protocol dictates that they pay a visit to the most important ambassadors in country: this 'ranking' is determined by the countries they represent, the relationship to either the sending or host country or by the personal longevity of an Ambassador in post. The longest-serving Ambassador is called the 'Dean' of the Diplomatic Corps. In many places, the United Kingdom is amongst one of the key countries on which Ambassadors wish to call. As a British diplomat, therefore, one of the key tools in one's armoury is that the UK is a permanent member of the UN Security Council, of the Commonwealth, of NATO, of various other diplomatic groupings and, as of

2017, a member of the European Union. As a result, one *had* to be invited to certain meetings as the protocol point of not doing so would be blasphemous in diplomatic circles. Thus, the nationality and job title often became more important than the gender/creed/colour of the person in that role.

In Yemen, one of the key political groupings was the 'G10', representing the five permanent members of the UN Security Council (China, France, Russia, the United Kingdom, and the United States of America), the EU representative and key Gulf countries. In Tehran, the EU grouping was one of the more important, although membership of the Commonwealth also gave insights into Iran's relationship with different African countries. In Sana'a, Yemen, a European diplomatic colleague wished to speak to a senior UK diplomat but initially refused to deal with Harriet Cross.[9] He had dropped in without prior communication and immediately assumed that she was an inexperience female junior member of staff: until she handed over her card, stating that she was the deputy British Ambassador.

Ambassadors are expected to call on other Ambassadors but it is the job of all newly arrived diplomats to embark on a range of contact-making and networking as a matter of priority. Most respondents found that on first impression, the expectations from interlocutors on them as women diplomats were significantly lower than their male counterparts; but the pressure from themselves and their Service to get it 'right' significantly higher. Respondents consistently perceived that if they got it 'wrong', their gender, rather than any personal failings, might be unfairly blamed. Being consistently under-estimated or even ignored upon first meeting a new interlocutor remained a regular feature for colleagues in their interactions with a range of cultures.

The author described how she would sometimes 'be looked up and down and given the impression that twenty points were deducted from my IQ'. A North African Foreign Minister once turned to a respondent, and not her male equivalent, to interpret at a meeting – being a smart woman, she could do it: but it was not her job any more than his. For the first few weeks after arriving in Namibia, High Commissioner Marianne Young regularly had to explain that *she* was the boss, not her husband.[10] Diplomat Nadia Hashmi, alone in a taxi, directing the driver to the compound of the British High Commission in Kuala Lumpur, was asked if her husband was the High Commissioner.[11] Frances Wood, due to brief Australian Defence Ministry colleagues on climate security, found that they immediately turned to her junior and younger male colleague to begin the meeting.[12] It was a not uncommon experience, although thankfully gradually less so, to have arrived at a meeting or function to find the name plate read 'Mr' instead of 'Ms/Mrs/Miss' or that the hosts expected a man when the nameplate read 'Dr'.

Gendered segregation

Respondents highlighted that another barrier to building trust and relationships as a female diplomat was the lack of admission into all-male venues or social arrangements or activities: be they the remaining clubs in Pall Mall where women can now be guests but not members, or all-male qat chews in Yemen.[13] Or, the inability to watch a football match in Iran, where the author wanted to watch Tehran's two local teams, Esteghlal F.C. and Persepolis F.C. – unsuccessful, she was denied the opportunity for a societal-bonding experience and participation in water-cooler discussions the following day.[14] High Commissioner Marianne Young was not invited to football matches hosted for her male colleagues by the Acting Chief of Protocol for Namibia's President: 'I don't think it's hampered my job and I'm not sure I would have donned shorts and boots if I had been invited' Marianne admitted, 'but I might have suggested a game of tennis instead'. Events and activities such as these provide opportunities for additional networking and strengthening trust and relationships between colleagues and interlocutors, and being isolated meant that female diplomats were occasionally disadvantaged by virtue of their gender in such trust and relationship building processes and had to find creative and alternative ways to build those contacts instead.

Moreover, social activities and events were not the only occasions female ambassadors and diplomats were isolated from their male colleagues. Some recounted experiences of being sat with the women in a separate room in order to respect purdah, or being invited to female-only dinners hosted by diplomatic wives.[15] However, this was not the case for most respondents, and junior female diplomats in a range of countries found themselves invited to more senior dinners in male-dominated diplomatic corps and sometimes host nation events than their junior male colleagues. Their gender and not their policy prowess may have been the primary reason they were on the invitation list, but respondents ensured they made the most of the opportunity afforded, making policy contributions, contacts and expanding their networks.

Respondents found that sometimes it was necessary to take a stance against this segregation. In Iran, for example, the author occasionally wanted to make a political point about being female and the value and participation of women in society that was in line with the UK's values; or else she wished to emphasise that her rank and role would define her, not her gender. In 2011, she attended an annual event to which Ambassadors were invited. Determined to be seated in the main function room and not the secondary chamber to where the women had been diverted, she decided to stand her ground as the only female Head present. Supportive (male) Spanish and Brazilian Ambassadors moved in closely as the line inched towards the security arches, making it clear that they were a pack and would – or would not – go through together. With only minor disgruntlement and confusion about the absence of a female body-searcher, the author was finally allowed into the room and attend the event sitting with her male colleagues. One could usually get to where one wanted and needed to be: it just took a lot more work than for others.

Making progress

Acknowledging and accepting that their role in the host country was going to be influenced by their gender was identified by respondents as an essential step towards building trust and relationships. The aforementioned issues may have provided initial barriers in their posting, but finding ways to transform these challenges into opportunities, and embracing their role as a 'different kind of woman' was important for all respondents. Showing that they were competent, credible, knowledgeable interlocutors and able to make a connection, regardless of their gender, would help build trust and strengthen relationships. For example, when the author was posted to a particular Middle Eastern country, she called upon that country's deputy Foreign Minister. At the end of the meeting, he pursed his lips, looking pensive: 'I'm sorry' he finally said, 'I completely underestimated you'. He escorted the author to the exit of the Foreign Ministry (an honour): 'Will you come back next week?' The meeting had been scheduled for thirty minutes, was closer to ninety and presaged regular contact for the rest of her posting, building up a strong working relationship.

A number of respondents also highlighted that male interlocutors would often answer their questions with an openness that would be less forthcoming if they were regarded as an equal (a man) and thus, potentially, a threat. This meant that once one had started the real content of the discussion, respondents found that their gender enabled them to move on to the real, substantive conversations quite quickly. By the time their male interlocutors realised their error, it was too late. They would also see – providing the diplomat was good at what she did – that there were not any negative repercussions for them and subsequent conversations would continue with the same openness and trust. In Basra, Consul-General Alice Walpole thought that 'The anti-British Basrawis put less energy into being nasty to me than I think they would have had I been male, because they simply didn't realise I was a player'.[16] By the time they did, Alice had already built the foundation of trust to enable future cooperation and engagement. Another respondent noted that '[interlocutors] will have real conversations rather than posturing statements because you probably remind them of a strong-willed sister or aunt they enjoy talking to'.

Engaging with local women

The most common advantage for female diplomats, however, was that in many societies, building relationships and trust with local women was something that, due to cultural norms, their male colleagues found much more challenging to do. For a long time, the importance of engaging with the women of the host nation has been widely undervalued by many foreign ministries. Diplomatic interaction with local women was often valued, if at all, as a way of eliciting information about their more important husbands, rather than for the views of the women in their own right. On other occasions, they offered useful insights into society that would have wider application. Pamela Gordon accompanied her husband to

Chile, where it was difficult for him to interact freely with locals, but Pamela found that:

> my joint spouse/teaching role was a real advantage as opposition members could come to my English language classes and talk freely (at a time when they were banned and not allowed to meet in groups) knowing that, with my background, I knew what was important to pass back to my husband in the embassy.[17]

US Department of State 2011 guidance noted that:

> Gender roles vary from country to country ... [but] the practice of actually separating men and women at any time during a dinner party is rare even in primarily gender biased societies. Be aware that this may happen and when it does, it is best to go along with these traditions ...
> (Leki 2011: 3)

Many respondents approached such situations in line with this advice and used their gender to access information and engage with local women. Whilst a young Third Secretary in Cuba, Pamela Gordon recalled being instructed by her Ambassador, after dinner, to join the 'wives' 'powdering their noses' whilst the men passed the port and talked. 'In fact it wasn't such a hardship' Pamela explained,

> as the Cuban wives were very high powered, including ministers in their own right, and many topics of political interest were talked about in the garden where we were. Afterwards my ambassador said he knew that would happen, which is why he wanted me to leave the dining room with them (although I suspect that was retrospective thinking to answer my complaint the next day).

Ailsa Terry also found that the best unofficial information could be found from behind the purdah screen at dinners in Kabul.[18] Other respondents reported finding out useful information by popping into the backrooms of events with the wives before re-appearing on the verandas where their husbands were having the official discussions. This highlights an interesting way in which embracing the role of being a 'different kind of woman', enabled female diplomats to move with relative ease between different parts of society, some of which were more difficult (or less of a priority) for male diplomats to engage. As women they were able to access women-only events and venues, but by being categorised as a 'different kind of woman' and by being the official representative of their country they were also able to transgress the gender segregation at certain events and venues and engage with male colleagues and interlocutors.

Other respondents noted that another advantage of being female was that there were often powerful women whom one could more easily access by being female oneself. As Consul-General, Walpole built good relationships with female members of Basra's Provincial Council, who would have been much more reserved about meeting with her male colleagues. Diplomat Alyson King took her young daughter to a women's group in Khartoum, which included an older generation of Sudanese feminists and young students and professionals, impatient with the accommodations of the past, and far more business and tech savvy than their elders.[19] Marianne Young's gender gave her a clear advantage in the matriarchal aspects of African society, gaining insights into the inner workings of cultural issues and often complex family networks and power plays.

Sian MacLeod was one of many who though that 'as an Ambassador who happened to be female, I was better placed to address my host country's record on representation of women politics and public life and support the cause of those trying to increase it'.[20] Certainly, the author reported how she enjoyed attending and hosting women-only salons in most of the countries where she had worked, opening up new networks of contacts for colleagues amongst entrepreneurial and reformist groups in particular.

Many respondents were also proactive in supporting their male colleagues to raise societal issues understood primarily as 'women's issues' – and therefore often ignored – such as child marriage, female genital mutilation and representation in constitutional systems. It was an appreciated rarity when men took the lead: former British Foreign Secretary William Hague, partnered with the UN Goodwill Ambassador, Angelina Jolie, role modelled such behaviour with his Preventing Sexual Violence Initiative (PSVI).[21] On a smaller scale, two (male) British Defence Attachés in Yemen accessed influential female-only circles in senior Sana'a society, facilitated by their foresight in employing a female Yemeni defence advisor.

Working in male dominated environments

Alongside the challenges arising from the role and status of being a female diplomat juxtaposed with the host country's political, legal, and cultural understandings of the role of women, respondents reported that working in an environment where most colleagues and interlocutors were men provided additional issues and challenges.

From feeling uncomfortable to sexual assault

Respondents reported a variety of situations in which they had been made to feel uncomfortable as a female working in a male-dominated environment: experiences shared more widely than within the diplomatic community of course. For example, one respondent reported that whilst at a business lunch, a foreign, male colleague pretended that he was having language comprehension issues about a phrase he had read in a novel and asked her to explain what a 'wet dream' was. She took control back by explaining that 'It is a nocturnal emission of semen, experienced by adolescent boys, and sometimes men who abstain from sex'.

Another respondent was called a 'whore' by an Asian academic after she had walked into their first meeting carrying the jacket of her dress suit over her arm.

In Russia, Alyson King whilst working on conflict diamond issues, attended a diamond-themed fashion show in Moscow during a global plenary meeting without the advance knowledge that the models would be wearing only diamonds. Not only feeling that this was entirely inappropriate, King felt further isolation from her male colleagues as they used their mobile telephones to document the models. Being in the position of feeling inherently uncomfortable themselves, but also not wanting to be seen as a malcontent or prude, spoiling others' 'fun', and thus being further isolated from their male colleagues and interlocutors, was seen by respondents as a difficult balance to achieve.

Respondents recalled that there were also times when working in a male-dominated environment did not only feel make them feel uncomfortable and an outsider, but in danger as a victim of verbal and, sometimes, physical assault. The author herself was sexually assaulted by a European military officer in Iraq. She alerted a (male) colleague and friend in Basra, who, with her permission, told the Commanding Officer, British Major-General, Andrew Stewart. Stewart's support helped her process and move past the ordeal. There are currently no existing or recorded statistics about how many British female diplomats have been assaulted in post[22] – although some colleagues gave the author their stories in person once she had spoken about her own experiences.

Appearance

Respondents also noted that not only were assumptions made about them on the basis of their gender, several reported that there was often an inherent assumption that, as a female diplomat, one would be interested in hearing what people thought about one's appearance: 'being offered heavy handed compliments on one's beauty and intelligence at the beginning of formal meetings is unnerving the first time it happens', commented Ambassador Thorda Abbott-Watt.[23] 'The only thing to do is to smile graciously, resist the temptation to suggest your new acquaintance buys new spectacles and get on with the business in hand'. The author has had a Foreign Minister tell her that his aim was to fatten her up. Another senior official commented, as the author, who has coeliac disease, was politely declining sandwiches, that it was no wonder she looked emaciated. In the author's experience, the (male) commentators did not intend to be disrespectful and she assessed that it was often their way of dealing with the relatively unknown – a woman. Respondents distinguished such exchanges from diplomatic small talk and relationship-building, based on the context of the remarks. They believed that such exchanges, unwittingly or otherwise, however, often left them on the back-foot, with the onus on them having to move the conversation on from their appearance and to the more important matters at hand.

Sian MacLeod was 'acutely aware of the opportunities and pitfalls of having your appearance constantly in the public eye – opportunities to promote UK fashion companies in the local market, balanced against the risk of criticism if one got it "wrong"'. In Swaziland, then Deputy High Commissioner Marianne Young found that trousers were not acceptable attire for a female diplomat. On exercise with the British military in Germany, Tiffany Kirlew politely declined the request of a retired British Colonel that she wear a skirt the next day to 'raise morale' – although otherwise had a positive experience.[24] Both Tiffany Kirlew and the author recalled putting a lot of thought into what they wore when attached to the military on operations, concluding that smart clothing – trousers and a shirt – was essential to show professionalism and to be culturally appropriate. Both decided to wear their long hair down on most occasions to bring a degree of femininity to their attire. 'Our value was in not thinking like the military, so I thought hard about how my image would reflect this', noted Kirlew. 'Not all female diplomats thought the same though, with one senior female diplomat memorably disembarking from a helicopter in wedge heels, a sun hat and a beach bag'.

Furthermore, in a number of host-countries – particularly in Asia where deference to age plays a part – being female and looking young was also reported as an often disadvantage. Harriet Cross found that most meetings in Morocco, when she was in her early 20s, started with exclamations regarding how young she looked, which she found patronising. Harriet stated: '[it] would never have happened to a man in his 20s – they would have just thought he was awesome [for] having "bagged" such a good job so young, not questioned his ability to do it'.

Others also found that the combination of their gender and age seemed to threaten their male colleagues and interlocutors. Frances Wood shared her experience of being taken out for dinner by a Korean contact as part of the preparation for a VIP visit.[25] Unnerved by the fact that he and Frances were the same level of seniority when she appeared much younger, he interrogated her about her life events to try and establish her age, and was angered when she did not reveal it – to do so would have made it easier to patronise her. No one else at the dinner had intervened, making the experience an isolating one. A senior Namibian official wryly accused HM The Queen of dispatching child soldiers to his country: the then High Commissioner, Marianne Young, took to making quips about her surname to deal with such incidents.

However, in Yemen, the author found that her relative youth was an advantage, allowing her to connect directly with civil society organisations and the youth movements born out of the 2011 revolution. Most of Yemen's senior leaders were in their 70s, whereas the Houthi movement that conquered the capital, Sana'a, in September 2014, were in their 20s and early 30s. They were fascinated by her age and not sufficiently used to diplomatic niceties as not to ask.

Standing out

With reference to their appearance and often being the only or one of few women representing her country overseas, respondents reported that a key advantage of being female – whether to the host nation or with their diplomatic colleagues – was that one was often remembered more easily than most, because one stood out. The author's first posting was with a British military brigade in Maysan, southern Iraq, in 2003. With 1,200 men in uniform but only a handful of women, the latter were more memorable. The author found that men in the same uniform looked somewhat similar and would regularly fall into conversations with a fatigue-clad man in the mess tent unsure if they were conversing for the first or fifth time, but the women were always remembered.

Being a female ambassador in most countries resulted also meant greater media attention and coverage. Sian MacLeod, when Ambassador to Prague, commented that she was likely to turn down interviews that she feared would reinforce gender stereotypes, 'such as the dreaded "lifestyle" interview', unless journalists were also willing to include policy relevant content. The Yemeni Foreign Minister once told the author that a meeting with her was guaranteed to feature in the top three stories of the evening Yemen news slot which would open with camera footage of the meeting. Many respondents reported that they struggled with the concept of one's gender being used in such a way, but ultimately decided that it was a platform to promote and generate greater coverage of UK policies and ideas in the host country.

Personal life

For most ambassadors and diplomats, male or female, moving to another country and adapting to a new culture as an individual travelling alone or with a family is a challenging but essential part of the job. For female diplomats working in host-countries where the role of women has a primarily domestic focus, making adjustments to reconcile her personal life with her status as a working, and powerful, woman in the country was sometimes problematic.

Life as a single woman

Interestingly, with reference to their personal life, some respondents discussed the loneliness that occasionally arose from the lack of company of a partner or the inability to engage in social arrangements with other women in the community, who were mostly married with families, due to work. Nadia Hashmi said: '[you] find yourself unable to join cultural excursions or yoga classes because they happen at 10 am on a Tuesday and being told they had no activities at the weekend because that's when they spent time with their families'.

Whilst discussing their experiences with dating during their postings, including experimenting with internet dating, heterosexual respondents reported the difficulties of meeting men, particularly men who were not seemingly threatened or disconcerted by their status or experience as an ambassador or diplomat. Another issue that was identified was that fellow expatriates were more interested in and attracted to the local women. One respondent stated: 'I know what it's like to be invisible to expatriate Western men who only have eyes for the petite, pretty local population'. Thus, although embracing the categorisation of a 'different kind of woman' enabled respondents in building working relationships and trust with their male colleagues and interlocutors, they found it was often detrimental to their personal life.

Travelling with a partner

Respondents identified that travelling with a partner was not necessarily an easier adjustment. One of the most significant cultural challenges highlighted by respondents was the incredulity sparked by the male spouse, particularly if he was a 'stay-at-home' husband and father. Susie Kitchens reported her husband was viewed 'with great suspicion for being a stay at home dad' when they were posted in Central America.[26] Another respondent added that, whilst working in a strictly patriarchal African society, her partner felt isolated from the host and the expatriate community, particularly when it became clear that husbands were not comfortable for their wives to bring their daughters around for play dates.

Amassador Thorda Abbott-Watt, however, found that:

> having a male spouse allows one to model behaviour that is different, in a non-threatening way: I have taken great delight in taking my other half on regional visits and watching people's response as he walks a pace behind, clearly delighted to be there and with his masculinity visibly unimpaired by the fact that he is travelling as my consort.

LGBTI

Respondents who identified as LGTBI faced additional challenges and opportunities working in many countries overseas. Homosexuality[27] is illegal in 72 countries[28] and many more have anti-homosexual laws, although lesbianism can be 'a glorious omission from the statute book, which provides a rather grey area in which to operate'.[29]

Challenges included being limited in career choices: certain countries were unlikely to give Agrément (formal agreement to the appointment) to LGBTI Ambassadors, or they were stereotyped in advance as 'the lesbian diplomat or ambassador'. Being single at LGBTI had a different set of challenges to those in a relationship. One lesbian couple thought it would be possible to navigate a challenging Asian country, only to find that the officer's partner could only receive thirty-day visas, which required her to leave the country prior to each renewal. Another respondent noted that her partner had to be registered as 'a member of her household' rather than as her spouse.

Yet alongside the challenges, LGBTI diplomats were also determined to find opportunities. Dealing with host-country officials was seen as easier than dealing with the press or a minority of fellow diplomats: 'In my experience, a number of male interlocutors overseas find gay women intriguing (and often a legitimate challenge) rather than the threat that male homosexuality poses', commented Judith Gough. 'I am therefore, often met with curiosity and the odd bout of flirtation, rather than by hostility. That's fine by me – access is access, which is often half the battle'. Jo Adamson[30] believed that getting involved with LGBTI events overseas, whether private or public, could quickly help to establish tight-knit professional and personal networks and often open doors to different aspects of the diplomatic community or host countries.

Families and children

With reference to adjusting to the host country with children, some respondents found that their role as a mother helped them connect better with both the population and their male colleagues. Kara Owen reported that by opening her family life up to otherwise closed male Vietnamese colleagues allowed them to form swift bonds and confidences, but the opposite with the French, who, she found, tended to draw more clear distinctions between work and family life.[31] Speaking of her experiences in Tanzania, Alice Walpole stated:

> In a country where people were wary of authority, it was a definite advantage to appear relaxed and informal [as a mother]. I used to get out of the car to sit under a tree to breastfeed the baby and people would materialise to talk to us – I heard a great deal of interesting information about the government that way.

Race

For some respondents, race also played a part in their adjustment to the host country. One respondent noted that 'if you feel as though twenty IQ points are deducted on first sight for being female, it feels like double that as a black woman'. As a black female, Diane Smith would find that she was regularly asked 'but where are you from really?' ('Harlow, Essex' in the UK never seemed to satisfy them) and, without fail, was repeatedly stopped and searched at an Asian airport until she showed her diplomatic passport.[32] The darkness of a British diplomat's skin tone may also play a role: Diane characterised her time in one Asian country as 'mostly good', and noted that she could shop in the country's more elite shopping areas without any issues. A female diplomatic colleague who had darker skin, however, found that people would 'stare, point, and constantly take her picture without her consent', making her time there often uncomfortable.

The British High Commissioner to Kuala Lumpur, Vicki Treadell, was born in Malaysia. Her mother was Chinese whilst her father, who was born in Kuala Lumpur, traced his ancestry to the Dutch Burgher community of Sri Lanka.[33] She migrated to the UK when she was eight years old. As a Eurasian, she found she was often questioned on her diplomatic postings as to how she could be a British Diplomat representing HM The Queen and the United Kingdom. Her answer was that she is a legacy of the British Empire and that her family's Commonwealth antecedents and mixed race credentials are advantages in representing the United Kingdom.

Conclusion

Through focusing on the experiences of female diplomats working in host-countries where the political, legal, and cultural understandings of the role, status, and visibility of women differs significantly from their own, this chapter has examined the different issues and challenges they encounter working in these, sometimes difficult, environments.

Interestingly, in identifying the ways in which women working in the British Diplomatic Service overcame these issues and challenges, this chapter has also demonstrated that there can be specific advantages to working in particularly difficult host-country cultures as women. The UK's female diplomats who were interviewed overwhelmingly concluded that in spite of the challenges along the way, including hurdles that others may not have to face, they had ultimately been able to turn most situations to the UK's advantage, particularly when it came to building trust and managing diplomatic relationships with all members of the host country's community, including local women. The FCO's Political Director, Karen Pierce, regularly advises the new generation of diplomats to 'just go for it and don't overthink the obstacles'.[34]

As of 1 March 2016, the Board of the Foreign and Commonwealth Office was 55 per cent female and the number of female Heads of Mission had increased from around 8 per cent of Head of Mission posts in 2008 to nearly 20 per cent. Thirty per cent of senior staff were women. Of all staff, 4 per cent self-identified as BME and 5 per cent as LGBTI.[35] Significant progress has been made and more needs to be made: there have now been female ambassadors to Moscow, Beijing, and NATO, but the positions in Washington, Paris, Berlin, and the Permanent Representative to the United Nations have yet to be held by a woman. Over the last decade, the average number of female Ambassadorial appointments in the UK's posts to the Middle East and North Africa has remained stubbornly at one post.

As a preliminary and small-scale study into the role and lives of female diplomats who are posted to often-difficult host-countries, this chapter has only focused on a small number of female members of the British Foreign Service. The relatively small number of BME or LGBTI female diplomats means that significantly more research is required to begin to understand the additional complexities they face.

Notes

1 For example, see: Watson Foster (1910); Cowper-Coles (2013); Wright (2001 [1977]).
2 For example, see: Hickman (2011); King (2015); Keenan (2006).
3 Gertrude Bell was an English writer, traveller, political officer, administrator, spy, and archaeologist who explored, mapped, and became highly influential to British imperial policy-making due to her knowledge and contacts, built up through extensive travels in Greater Syria, Mesopotamia, Asia Minor, and Arabia; academics Nancy Lambton and Freya Stark were the first female attachés in Tehran and Baghdad respectively, and two of the first women honoured with diplomatic rank in the Middle East. For more information, see McCarthy (2015) and Bell (2015).

4 Acting Ambassador – the additional 'e' denoting a female acting Ambassador.
5 Different cultures and schools of academic thought understand different things by the term 'Third Gender'. Female diplomats adopted the term as shorthand to refer to the social category where societies recognise 'male'; 'female' and see the diplomats as biologically female, but are treated by some host cultures as if they possessed the social attributes of both men and women as the host society understands its own culture.
6 The Houthis have their roots in a movement that started in northern Yemen in the late 1980s to protect and revive Zaydi religious and cultural traditions. Zaydism is a branch of Shia Islam different from the Twelver Shiism of Iran, Iraq, and Lebanon. The Zaydis make up the majority in the far north but they're a minority in Yemen.... The Houthis became politicized under [their late leader] Hussein Badreddin al-Houthi [who] shifted the movement toward political activism.
Source: www.cfr.org/yemen/yemens-houthis/p36178.
Accessed 10 November 2016
7 Islamic codes of behaviour and dress are strictly enforced. In any public place women must cover their heads with a headscarf, wear trousers (or a floor length skirt), and a long-sleeved tunic or coat that reaches to mid-thigh or knee. Men should wear long trousers and long-sleeve shirts. There are additional dress requirements at certain religious sites. Women may be asked to put on a chador (a garment that covers the whole body except the face) before entering. Source: www.gov.uk/foreign-travel-advice/iran/local-laws-and-customs. Accessed 10 November 2016.
8 It is illegal for women to drive in Saudi Arabia (source: www.gov.uk/foreign-travel-advice/saudi-arabia/local-laws-and-customs). Accessed 10 November 2016.
9 Harriet Cross is currently (from August 2016) Britain's Consul General to New England. Previously she was posted to Sana'a, Yemen as Deputy Head of Mission at the British Embassy in Sana'a, though due to the conflict in Yemen, she was mainly based in the Kingdom of Saudi Arabia. She has also been posted to Morocco as Second Secretary at the British Embassy in Rabat, and as First Secretary at the UK Mission to the UN in New York.
10 Marianne Young is currently Deputy Head of Global Economic Issues. Previously, she was British High Commissioner to Namibia from June 2011 to August 2015. She has also served as Deputy High Commissioner to the Kingdoms of Lesotho and Swaziland, and served as Head of the External Political Section at the British High Commission in Pretoria.
11 Dr Nadia Hashmi is a member of Her Majesty's Diplomatic Service and has served in Malaysia, Turkey, and France.
12 Frances Wood is Head of the Economics Unit at the Foreign and Commonwealth Office. Previously she has served in the UK Embassy in Seoul, Republic of Korea.
13 A leafy plant called qat, khat, or miraa or – more mystically – 'Tea of the Arabs'. Socially, users chew the bitter leaves of this natural stimulant. It is supposed to make them more alert and raise energy levels. (source: www.bbc.co.uk/news/uk-27921832). Accessed 10 November 2016.
14 Women are banned from attending male football matches in Iran, at least partly down to the theory that women shouldn't hear male fans swear and curse (source: www.hrw.org/news/2016/06/30/banned-stadiums-being-woman-iran). Accessed 10 November 2016.
15 Purdah is the practice in certain Muslim and Hindu societies of screening women from men or strangers, sometimes by means of a curtain.
16 Alice Walpole is currently the British Ambassador to Mali and Niger. Previously she served as the British Ambassador to Luxembourg. Immediately before that, she was the British Consul General in Basra and has had postings to the UK Mission to the United Nations in New York (twice), the UK Representation to the European Union

in Brussels (twice), the UK delegation to NATO, and in the British High Commission in Dar es Salaam.
17. Pamela Gordon retired from the Diplomatic Service in 2014 and has been the Chair of the Diplomatic Families Association (DSFA) since 2012. She has served in Cuba, Brussels, and Strasbourg and accompanied her husband on his diplomatic postings to Santiago, Paris, Warsaw, Rangoon, and Hanoi. During those times, she worked as a teacher and English examiner in most posts and as Director of the EU Chamber of Commerce and in the EU delegation, in Hanoi.
18. Ailsa Terry is currently a first secretary of the United Kingdom to the European Union.
19. Alyson King is currently the Deputy Director for Policy in Scotland. Her previous roles included conflict resolution work in Sudan, a secondment to the European Commission working on sanctions and conflict diamonds, and legal advisory roles on international and EU law in both Brussels and London.
20. Sian MacLeod is currently Head of UK Delegation to the Organization for Security and Cooperation in Europe, Vienna. She has previously been posted to Moscow (twice), The Hague, and was Ambassador in Prague from 2009 to 2013.
21. William Hague and Angelina Jolie spearheaded the FCO's Preventing Sexual Violence in Conflict Initiative (PSVI) which aims to address the culture of impunity, ensure more perpetrators are brought to justice and ensure better support for survivors. For more information, see: www.gov.uk/government/policies/sexual-violence-in-conflict.
22. The FCO offers a counselling service to staff.
23. Thorda Abbott-Watt is currently Her Majesty's Ambassador to Ashgabat, Turkmenistan. Previously she has been posted to Ulaanbaatar and Yerevan, as Ambassador; Kabul as Acting Head for the Political/Military Section, Dushanbe as Chargée d'Affaires, Belgrade as First Secretary Political, and Kiev as First Secretary, Head of Commercial Section, as well as serving in multiple roles in the UK and Europe.
24. Tiffany Kirlew is currently the North Africa Team Leader in the Joint International Counter-Terrorism Unit. Previously, she has been posted as Private Secretary to HMA Washington, First Secretary Political in Moscow and as Provincial Reconstruction Team liaison to the international military forces in Helmand Province, Afghanistan.
25. Very Important Person: usually a junior Minister or Secretary of State.
26. Susie Kitchens is currently Head of Economic Growth and Business Department in the FCO. Previously, she has served in Boston, Tanzania, and Guatemala.
27. As of late 2016, 21 countries recognised gay marriage. Others recognised civil unions and registered partnerships; unregistered cohabitation accounts for several more places for potential postings for LGBTI officers.
28. https://en.m.wikipedia.org/wiki/LGBT_rights_by_country_or_territory. Accessed 10 November 2016.
29. Judith Gough is currently Her Majesty's Ambassador to Ukraine and has previously served as Director for Eastern Europe and Central Asia, Her Majesty's Ambassador to Georgia and in Seoul, Republic of Korea.
30. Jo Adamson is currently Deputy Head of the European Union Delegation to the United Nations. Previously, she was Her Majesty's Ambassador to the Republic of Mali and has also served in Geneva, Washington and Jerusalem.
31. Kara Owen is currently FCO Director of the Americas. Previously, she was Deputy Head of Mission at the British Embassy in Paris and has also served in Vietnam.
32. Diane Smith is currently posted to the British Embassy in Baghdad and was previously the Tunisian Desk Officer in the Joint International Counter-Terrorism Unit.
33. Vicki Treadell CMG MVO is currently the British High Commissioner to Malaysia. Previously, she has served as the British Deputy High Commissioner in Mumbai, covering Western India, and then as High Commissioner to New Zealand. She has been posted in Pakistan and once before to Malaysia. She won the UK Asian Women of Achievement Award in 2009.

34 Karen Pierce CMG is currently the FCO's Political Director and former Chief Operating Officer. Previously, she was British Ambassador to Kabul, Afghanistan; Permanent Representative to the United Nations and the World Trade Organisation in Geneva; Deputy Permanent Representative to the United Nations in New York and has also served in Washington and Tokyo.
35 Letter from Sir Simon McDonald KCMG KCVO, Permanent Under Secretary of State to Crispin Blunt MP, Chair of the Foreign Affairs Committee, 26 April 2016.

References

Bell, Gertrude. 2015. *A Woman in Arabia: The Writings of the Queen of the Desert*. Penguin Classics.

Cowper-Coles, Sherard. 2013. *Ever the Diplomat: Confessions of a Foreign Office Mandarin*. Harper Press.

FCO Historians. 1994. 'Women in Diplomacy: The FCO 1782–1999'. *History Notes* 6. https://issuu.com/fcohistorians/docs/history_notes_cover_hphn_6. Accessed 24 February 2017.

Hickman, Katie. 2011. *Daughters of Britannia: The Lives and Times of Diplomatic Wives*. Flamingo.

Keenan, Brigid. 2006. *Diplomatic Baggage: The Adventures of a Trailing Spouse*. John Murray.

King, Mary. 2015. *Letters of a Diplomat's Wife, 1883–1900*. Create Space Independent Publishing Platform.

Leki, Ray S. 2011. *Protocol for the Modern Diplomat*. Foreign Service Institute: US Department of State, Transition Center. www.state.gov/documents/organization/176174.pdf. Accessed 2 February 2017.

Linse, Caroline. 2004. 'Challenges Facing Women in Overseas Diplomatic Positions'. www.diplomacy.edu/sites/default/files/IC%20and%20Diplomacy%20(FINAL)_PPar16.pdf. Accessed 2 February 2017.

McCarthy, Helen. 2015. *Women of the World: The Rise of the Female Diplomat*. Bloomsbury Press.

Watson Foster, John. 1910. *Diplomatic Memoirs*. Houghton Mifflin.

Wright, Denis. 2001 [1977]. *The English Amongst the Persians*. I. B. Tauris.

8 Women in global economic governance
Scaling the summits

Susan Harris Rimmer

Introduction

This chapter provides an examination of the roles of woman participating in global economic governance, with a particular focus on women representing their state in Group of 20 processes. This examination is for the purpose of understanding more deeply how gender dynamics play out in different aspects of diplomatic practice. Ideas explored include how women use their *agency* in the context of a leader-led economic summit often focused on crisis response; how *gender* issues are framed in the field of economic diplomacy; questions of *institutional power* where actors involved are frequently from central banks or treasuries rather than foreign ministries; and *leadership* on behalf of actors pursuing women's economic rights and inclusive economic growth that reduces inequality between men and women, rich and poor.

This chapter takes a feminist approach to diplomacy as a social practice,[1] and therefore examine women's lived experiences of economic summitry, but also interrogates how masculine values and worldviews, such as the assumptions of mainstream economics, have shaped this area of diplomacy. The central argument posited is that economic diplomacy and trade are areas extremely resistant to the participation of women, as of 2016. Currently, 15 per cent of the heads of state of the G20 member countries are women.[2] The figure for finance ministers, central bank governors, and 'sherpas' (a leader's personal representative) is also low, with roughly 15 per cent women. The official photo of finance ministers and central bank governors from the Sydney meeting in 2014 shows 10 per cent representation. This already represents a positive shift with Janet Yellen as the first female head of the US Federal Reserve and Christine Lagarde the first female head of the International Monetary Fund.

The rise of economic diplomacy internationally and the investment of emerging economies in economic fora is both an opportunity and a threat to women in traditional diplomatic roles in foreign ministries. It is an opportunity because it is a traditionally 'soft' area of international relations, theoretically more open to women than traditional intelligence or security. It may be a threat because current economic summitry draws on technical personnel outside foreign ministries, such as finance and treasury officials, central banks, and the corporate sector, with low representation of women. Anne Marie Slaughter posits that these regulators are the 'new diplomats' (2004: 14). Summit processes also operate informally without scrutiny from the broader women's movement that organs such as the UN Security Council attract.

This chapter takes the form of three distinct, but interlocking, sections. Part I presents a theoretical analysis of gender and diplomacy to date. Based on this analysis, Part II puts forth a central case study concerning the particular context of women involved in economic diplomacy at the most senior levels, as represented by the G20 forum. Here, I offer snapshots of some of the key women involved as sherpas, central bank governors, leaders, and heads of international financial institutions (IFIs). Cases of female representatives are presented showing great agency and leadership skills in influencing the G20 Summit outcomes. Part III then moves to outline the development of the outreach group that seeks to promote gender equality within the G20 processes, called the 'W20' (Women 20), as well as female leadership in the official engagement groups that seek to influence the Summit. I then conclude with some warnings to heed for progress on gender equality goals and diversity of actors in this increasingly important but quasi-informal summitry space.

Part I: theorising gender and diplomacy

This Part examines the role of gender in the past, present, and possible future activities, and roles and relations between the diplomatic actors of the global society. I consider briefly:

- Gender dimensions to theories of diplomacy;
- Gender dimensions to diplomatic practices;
- Feminist methodologies of diplomacy;
- The changing role of the diplomatic spouse; and
- Sex, sexuality and diplomatic cultures.

As Nigel Gould-Davies has stated:

> [t]hose who study international relations pay little attention to those who practise them. But the terms of scholarly explanation – the great abstractions of state, interest, power and so on – are always embodied in human representatives, and their interactions mediated through human relationships. The daily experience, lived and felt, of diplomats thus offers a valuable perspective on how international relations work.
>
> (2013: 1459)

If this is so, then the new representation of women and LGBTI+ persons in the practice of diplomacy since the mid-twentieth century, as well as changes in gender relations in society and in foreign policy, should have made a profound impact on the field of diplomacy studies. Much progress has been made, celebrated in this volume. But often, energy has focused on inclusion of some limited diversity in diplomatic personnel, rather than more transformational reform of the vocation.[3] The 'business model' of diplomacy has been resistant to transformation on gender equality grounds thus far.

There has been insufficient gender analysis of diplomacy as a social practice, despite significant attention to gender in the fields of international relations and international law over the past two decades. Why the academy has broadly ignored this topic is unclear, but partly due to reliance on official records, which formally excluded women until recent times. I argue that one of the most important changes to modern diplomacy is the increased participation of women, both as foreign policy elites and in wider transnational networks. This advent could be even more significant as the Internet or the rise of NGOs for the practice of diplomacy.

Moreover, the representation of women and people identifying as LGBTI+, and acceptance that gender equality norms are changing, should be changing the diplomatic agenda. We would expect to see change occurring in terms of who should be at the table, what is discussed, and whether a diversity of negotiation styles can be accepted. This is occurring very slowly but the fundamentals of diplomacy and foreign policy are not demonstrably altered. We could describe this as a transition, not transformation of the 'business model'. More data is required to investigate specific areas of diplomatic practice (peace negotiations, trade talks, summitry) to see how the participation of women and LGBTI+ persons is shifting the practice of diplomacy.

Gendered theories of diplomacy

Most theoretical perspectives of women in diplomacy focus on exclusion and the limited form of citizenship women are allowed to demonstrate in terms of public life and the representation of the state in international affairs. Eleanor Roosevelt told the United Nations General Assembly in 1952 that:

> Too often the great decisions are originated and given form in bodies made up wholly of men, or so completely dominated by them that whatever of special value women have to offer is shunted aside without expression.
> (Crapol 1992: 176)

A majority of the scholarship in the field of feminist international law and international relations since the 1970s has been devoted to exploring this gender dynamic. As J. Ann Tickner describes:

> Conventional international relations theory has concentrated on the activities of the great powers at the centre of the system. Feminist theories, which speak out of the various experiences of women – who are usually on the margins of society and interstate politics – can offer us some new insights

on the behaviour of states and the needs of individuals, particularly those on the peripheries of the international system.

...

However, feminist theories must go beyond injecting women's experiences into different disciplines and attempt to challenge the core concepts of the disciplines themselves. Concepts central to international relations theory and practice, such as power, sovereignty, and security, have been framed in terms that we associate with masculinity.

(Tickner 1992: 18)

Feminist approaches to diplomacy would therefore examine women's experiences of diplomacy, but also interrogate how masculine values and worldviews have shaped diplomacy, or how 'normative ideas about manhood' inform policymakers' decision making in both domestic and international contexts, such as liberation movements or militarism (McEnaney 2010: 14; Pettman 1996; Enloe, 1989). For example, we could examine texts like Thomas Schelling's (2008) famous 'The Diplomacy of Violence' and theorise that diplomacy itself is a feminised representation of the state as compared to the soldier and the spy; based on feminised skills of communication, non-violent conflict resolution, and relationship building, but still underwritten by the threat of armed violence. This would explain why women are often essentialised as peaceful, but excluded from formal peace processes, as one example (Fukuyama 1998; Ehrenreich et al. 1999).

Queer theorists would interrogate the heterosexual norms displayed in diplomatic practice in the same manner. Both approaches would make visible the intersections between diplomats from developing countries compared to strong economies, gender roles, sexual preference, class, ethnicity, race, and migration status. Both approaches would consider discourse seriously. As Laura McEnaney notes, '[g]endered metaphors and tropes are not just casual talk; they are the stuff of politics' (2009).

The same arguments can be made forcibly about diplomacy leading to the adoption of international law. As feminist international lawyers argue:

Our argument is ... that international law does not provide even momentary distance from subjectivity. It is intertwined with a sexed and gendered subjectivity, and reinforces a system of male power. Until international law focuses on all people and peoples, not just a powerful few, it will always be subject to geopolitical agendas inimical to genuine security ...

(Chinkin, Charlesworth, and Wright 2005)

Dianne Otto highlights the tensions of an approach which focuses on the transformative potential of a gendered approach to diplomacy, asking 'whether it is possible to work for progressive outcomes for women, while also being deeply critical of the same institutions, laws and policies that we expect to produce those outcomes?' (2010: 98). In one sense it could be argued that feminist scholarship has made inroads into international law: success stories include the adoption of Security Council Resolution 1325 in 2000, which called on UN members to include women and children when considering issues of peace and conflict; the attention to women's lives in the work of the UN human rights treaty bodies; and the development of international criminal law to recognise sexual crimes.

But women's lives have also been invoked as justifications for the use of force in international relations, for example in the United States-led invasion of Afghanistan in 2001. Once an intervention is underway, however, women's lives are typically pushed off the agenda. Although the politics of masculinity and femininity are deeply implicated in international interventions, such as the contributions interventions make to the sex trade and to violent war economies, they are not often taken into account. Dyan Mazurana (2005) observes that women and gender are seen as 'soft' or peripheral issues in conflict and post-conflict situations and can therefore be postponed until after the 'hard' problems of establishing new governmental or economic structures are resolved. In this sense, interventions regularly reinforce the unequal and oppressive political and social systems that have caused and sustained the immediate conflict (Charlesworth and Harris Rimmer 2010).

The state of the field at present is more attuned to diverse experiences of diplomacy since women and LGBTI+ persons have entered the vocation in serious numbers, an approach more in common with a cultural diplomacy approach (Iriye 1979). But as McEnany notes, 'we are past the question of "whether?" and on to the business of "how?" when it comes to understanding gender and sexuality's relationship to international relations' (McEnaney 2010).

Feminist methodologies for diplomacy studies

In the influential 2015 text, *Women, Diplomacy and International Politics Since 1500* edited by Glenda Sluga and Carolyn James, there is an approach to diplomatic studies that could be described as utilising a feminist methodology. Instead of relying solely on diplomatic archives and other embassy or consular official documents, the volume looked at letters and biographical detail of many women in informal positions of power who nonetheless had significant impact (including through networks, alliances, and discussions) in the diplomatic world, as well as oral interviews with official female diplomats.[4] Helen McCarthy argues that the task is of 'historical recovery' and acknowledgement of agency and impact in a broader investigation of diplomatic practice (Sluga and James 2015: 168).

Gender dimensions to diplomatic practice: start royal and work your way down

The origin story for women in diplomacy is instructive for our examination of the gender dynamics of the G20 as a leaders' forum. There are two clear trends:

the legitimacy of female diplomats based on their aristocratic status to embody the nation, and the unacknowledged contributions of women as core low-level workers and diplomatic spouses.

Ambassador Claudia Fritsche (2002) posits that Spain appears to have pioneered the employment of women as diplomats. According to the British Foreign Office documents, in 1507, Ferdinand of Aragon sent his widowed daughter Catherine with formal credentials as his ambassador in England and instructions to negotiate with Henry VII about the delay in her proposed marriage to Prince Henry.

Ambassador Fritsche further notes:

- The Treaty of Cambrai (1529) was popularly known as 'The Ladies' Peace' because it had been negotiated and drafted by Louise of Savoy, mother of King Francis I, and Margaret of Austria, aunt of the Emperor Charles V, on behalf of their respective countries.
- Madame Delahaye-Vautelaye was appointed French Ambassador to Venice in the sixteenth century.
- The Maréchale de Guébriant became the French Ambassador to Poland in the early years of the seventeenth century.
- The Duchess of Orleans acted as Louis XIV's representative when negotiating the secret Anglo-French Treaty of Dover with her brother in 1670.
- In the eighteenth century, there are two examples of a woman acting as her country's representative, both British. One was the widow of the British Consul at Tripoli, Mrs White. When her husband died in office in November 1763, Mrs White took on the management of consular affairs. Around the same time, following her husband's death in 1771, Mrs Marguerite Wolters carried on the British spy network in Rotterdam.

From other sources, we can note a flurry of progress in the 1930s with mainly political appointments of women to posts. By 1933, 13 countries including Nicaragua and Turkey had admitted women to their diplomatic and consular Services. During the inter-war period, the United States and the Soviet Union were the most enterprising in the appointment of women as diplomats, even if the numbers involved were small. Russia lays claim to the first female Ambassador. From 1930–1945 Alexandra Mikhailovna Killontai worked at first as the envoy and then as the ambassador in Sweden and was also a member of the Soviet delegation in the League of Nations.[5] Congresswoman Ruth Bryan Owen Rohde became the first American woman appointed to a major diplomatic post when she was named minister to Denmark in 1933.

Career diplomats took longer to become Ambassadors, and women began to join the ranks of foreign services in the 1940s. For example, Frances E. Willis was appointed US Ambassador Extraordinary and Plenipotentiary to Norway by President Dwight Eisenhower in 1957. Willis was the first female career Foreign Service officer to serve as an Ambassador, and later served as Ambassador to Norway from 1957 to 1961. During her 37-year-long career, she held posts in

Sweden, Belgium, Spain, Norway, Britain, Sri Lanka, and Finland, and was the first woman chargée d'affaires, the first woman deputy chief of mission, the first US Ambassador to Switzerland, and the first woman to serve as ambassador at three of her posts. In 1962 she became the first woman to be designated Career Ambassador. In the 1960s, the diplomatic services of Nordic and Latin American countries started admitting women as 'normal' candidates, who then develop into diplomats.

The UK were late bloomers. It was not until 1946 that women could officially represent their country abroad. It was not until 1973 that a UK woman could have both a diplomatic post and a husband. No woman was appointed Head of a British diplomatic post before the early 1970s, and the appointment of the first married female Head of Consulate took until 1987. However, as documented by Helen McCarthy, in both world wars women were temporarily recruited to the Foreign Office as typists, clerks, code breakers, and translators (McCarthy 2014). Among the more famous was the mountaineer, traveller, and author Gertrude Bell, who, in 1915, aged 47, worked in the fledgling Arab Bureau in Cairo. Yvonne Roberts notes that Bell was called by one male MP 'a flat-chested, man-woman blathering ass', but held in esteem by others (Roberts 2014).

However, since that wave of 'firsts', the inclusion of women in senior positions in foreign services has seemed to plateau despite the more even recruitment practices. The make up of the new EU diplomatic corps has come under scrutiny after a study found that just 11 of the current 115 ambassadors are women (9.6 per cent) (Banks 2010).

Thirty of the UN's 193 members had female ambassadors in 2014, the most since the international body was created in 1945 (15.5 per cent). In 2014, Nigeria's Joy Ogwu and Lithuania's Raimonda Murmokaite began their two-year terms on the Security Council, joining three other female ambassadors: Samantha Power of the US, Maria Cristina Perceval of Argentina and Sylvie Lucas of Luxembourg. They have been dubbed the 'W5', a play on the Permanent Five members of the Council with veto powers (Yoon 2014).

In terms of political leadership, the number of women heads of state or government declined to 18 from 19 in 2012 (9.3 per cent). The number of female Ministers of Foreign Affairs is similarly low, although some have held a very high global public profile including Madeleine Albright, Hillary Rodham Clinton, and Catherine Ashton. Female leadership in the UN system is growing with Baroness Amos (Office for the Coordination of Humanitarian Affairs), Helen Clark (UN Development Programme), Margret Chan (World Health Organisation), Ertharin Cousin (World Food Programme), and the creation of a new agency, UN Women, in 2010.

The roadblocks

If we concentrate on the United Kingdom as a case study, we can analyse the reasons women have been generally regarded as either uninterested or unfit for diplomacy. The UK held the Schuster committee on the admission of women in

February 1934, which canvassed an array of objections, as summarised by Susan Pedersen.

- The 'nuisance and expense' argument: employing women would require building separate accommodations, worrying about protocols and dress, and generally re-examining practices that were working perfectly well.
- the 'backward foreigners' argument: the claim that, while Britons might treat women as equals, 'less civilised' Arabs and Orientals would never do so.
- the 'reverse discrimination' argument: if women couldn't be posted in 'backwards' areas, male officials would be stuck with an unfair share of those undesirable posts.
- the 'drunken sailor' problem: the question of whether women could handle the unruly locals and weaving and belligerent British sailors who absorbed much consular officials' time.
- the 'diplomatic husband' problem: the fear that women officials would acquire loose-lipped husbands who, unlike useful wives, could never be controlled.
- the 'Foreign Service as matrimonial bureau' argument, noting that single women who married diplomats would have to leave the service due to the marriage bar (Pedersen 2014).

We can add to this list the 'battleaxe' argument contained in the infamous minute on why Australian women were unfit to be trade commissioners, dated 13 March 1963:

> A spinster lady can, and very often does, turn into something of a battleaxe with the passing years. A man usually mellows.[6]

By 1962, the Plowden Report finally introduced gender equality measures into the UK diplomatic service. The report surmised, 'women officers should be employed as widely as possible in the Diplomatic Service [as] we received no evidence which would suggest that women in the Foreign Service have proved "tender plants"' (FCO Historians 1994: 18).

Equal pay for women became fully implemented, and the marriage bar was finally withdrawn in 1972, which enabled married women to become employable again without discriminatory stipulation. However, the policy was slow in practice as women in the most senior posts were all unmarried even as far as 1985 (Pedersen 2014).[7]

We can still see some of these roadblocks as live for women engaging in economic diplomacy in the present day – that less 'advanced' states may not accept a female finance official, or a crisis response requires full 24/7 commitment incompatible with a female set of carer responsibilities. But there is also still an element of who is allowed to embody the state on the global stage when the stakes are the highest. In an era of globalisation, economic crisis can represent an existential threat to a state on a par with armed conflict. At that point, as Walter Bagehot once wrote, '[a]n ambassador is not simply an agent; he is also a spectacle' (1873: 112).

Impact of female representation on issues and practice

There are some areas of diplomatic practice that seem particularly resistant to female representation. One is the conduct of peace negotiations, as noted. For example, Charlesworth (2010) cites a UNIFEM study in 2009, which found that only 2.4 per cent of signatories to peace agreements since 1992 had been women and that no woman had ever been designated as a 'chief mediator' by the United Nations. The International Women Leaders Global Security Summit was held on 15–17 November 2007 in New York City, co-hosted by H.E. Mary Robinson, President of Ireland (1990–1997), and the Rt. Hon. Kim Campbell, Prime Minister of Canada (1993). This Summit brought together 68 women leaders from 36 countries. They declared:

> Women leaders have been particularly effective in mediating complex conflicts and are acutely aware of the social, economic and political effects of mass atrocity and armed conflict.
>
> (Potter and Peters 2008: 6)

The recommendations from the women leaders emphasised political leadership, non-violent resolution of conflict, humanitarian values, a consistent and agreed threshold for intervention, and female participation and agency (Ibid., 9).

The appointment of former President of Ireland and UN High Commissioner for Human Rights, Mary Robinson, as Special Envoy for the Great Lakes Region on 18 March 2013 was notable, her term ending on 17 July 2014. Robinson deployed considerable energy and political capital in bringing the suffering and the potential contribution of the women of DRC to international attention. As Charlesworth (2013) notes:

> [i]t is all too rare that women are appointed to such positions and it brings some substance to the Security Council's urging of the UN Secretary-General in SCR 1325 (2000) 'to appoint more women as special representatives and envoys to pursue good offices on his behalf'.

There are a number of female Special Representatives of the Secretary General.

Economic diplomacy and trade is another area resistant to the participation of women, as argued below, and does not attract the same level of external pressure as the Women Peace and Security agenda. This leads to the question of whether the participation of women has influenced the diplomatic agenda. There have been some key diplomatic moments for gender equality since World War II, which have often featured female representatives and male champions.

One key moment would be the negotiation of the Universal Declaration of Human Rights, the capstone of the modern human rights law system. Hansa Mehta of India and others insisted that gender equality be made explicit in the document in 1948 (Morsink 1991). Another moment was the creation of the Commission on the Status of Women in 1946. CSW as a body led to the eventual adoption of a specific treaty for women. The Convention for the Elimination of All Forms of Discrimination Against Women (CEDAW) was adopted by the UN General Assembly in 1979 and now has 187 state parties (but with many states making serious reservations to certain provisions). The United States is among seven countries that have not ratified – along with Tonga and Palau, Iran, Somalia, South Sudan, and Sudan. The 23-member elected expert Committee overseeing the Convention puts out opinions ('general comments') about how the treaty should be interpreted, and responds to periodic state reports about compliance with the Convention.

Other key diplomatic moments include

- The Cairo Programme of Action at the International Conference on Population and Development in 1994.
- The Beijing Declaration and Platform for Action from the Fourth World Conference on Women in 1995.
- The adoption of MDGs 3 and 5 at the Millennium Summit; the 2005 World Summit; the 2010 high-level plenary meeting on the Millennium Development Goals, and the 2013 Special Event on the Millennium Development Goals.
- The Declaration on the Elimination of Violence Against Women by a resolution of the General Assembly in 1993.
- The adoption of the Women Peace and Security Agenda at the Security Council. A cluster of UN Security Council Resolutions (UNSCR) comprise the WPS agenda. Those resolutions are UNSCR 1325 (2000), UNSCR 1820 (2008), UNSCR 1888 (2009), UNSCR 1889 (2009), UNSCR 1960 (2010), UNSCR 2106 (2013) and UNSCR 2122 (2013).[8] In essence, the 1325 agenda states that women and girls experience conflict differently from men and boys.[9] Women have an essential role in conflict prevention, peace building, and post-conflict reconstruction, and States are required to ensure women are represented in all decision-making.[10] The later resolutions focus on ending impunity for sexual violence in conflict, and increasing the participation of more women in the UN's own 'good offices' roles in mediating conflict and negotiating peace.
- The establishment of the International Criminal Court, with gender provisions in the Rome Statute in 1998.
- The establishment of UN Women in 2010.
- The creation of Ambassadors for Women in the US (2009), Australia (2011), and Norway (2010).

Much of this progress has been in the multilateral realm, with a UN focus, and focused on non-discrimination and recognition of the issue of violence against women. Very few of the key moments have focused on women's economic rights and status.

Despite all of the progress noted above, most of the female diplomats around the world interviewed about challenges they face note that balancing work and family lives is the biggest challenge (Yoon 2014). This brings us to consider the evolving role of the diplomatic spouse.

The diplomatic spouse

As noted above, the hierarchy and practice of diplomacy has been resistant to change, not just with the inclusion of a more diverse recruitment base in terms of gender, but also sexual identity, migrants, and class. A clear symbol of this resistance has been the role of the diplomatic spouse, as Cynthia Enloe (1989) pointed out in one of the first feminist IR texts. President Theodore Roosevelt made the connection between the domestic and international explicit in 1899:

> Exactly as each man, while doing first his duty to his wife and the children within his home, must yet, if he hopes to amount to much, strive mightily in the world outside his home, so our nation, while first of all seeing to its own domestic well-being, must not shrink from playing its part among the great nations without.
>
> (Roosevelt 1899: 133)

From the earliest years to the mid-twentieth century, the most extensive contribution made by women to diplomacy was as the wives of diplomatic and consular officers. In this capacity they supported their husbands by running large diplomatic households presiding as hostesses, making their own range of contacts to complement the official work of the embassy and, in many instances, distinguishing themselves by local voluntary and community work.[11] Diplomacy then can be criticised, as many other professions have been, as exploiting the unpaid and unrecognised labour and skills of women. Madeleine Albright once quipped that it used to be that the only way a woman could truly make her foreign policy views felt was by 'marrying a diplomat and then pouring tea on an offending ambassador's lap' (Bloch 2004).

As Susan Pedersen points out regarding the diplomatic spouse in her review of Helen McCarthy's book length treatment on the rise of the female diplomat *Women of the World*:

> The state governed men, and men were to govern women a *he-for-God-only-and-she-for-God-in-him* theory of politics that made women's service to the state and marriage genuinely hard to reconcile. This is why interwar women (but not men) lost their nationality when marrying a foreigner, why postwar wives (but not husbands) accessed state insurance through their spouse, and why women were for so long considered most useful to the diplomatic enterprise as wives.

Male government officials relied on women's unpaid labour in maintaining relations with their political counterparts. By the end of the 19th century, diplomacy and hostessing became tightly intertwined to the extent that women married to diplomats were unable to do little else.

(2014)

The contribution of the diplomatic spouse to the overall success of the relationship between capitals was often extensive and given insufficient recognition, Lady Palmerston in the UK and her 'sympathetique' reputation being one possible exception. Many Foreign Ministries had shadow counterparts in diplomatic spouse associations, formed to offer support and advice to each other.

Many of the attributes of the traditional diplomatic spouse have been put forward in modern times to justify the special qualities of female diplomats. These include their function as an emblematic symbol of national values (such as modernity), access to other women in the local population, an ethic of care, and specific communication skills. I argue that the origins of female diplomats remain current: that the diplomatic spouse has morphed into the junior career diplomat. This has some implications for areas of diplomatic practice that are informal and technical, such as the G20 space. The G20 processes often feature hard-working women in more support-style roles and few in leadership/decision-making roles.

Why focus on the Group of 20 and summitry?

The Group of 20 (G20) is currently the 'premier forum for international economic cooperation', with political leaders from the nations that provide over 80 per cent of the world's output meeting to face the complexity of globalised markets. It was designed to create a leader-level response to the Global Financial Crisis, in recognition that the Group of 7 (G7) no longer adequately reflected global economic power.

The Group of 20 Leaders' Summit is a new entity in international relations, only eight years old (previously finance ministers met, since 1999). The G20 can itself be seen as the product of outreach by the G8, as the G8 faced challenges to its own legitimacy during the Asian financial crisis. It has become an important new global governance actor, more than a forum, dealing with crises, urging coordination to promote growth with a more representative group of states.

The G20 Leaders meet annually, the Finance Ministers and Central Bank Governors meet twice a year, the Sherpas (or the senior officials representing the Leaders) meet four times a year, and there are over 100 working level meetings in the lead-up to the Leaders' Summit, as well as side summits held by business, labour, think tanks, youth, civil society, and women. The G20 works on a loose troika arrangement between the past, present, and future hosts, with no secretariat. For example, Turkey's troika partners in 2015 were Russia (2013), Australia (2014) and China (2016). The President can set the agenda for the Leaders' Summit, and the Leaders release a communiqué at the end of the Summit.

The G20 'outreach strategy' refers to the diplomatic meetings and communications strategies used by the host state to let the rest of the international community know the priorities of the G20 Summits, to consult with non-members and take on board their suggestions and reactions. The strategy aims to address the tension between effective crisis management by a small number of key G20 members and the long-term objective to be a legitimate global actor whose decisions are supported by non-members.

This chapter argues that the G20 deserves our feminist attention because it has evolved as the most important site of global economic governance, despite legitimate critiques of its effectiveness. The G20 can act as 'constructed focal point' for rebalancing economic power and governance reforms that promote international cooperation and offer reassurance to markets. Despite only eight years and 11 summits passing since the first leaders' meeting, the G20 is suffering a loss of confidence in its ability to successfully promote policy coordination between its members and achieve global economic stability and sustainable balanced growth, design financial regulation that prevents the next crisis, and progress financial architecture reform. Until now, the G20 has been seen as a nascent and 'informal' economic forum with effectiveness issues, and thus the main criteria for success focus on effectiveness. Effectiveness appears to be limited to evaluating whether a coordinated response to the 2008 crisis occurred, as debated by experts such as Daniel Drezner (2014) and Eric Helleiner (2014). Even on this limited but still complex criterion, eminent commentators such as these come to exactly the opposite conclusions. Nevertheless, leaders still engage with the Summits and the preparatory meetings grow in importance.

The glue of the whole G20 process is the sherpas, who lead the 'sherpa track' negotiations. The sherpa is the personal representative of the leader, helping them to reach the summit. The sous sherpa and yak are senior public officials helping the sherpa or the Finance Minister. The Leaders' Meeting is crucial to fostering the political support necessary to coordinate and solve problems that cross state borders, like corporate tax evasion. But public officials are also crucial to the long-term development of the G20 as an institution, and problems that take a long time to fix.

The G20 aims:

- to promote policy coordination between its members in order to achieve global economic stability, and sustainable balanced growth
- to promote financial regulations that reduce risks and prevent future financial crises
- and to modernise international financial architecture.

We could see the G20 as an example of 'club' diplomacy which focuses on transnational elites who are culturally similar with only very powerful countries at the table (minilateralism), acting in secret, and focused on written agreements (Cooper, Heine, and Thakur 2013). The G20 in 2015 is not quite the ultimate 'club' compared to the G7, but it is still very opaque in its processes. But there are also aspects of 'network diplomacy' due to the evolving outreach parallel to the G20.

As the previous Australian Sherpa Heather Smith noted:

> Governments alone cannot solve the economic challenge. All parts of society have a part to play and have a significant stake in G20 outcomes. This was recognised in the 5th Anniversary Vision Statement that Leaders agreed upon at the Saint Petersburg Summit last year
>
> (Harris Rimmer 2015)

Women in the G20

This section gives a snapshot of the most prominent women involved in the formal G20 processes. An interesting fact is that despite the few women involved in the overall G20, there was a series of successful female sherpas leading the consecutive summits in Mexico, Australia, and Turkey.

i Los Cabos Summit, Mexico 2012

Lourdes Aranda Bezaury was the Mexican Sherpa for the G20 from 2008 to 2012 and was the sherpa for the Mexican Presidency in 2012. She was known for being open to civil society actors in an expanded outreach program and a broader agenda that incorporated 'green growth'. She had been undersecretary of foreign affairs of Mexico since December of 2003, where she is president of the Mexican diplomatic academy, *Instituto Matías Romero*. Previously, she was director general of the *Instituto Matías Romero* in 2003 and director general of global affairs from 2001 to 2003 at the Foreign Affairs Ministry. Ambassador Aranda was also deputy representative at the Mexican Permanent Mission to the Organization of American States from 1995 to 2001. She has also held various positions in the Directorate for North American Affairs, Administrative and Budgetary Issues, Environmental and Natural Resources Issues, Human Rights and Narcotics Affairs, and the Office for Multilateral Economic Relations from 1983 to 1995. Ambassador Aranda holds a Bachelor's degree in International Relations from *El Colegio de México* and completed her graduate studies in History and Foreign Policy at the *Institut Universitaire de Hautes Études Internationales* of Geneva and a Continental Defense Graduate Course at the Inter-American Defense College (IADC) in Washington, DC.

ii St Petersburg Summit, Russia 2013

Svetlana Lukash was appointed as the new Russian G20 Sherpa immediately after the Leaders' Summit, one of the youngest sherpas. She was the Deputy Chief of Presidential Experts' Directorate, after having worked for six years as Head of the Russian G8 and G20 Sherpa Office.

In her capacity as the Russian Sherpa Assistant and Deputy Sherpa in the G20 Ms. Lukash was in charge of managing substantive preparation of five G8 and seven G20 summits at the Sherpa's Track, promoting Russia's initiatives and representing Russia in the G8 and G20.

Svetlana Lukash graduated in 1999 from the Russian State University for Humanities (RGGU), faculty of management, continued post-graduate studies in the Institute for Social and Political Research, Russian Academy of Sciences, and started to work in the Federal Energy Commission of Russia (Federal Tariff Service at present). In 2001 she moved to the consulting business to continue work on reforming Russian natural monopolies. In 2003 Ms. Lukash joined the 'Expert' Analytical Centre, a think tank within the *Expert* magazine, until in 2005 she was called to the Expert Council on Russia's G8 Presidency in 2006 and later in 2007 – to the Presidential Executive Office.

iii Brisbane Summit, Australia, 2014

Dr Heather Smith was the Australian sherpa for the 2014 Presidency, and was awarded a Public Service Medal (PSM) in the Queen's Birthday 2015 Honours for her outstanding public in this role. The G20 Leaders' Summit was the largest international meeting ever held in Australia. Subsequently she was appointed as Secretary of the Department of Communications and Arts, one of the few women to be appointed to this senior level of the Australian Public Service.

Dr Smith has had a public service career as an economist in the Treasury, Office of National Assessments, the Department of Foreign Affairs and Trade, and the Department of the Prime Minister and Cabinet. As sherpa, she was widely perceived to be a stable, accessible, and respected expert who shepherded the new government to a substantive agenda and communiqué. Dr Smith as sherpa successfully facilitated agreement of the G20 leaders to include the female labour participation target in the Brisbane Leaders Declaration.

Dr Smith graduated with a PhD in 1994 and a Masters of Economics in 1990 from the Australian National University. She also holds a Bachelor of Economics (Honours) from the University of Queensland. Before joining the public service, Dr Smith was an academic working on North Asia at the Australian National University, holding various positions from 1994–2000. She also worked at the Reserve Bank of Australia from 1988–1990.

iv Antalya Summit, Turkey 2015

Ambassador Ayşe Sinirlioğlu is the Deputy Undersecretary, Economic Affairs in the Ministry of Foreign Affairs of Turkey and was the G20 Sherpa of Turkey in 2015. She received her Bachelor's Degree from the Faculty of Economics and Administrative Sciences at the University of Marmara, Master's Degree in European Integration law from the University of Amsterdam, and PhD in Political Science from Boğaziçi University.[12]

Ambassador Sinirlioğlu is arguably the female sherpa with the most senior diplomatic experience with postings in Rotterdam, Aleppo, New York, Amman, and Geneva, before serving as Ambassador of Turkey to Romania, and then Spain and Andorra. With assistance from other sherpas, Ambassador Sinirlioğlu also drove the launch of the W20 during the Turkish Presidency as discussed below.

Central Bank Governors

i USA

Dr Janet Yellen took office as Chair of the Board of Governors of the Federal Reserve System on 3 February 2014, for a four-year term, which will end in February 2018. Dr Yellen also serves as Chairman of the Federal Open Market Committee, the System's principal monetary policymaking body. Prior to her appointment as Chair, Dr Yellen served as Vice Chair of the Board of Governors, taking office in October 2010, when she simultaneously began a 14-year term as a member of the Board that will expire 31 January 2024.

Dr Yellen is Professor Emeritus at the University of California at Berkeley where she was the Eugene E. and Catherine M. Trefethen Professor of Business and Professor of Economics and has been a faculty member since 1980. Dr Yellen took leave from Berkeley for five years starting in August 1994. She served as a member of the Board of Governors of the Federal Reserve System through February 1997, and then left the Federal Reserve to become chair of the Council of Economic Advisers through August 1999. She also chaired the Economic Policy Committee of the Organization for Economic Cooperation and Development from 1997 to 1999. She also served as President and Chief Executive Officer of the Federal Reserve Bank of San Francisco from 2004 to 2010.

Dr Yellen is a member of both the Council on Foreign Relations and the American Academy of Arts and Sciences. She has served as President of the Western Economic Association, Vice President of the American Economic Association, and a Fellow of the Yale Corporation. Dr Yellen graduated summa cum laude from Brown University with a degree in economics in 1967, and received her PhD in Economics from Yale University in 1971. She received the Wilbur Cross Medal from Yale in 1997, an honorary doctor of laws degree from Brown in 1998, and an honorary doctor of humane letters from Bard College in 2000.

An Assistant Professor at Harvard University from 1971 to 1976, Dr Yellen served as an Economist with the Federal Reserve's Board of Governors in 1977 and 1978, and on the faculty of the London School of Economics and Political Science from 1978 to 1980. Dr Yellen has written on a wide variety of macroeconomic issues, while specialising in the causes, mechanisms, and implications of unemployment.[13]

ii Malaysia (representing ASEAN at the G20 Turkey, 2015)

H.E. Tan Sri Dr Zeti Akhtar Aziz was the 7th Governor of Bank Negara Malaysia, Malaysia's central bank. She was governor from 2000 to 2016, and was the first woman in the position.[14]

The daughter of celebrated Malaysian Royal Professor Ungku Abdul Aziz Ungku Abdul Hamid and famed cultural/social activist Sharifah Azah Syed Mohamed Alsagoff, Zeti became acting governor of the central bank at the peak of the Asian financial crisis in 1998 (a possible example of the 'glass cliff' syndrome), and appointed governor in May 2000.

Over time she pushed for more autonomy for the central bank, achieving a certain amount of independence by the end of her term and the successful passage of the Central Bank of Malaysia Act 2009. In Bank Negara, Dr Zeti presided over the formulation of the Financial Sector Master Plan, a 10-year road map for the development of the Malaysian financial system. As Governor, Dr Zeti oversaw the transformation of the financial system, which included wide-ranging financial reforms, evolution of new financial institutions, strengthening of the financial markets and the rapid expansion of Islamic finance, and the transition to a managed float of the Ringgit exchange rate. Global Finance awarded her the title of 'World's Best Central Bank Governor' in 2005 for overseeing successful financial reforms.

In 2012, she was awarded the Islamic Development Bank Prize in Islamic Banking and Finance, for her contributions to the development of Islamic banking and finance. Under the Turkish presidency in 2015, she highlighted the regulatory issues for Islamic banks with the Financial Stability Board.

Zeti received the Lifetime Achievement Award at the Central Banking Awards 2016.[15] Dr Zeti received her B.Sc in Economics from the University of Malaya and her PhD from the University of Pennsylvania. As part of her dissertation, Dr Zeti did pioneering work on capital flows and the implications for policy. She has written extensively in the areas of monetary and financial economics, Islamic finance, capital flows, macroeconomic management, financial reform, and restructuring. Prior to her career in the Bank, Dr Zeti had served in the South East Asian Central Banks (SEACEN) Research and Training Centre from 1979–1984, where she conducted research in the area of financial policies and reform in the South-East Asian region.

G20 International Financial Institutions

Ms Christine Lagarde was Chairman of the G20 when France took over its presidency for the year 2011, with an ambitious reform agenda for the international monetary system. In July 2011, Lagarde became the eleventh Managing Director of the IMF, and the first woman to hold that position. In February 2016, she was selected by the IMF Executive Board to serve a second five-year term until 5 July 2021.

Born in Paris in 1956, Christine Lagarde completed high school in Le Havre and attended Holton Arms School in Bethesda (Maryland, USA). She then graduated from law school at University Paris X, and obtained a Master's degree from the Political Science Institute in Aix en Provence.

After being admitted as a lawyer to the Paris Bar, Lagarde joined the international law firm of Baker & McKenzie as an associate, specializing in Labour, Anti-trust, and Mergers and Acquisitions. A member of the Executive Committee of the Firm in 1995, Lagarde became the Chairman of the Global Executive Committee of Baker & McKenzie in 1999, and subsequently Chairman of the Global Strategic Committee in 2004.

Lagarde joined the French government in June 2005 as Minister for Foreign Trade. After a brief stint as Minister for Agriculture and Fisheries, in June 2007 she became the first woman to hold the post of Finance and Economy Minister of a G7 country. From July to December 2008, she also chaired the ECOFIN Council, which brings together Economics and Finance Ministers of the European Union, and helped foster international policies related to financial supervision, regulation, and strengthening global economic governance. Lagarde was named Officier in the Légion d'honneur in April 2012.

Ms Lagarde has been prominent in her support for gender equality and inclusion of women in the G20, writing prominent opinion pieces and speaking at the launch of the W20 in Turkey. She has been outspoken about her own role, noting that women in leadership need 'skin as thick as an old crocodile'.

> I regret to say that the crocodile skin is unfortunately a *sine qua non* for a period of time. But once a woman is established, she can take off the crocodile skin and become a normal human being, without having to shield against horrible attacks and below the belt punches.[16]

She has made public statements about gender during G20 processes; for example, as Lagarde left the Sydney meeting of the G20 Finance Ministers and Central Bank Governors in March 2013, she commented that the 'two genders' will have to contribute if the G20 was to achieve its aim of lifting economic growth targets by 2 per cent. She consistently makes the economic case for gender inclusion, calling it a 'no-brainer', and also famously told a reporter in 2011: 'I honestly think that there should never be too much testosterone in one room'.[17]

Lagarde is facing serious legal charges. In December 2016, she was ordered to stand trial at the Cour de Justice de la Republique, a special court that tries ministers for crimes in office. Under investigation is her role in a €400 million ($440 million) payout as French finance minister in 2008 to businessman Bernard Tapie (Reuters 2016).

The OECD

Gabriela Ramos is the OECD Chief of Staff and Sherpa to the G20 since 2006, one of the longest serving sherpas. She has been advising and supporting the strategic agenda of Secretary-General Angel Gurria, who has himself been a strong gender advocate in the G20. She is responsible for the contributions of the Organisation to the global agenda, including the G20 and G7, and oversees the preparations of the yearly OECD Ministerial Council Meeting. She has contributed to the launch of major OECD initiatives related to gender, skills, and development, has also launched and supervises the New Approaches to Economic Challenges and the Inclusive Growth initiatives, and oversees the activities of the Directorate for Education and Skills. Previously, she served as Head of the OECD Office in Mexico and Latin America, where she promoted OECD recommendations in many areas including health and education. She helped in the preparations of several OECD reports on Mexico, developed the OECD Forum there and launched the 'Getting it Right' flagship publication series.

Prior to joining the OECD, Ms Ramos held several positions in the Mexican Government, notably as advisor to the Minister of Foreign Affairs and Director of OECD Affairs. She has also held several positions as Professor of International Economy at the Universidad Iberoamericana and at the Instituto Tecnológico Autónomo de México. Ms Ramos holds an MA in Public Policies from Harvard University, and was a Fulbright scholar.

Leaders

When Chancellor Angela Merkel, Germany presides over the Hamburg Summit in 2017, this will represent the first time a female head of state has presided over an economic summit of this breadth and significance. She has had experience of hosting G7 and G8 meetings, and high-level economic processes within the European Union. Her approach to austerity in economic policy during the Eurozone crisis has sometimes been criticised by Lagarde and the national leaders of Greece and Spain (Fischer 2015). She is also the G20 leader with the most summit experience, having attended them all.

What this brief examination of the most senior women in the G20 processes has shown is their path-breaking careers and exceptional status. Only two have traditional diplomatic backgrounds. All of these women have sought to progress the rights of women within the remit allowed by their role, sometimes in creative coalition, as we will see below. They are a diverse group, with only one common denominator being that they have generally been interested in listening to a broad range of voices during their G20 work.

Many of these women have used their agency in the context of a leader-led economic summit often focused on crisis response to promote gender outcomes, such as gaining agreement for the female labour participation target or the W20. Very few of these women overtly comment on gender issues in the field of economic diplomacy, with the notable exception of Christine Lagarde, but display behaviour that supports more junior colleagues and each other, such as the cooperation between sherpas to build agreement for the Brisbane gender target. The biographies of these women raise questions of institutional power where the actors involved are frequently from central banks or treasuries rather than foreign ministries but, due to their technical expertise, are elevated to significant representational roles. These women also demonstrate leadership on behalf of their nations' pursuit of women's economic rights and inclusive economic growth that reduces inequality between men and women, rich and poor. To a certain extent, their ability to exercise leadership in the G20 space is often constrained by these institutional and technical factors.

Part II: influencing the G20 from the outside – feminist leadership and the struggle to define feminist economic agendas

In this Part, having examined the role of women inside the formal G20, we can turn to the examination of the status of the newest G20 engagement group – the W20 – and what the challenges of economic diplomacy might be from this network diplomacy perspective. I then establish a basic feminist agenda for economic diplomacy, in which leaders of G20 countries need to demonstrate awareness of, and accountability for, the gendered consequences of their decisions.

The G20 has been affected by two trends, inequality and 'womenomics', leading to the acceptance of the W20. The world of economics is increasingly talking about the impact of inequality on economic growth at a national and regional level, spurred by the global interest in the work by French economist, Thomas Piketty (2014). The World Economic Forum (WEF) in 2013–2014 focused on inequality as a key systemic risk to global financial stability.[18] Of the types of inequality to have national economic impact, gender inequality is one of the most pervasive types, leading to gaps in opportunity across the globe (often intersecting with other kinds of discrimination, such as disability, age, sexuality, or ethnic minority status).

The evidence of gender inequality is accepted. The monitoring of progress across the globe against the Millennium Development Goals has found persistent gender gaps in secondary and tertiary education enrolment; the lack of economic autonomy of women including lack of integration into the formal economy, unequal access to full and productive employment and decent work, under-representation in non-agricultural wage employment, over-representation in low paid jobs and gender-stereotyped jobs like domestic and care work, and unequal pay for work of equal value; the unequal burden of unpaid care work and lack of measures to reconcile paid work and care responsibilities; the persistence of discriminatory attitudes, social norms, and stereotypes; the lack of social protection and insurance coverage for women; and the low proportion and unequal participation and representation of women at all levels of decision making, including in national parliaments and other governance structures (UNDP 2014).

At the same time as this focus on inequality, the world has seen a surge of interest in 'womenomics' or the idea that women's participation in the formal economy can stimulate growth (The Economist 2006). The United Nations Secretary-General states that investment in girls translates into an average GDP growth of 0.3 percentage points for each per cent increase in female education. The World Bank, Organisation for Economic Cooperation and Development

(OECD), the International Labour Organisation (ILO), and the International Monetary Fund (IMF) have all released reports pointing to the economic case for promoting equitable economic opportunities to both men and women.

These initiatives generally rely on a blend of two bases, that investments in gender equality are both a good thing to do (a human rights and moral argument), and the 'smart' thing to do (an economic productivity argument). Most economic diplomacy in this area provides a blend of arguments with the 'smart choice' narrative dominant.

These conventional economic approaches to gender inequality also accept that there are additional cultural and structural barriers that have held women back, including perceptions of competence, entrepreneurial flair, and leadership.

The evolution of the W20

The W20 grouping represents an entirely new space in economic governance. It is a group tasked with the mission of promoting global, gender-inclusive economic growth by presenting policy recommendations to leaders. Given time, it could be the economic equivalent of the UN Security Council's Women Peace and Security Agenda (Resolution 1325). The evolution of the W20 has shown the potential for three distinct areas: agenda-setting, new perspectives, and being taken seriously.[19]

There is a strong argument that economic governance should reflect the citizenship of member states and that diverse teams will make better decisions. As 'womenomics' took the rest of the economic world by storm, the G20, as a premier economic forum, looked decidedly old-fashioned. The W20 has, from the beginning, shown the potential for agenda-setting at the G20, notably in recognising unpaid labour in national accounts or investment in more social infrastructure.

The W20 also represents the potential of fresh thinking and new solutions for the current G20 agenda, casting a gender lens over infrastructure, anti-corruption, trade, financial regulation, development, and tax. The group can challenge mainstream economic thinking in which the differentiated gender impacts of macroeconomic and microeconomic policy are not sufficiently considered. It can add balance to, and highlight the lack of, female membership in national chambers of commerce, finance ministries, or other industries.

The W20 has a clear preference towards business-women, specifically at the small and medium enterprise and entrepreneur levels, as well as women in global corporations. The few female or feminist leaders within the G20 members can use the forum to showcase their economic credentials. G20 nations can use the forum to gain attention for the economic potential of their female population, as China and Turkey have.

There is a clear opportunity for the W20 to monitor and ensure accountability for the G20's past commitments to women, and this is how it has evolved. The W20 mandate includes helping achieve progress on the G20's commitments to 'women's full economic and social participation', which was made in the Los

Cabos Leaders' Declaration in 2012, 'women's financial inclusion and education' which was made in the St Petersburg Leaders' Declaration in 2013, and finally to 'reducing the gap in participation rates between men and women by 25 percent by 2025', which was agreed upon in the Brisbane Leaders' Declaration in 2014.

The progress of the W20

Turkey's W20 year: origins

The G20 Summit in Brisbane 2014 made history by including a specific target to reduce the gender participation gap in formal labour markets in G20 economies by 25 per cent by 2025, whilst also outlining country strategies to achieve growth. This promise could bring more than 100 million women into the labour force, and yet it garnered little media or civil society attention.

This goal could be seen as the first of the 'concrete actions to overcome the barriers hindering women's full economic and social participation' called for in the Los Cabos Declaration in 2012. Indeed the Turkish Presidency followed by setting up the W20 engagement group to provide policy advice to leaders. The W20, the G20's gender engagement group, launched in Ankara on 6 September 2015 and its summit took place on 15–16 October.

The W20 Communiqué was also influenced by an open poll and delegate submissions. It contains a monitoring system for future W20 Summits.[20] China consolidated this process with the W20 Summit in Xi'an where the representatives of G20 countries and invited guests agreed a communiqué to be presented to the G20 leaders in the lead-up to the Hangzhou Summit.

China's W20 year: scale

China continued Turkey's investment in the W20, having just hosted a successful APEC Women in the Economy Forum with discussions on women and green development as well as women and regional trade in 2015.

The Vice President of China, Li Yuanchao, opened the W20 Summit in Xi'an on 26 May 2016 alongside host, the All-China Women's Federation. His words showed the increasing legitimacy and urgency of the gender and growth agenda, which the Chinese term 'She-Power'.

> It is all the more important to pool women's wisdom and strength at a time when the global economic recovery remains fragile. As the Chinese economy moves into a New Normal, efforts are made to encourage mass innovation and entrepreneurship and women are essential in this endeavour.
> (G20 China, n.d.)

W20 delegates underlined the importance of seeing demonstrable progress by the G20 Employment and Labour Ministers and the Employment Working

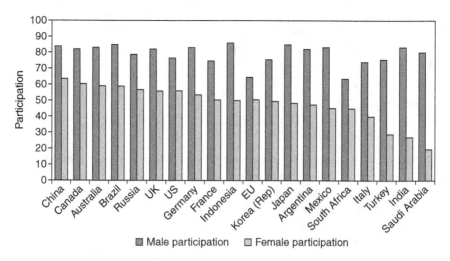

Figure 8.1 2015 labour participation in G20 countries by gender.[21]

Group. In debates during the Turkish Presidency, the members have opted for self-reporting against a template on a biennial basis. The ILO and OECD will compile a report on new policy initiatives, which may or may not be made public.

W20 delegates urged member states to update and publish their strategies towards the target, and adopt a transparent and rigorous monitoring process with, if necessary, the technical support of international organisations to make the data more comparable and more accessible to the public.

China has good female labour participation rates already, as the data indicates and the Vice President underscored in his speech. However, women are often in low skilled jobs, are under-paid and suffer from many forms of discrimination and stereotyping, as is the case in most of the G20 nations. The issues for the host in this area are still manifold, with the lifting of the one-child policy, and accompanying childcare and aged care concerns. China may soon increase the retirement age of women to be equivalent to that of men. The passage of the domestic violence law this year also has positive implications for women entering the workforce.

China went one step further at the W20 by linking the female labour participation debates to their headline outcome of a G20 Blueprint for the Innovative Growth, to be released in Hangzhou. The Vice President noted with pride that 55 per cent of e-commerce in China is conducted by women, and that the majority of online purchasing power is also female-dominated.

The focus on women in the digital economy by China has implications for the G20 Skills Agenda. The W20 recommended that the G20 Leaders should work to narrow and remove the digital divide, help women to gain equal access to the internet, provide effective digital skills training for women, set targets for women and girls to study STEM, and strengthen the capacity of women to undertake internet-based entrepreneurship and employment.

G20 members could take special measures to encourage inclusive sourcing policies by governments and by corporations, to include more women as suppliers in global value chains by establishing baseline data, setting targets and reporting on progress. They could support women's entrepreneurship and launch specific G20-wide programs to help women overcome business start-up barriers, grow and sustain their businesses, including through trade. Governments can improve women's access to and credit and investor networks, training, information services, and technical support. Governments can provide economic and trade incentives for businesses that are at least 51 per cent owned, managed, and controlled by one or more women. There are excellent precedents for these policies in Malaysia, the US, and Israel.

Time is of the essence as the world moves into the Fourth Industrial Revolution. Just as some developing countries were able to 'leap-frog' developed nations in infrastructure terms – straight to mobiles with no need for laying cables, renewables without power stations – China went straight to DVDs without VHS. There must be the potential for increased female labour participation to move straight to decent quality work in the new skills economy, supported by adequate social protections.

G20 members are debating how best to recalibrate Gross Domestic Product to include activity in the digital economy. This presents an opportunity to systematically recognise and measure all forms of work and value, including creating a national income accounting that includes unpaid care work. The W20 also called on the G20 leaders to consider 22 recommendations. The full communiqué can be found in English and Chinese.[22]

The best focus for the W20 may be to solidify the commitment of national leadership, alongside efforts to develop and monitor concrete measures at the country level, against the agreed country growth targets. How can G20 member countries encourage investment in social infrastructure to reduce the labour gap? Can public–private partnerships accelerate women's skills to meet the needs of the twenty-first century globalised economy and leapfrog women and girls into sectors like STEM? How can governments use levers like a procurement policy, tax, and regulation of corporate boards to encourage gender equality?

The challenges of the W20

The challenge for the W20 is to be strategic and add value to the diffuse and crowded G20 policy space. There is no reason the W20 cannot work with or enhance the policy work of the other engagement groups. The W20 should also be making sure the young women involved in the Girls20 and Youth20 feel there is a pathway into economic governance space.

The other major challenge for the W20 is legitimacy, due to the structural exclusion of women from the formal economy, reflected in economic governance. Economists talk of women as a resource to be better 'utilised', but others try to focus attention on women in economic governance. The World Bank, UN Women, and others point out the structural and cultural barriers to participation in the formal economy. Women experience more obstacles in accessing land, financial services, technology, information, and markets. In many countries, legal, social, and cultural barriers to joining the labour market restrict women's options for paid work. Women's unpaid work in the care economy is not valued or measured by mainstream economic theory. The solution is to recognise and value women's dual roles as breadwinners and caregivers and to provide incentives for further participation in the formal workforce.

A further challenge is the rights basis of the W20 agenda, and the relationship between the G20 and the UN. The full recognition of women's human rights requires the full integration of women into the formal economy, in particular, into economic decision-making. This means changing the current gender-based division of labour into new economic structures where women and men enjoy equal treatment, avoiding exploitation. In 2015 we marked the twentieth anniversary of the Beijing Declaration and Beijing Platform for Action agreed by 189 United Nations (UN) Member States during the Fourth World Conference on Women in 1995. The Beijing Platform recognises that women make significant contributions to the economy and calls for the promotion of women's economic rights and independence, including access to employment, appropriate working conditions, and control over economic resources, as well as equal pay for equal work and work of equal value. The global economy looks very different in 2017, but these fundamentals go unaddressed in all G20 economies.

The 'size of the prize' for G20 economies for investing in gender equality in growth terms is very large, as well as the potential for sustainable growth and more equality in growth. A new McKinsey report puts the figure at $12 trillion extra GDP by 2025 by simply giving more women the same opportunities as men.[23] The W20 represents a grouping that sees women as crucial actors in economic governance, not just as unrealised economic assets, and as such is unique.

The next W20 Summit will be hosted by Germany in 2017 with the full support of Chancellor Merkel. This may be the best opportunity the W20 has to influence the Leaders' Summit.

Part III: towards a feminist G20 agenda

The G20 is aiming for sustainable and balanced economic growth that minimises structural risk. Those engaging in the G20 need to both promote their national interest and reframe that aim of the G20 to encompass inclusive growth that respects women's economic rights. This is a challenging enterprise but some initial steps are presented here, as well as a conceptualisation of the long-term aim.

The G20 should itself model good gender practices. For instance, Chatham House has recommended undertaking a gender audit of public-sector employees – prioritising finance ministries and central banks and continuing to all G20 delegations.

There is also a need for good diagnostic data to encourage governments to improve outcomes. The G20 should also showcase good gender practice and the good practices of women and men, including companies and government programs committed to gender inclusive growth. Whatever is agreed by G20 members to promote gender-inclusive growth should be consistent with the new Sustainable Development Goals and UN human rights system.

The W20 should be actively supported by G20 leaders. The G20 leaders have selected an economic governance group for the first time to focus on these crucial gender equality issues at the strategic level. Unlike other international groupings with a gender focus, this is a group dedicated to making the premier economic forum accountable to taking women seriously and improving women's lives.

A feminist agenda at the G20 should surface the current empiric evidence of the exclusion of women from the benefit of their economic activity. Economic policies and institutions still mostly fail to take gender disparities into account, from tax and budget systems to trade regimes. Women are more likely than men to be in precarious, vulnerable, gender-stereotyped, and low-paying forms of employment, and to be engaged in the informal economy. They have less access to full and productive employment and decent work, social protection, and pensions. Evidence of the gendered impact of austerity measures is still emerging from Greece and Spain, from the high representation of female public sector employees laid off, to the mass closure of domestic violence refuges. The UN has now released a report from the new High Level Panel on Women's Economic Empowerment, which takes this approach.[24]

But it could go further towards a more transformational approach. A nascent G20 discussion on 'inclusive' growth, the financial inclusion agenda, and investing in gender equality measures for employment could accelerate, and the policy could expand beyond the formal employment sector and replace it with an emphasis on interventions throughout the life cycle, noting women's disproportionate burden of unpaid care. My proposal for the G20 is rights-based: that the international community should address the multiple and intersecting factors contributing to the disproportionate impact of poverty on women of and girls over the lifecycle and intra-household gender inequalities in allocation of resources, opportunities, and power by realising women and girl's civil, political, economic, social and cultural rights. For this kind of vision, the idea of a diplomat may also have to transform.

Conclusions

In Part I, this chapter presented a theoretical analysis of gender and diplomacy to situate the central case study in Part II of the particular context of women involved in economic diplomacy at the most senior levels, as represented by the G20 forum. This chapter offer snapshots of some of the key women involved as sherpas, central bank governors, leaders, and heads of international financial institutions (IFIs). Cases of female representatives are presented showing agency and leadership skills in influencing the G20 Summit outcomes under constrained circumstances. Part III outlined the development of the outreach group that seeks to promote gender equality within the G20 processes, called the W20, as well as female leadership in the official engagement groups that seek to influence the Summit.

The chapter concludes with some warnings to heed for progress on gender equality goals and diversity of actors in this increasingly important but quasi-informal summitry space. Citizens who wish for gender-inclusive economic policy must begin to display a level of interest in the G20 space and place pressure on their representatives. The long march of progress for the equal role of women in diplomatic representation faces some serious challenges in the area of economic diplomacy.

Notes

1 Inspired by the work of Cynthia Enloe and Judith Butler, I ask questions like 'where are the women?' and 'what work is gender doing in this particular context?'
2 These female leaders represent the United Kingdom, Germany, and South Korea. G20 members are Canada, France, Germany, Italy, Japan, Russia, the United Kingdom, the United States of America (G8) plus 'structurally important' states: Australia and Saudi Arabia and nine emerging market countries: Argentina, Brazil, China, India, Indonesia, Mexico, South Africa, South Korea, and Turkey. The European Union, IMF, OECD, and the World Bank are permanent members, acting as an informal secretariat, and Spain is a 'permanent guest'.
3 This is no small achievement in itself. 'Women ... cannot wait for men to open the door and invite them into the foreign policy process' (McGlen and Reid Sarkees, 1995).
4 See further Faucher (2016).
5 'The first woman diplomat Alexandra Kollontai born'. www.prlib.ru/en-us/history/pages/item.aspx?itemid=47. Accessed 3 February 2014.
6 Included as Appendix A in Miller (2013).
7 See also Conley Tyler, Blizzard, and Crane (2014).
8 The full texts of the WPS core resolutions are available under the year of adoption from www.un.org/documents/scres.htm. Accessed 1 February 2015.
9 See further Special Issue: Australia on the UN Security Council: Progressing the Women, Peace and Security Agenda, *Australian Journal of International Affairs* 68 (3) 2014. Accessed 1 February 2015.
10 See Olsson and Gizelis (2013). Resolution 1325 was ground-breaking and the agenda led to the appointment of a new Special Rapporteur on Sexual Violence in Conflict, Margot Wallström, in 2010 (now Zainab Bangura), as well as annual reporting by the Secretary-General. One of the key actions is for states to design and implement National Action Plans. As a piece of polylateral diplomacy, linked to both regional and global social movements, the Women Peace and Security agenda is strong, despite wide acknowledgement of its flaws. Advocates argue that the core premise of the WPS agenda remains being attentive to the security needs of half the world's population, and thereby builds the legitimacy of the Security Council as a normative actor.
11 See further the excellent treatment of this issue by Miller (2013).
12 For full CV, see further www.developing8.org/image/Booklet/Sinirlioglu.pdf. Accessed 1 February 2015.
13 See further www.federalreservehistory.org/People/DetailView/284. Accessed 1 February 2015.

14 See further www.nst.com.my/news/2016/02/125168/malaysian-central-bank-chiefs-imminent-exit-highlights-succession-risks. Accessed 1 February 2015.
15 www.centralbanking.com/central-banking-journal/feature/2440199/lifetime-achievement-award-zeti-akhtar-aziz. Accessed 1 February 2015.
16 See the original interview here at https://youtube/FyeFDwObjh4. Accessed 1 February 2015.
17 See further www.independent.co.uk/news/people/profiles/christine-lagarde-there-should-never-be-too-much-testosterone-in-one-room-2206357.html. Accessed 1 February 2015.
18 World Economic Forum, available at www3.weforum.org/docs/WEF_GlobalRisks_Report_2014.pdf. Accessed 1 February 2015.
19 See further www.chathamhouse.org/expert/comment/17507. Accessed 1 February 2015.
20 Available at http://w20turkey.org/event/october-16-17-w20-summit/. Accessed 1 February 2015.
21 Sources: 'World Bank and International Labour Organization, Key Indicators of the Labour Market database', compiled by Hannah Wurf; 'Reconsidering the G20 Approach to Setting Targets', *G20 Monitor*, May 2016, available at www.lowyinstitute.org/publications/g20-monitor-new-considerations-chinas-2016-presidency. Accessed 1 March 2017.
22 Available at www.g20.org/English/Documents/Current/201606/t20160628_2346.html. Accessed 1 February 2015.
23 Available at www.mckinsey.com/global-themes/employment-and-growth/how-advancing-womens-equality-can-add-12-trillion-to-global-growth. Accessed 1 February 2015.
24 'Leave No One Behind' report, 2016, available at www.womenseconomicempowerment.org/reports/. Accessed 1 March 2017.

References

Bagehot, Walter. 1873. *The English Constitution*. London: Chapman and Hall.
Banks, Martin. 2010. 'EU Diplomatic Service a "Western European Old Boys Club"' *Telegraph*, 1 September, available at https://history.state.gov/about/faq/women-in-the-foreign-service. Accessed 1 June 2014.
Bloch. Julia Chang. 2004. 'Women and Diplomacy' Council of American Ambassadors, *The Ambassador Review*, Fall 2004, available at https://s3.amazonaws.com/caa-production/attachments/287/93-100_Bloch.pdf?1366918904. Accessed 1 June 2014.
Charlesworth, Hilary. 2010. 'Feminist Reflections on the Responsibility to Protect' *Global Responsibility to Protect* 2(3): 232–249.
Charlesworth, Hilary. 2013. 'New Forms of Peacekeeping' Regulating Rights blog, available at http://asiapacific.anu.edu.au/regarding-rights/2013/04/12/new-forms-of-peacekeeping/. Accessed 1 February 2015.
Charlesworth, Hilary, and Susan Harris Rimmer. 2010. 'Feminist Internationalisms' *Australian Feminist Law Journal* 32(1): 3–7.
Chinkin, Christine, Hilary Charlesworth, and Shelley Wright. 2005. 'Feminist Approaches to International Law: Reflections from Another Century' in Doris Buss and Ambreena Manji (eds) *International Law: Modern Feminist Approaches*, 19–23. Oxford and Portland, OR: Hart Publishing.
Conley Tyler, Melissa H., Emily Blizzard, and Bridget Crane. 2014. 'Is International Affairs too "Hard" for Women? Explaining the Missing Women in Australia's International Affairs' *Australian Journal of International Affairs* 68(2): 156–176.
Cooper, Andrew F., Jorge Heine, and Ramesh Thakur, eds. 2013. *The Oxford Handbook of Modern Diplomacy*. Oxford: Oxford University Press.

Crapol, Edward, ed. 1992. *Women and American Foreign Policy: Lobbyists, Critics and Insiders*. New York, NY: Rowman and Littlefield.

Ehrenreich, Barbara, Katha Pollitt, R. Brian Ferguson, Lionel Tiger, and Jane S. Jaquette. 1999. 'Fukuyama's Follies' *Foreign Affairs* 78(1) January/February: 118–129.

Enloe, Cynthia. 1989. *Bananas, Beaches and Bases: Making Feminist Sense of International Politics*. Berkeley, CA: University of California Press.

Faucher, Charlotte. 2016. 'Book Review: Women, Diplomacy and International Politics since 1500' *Women's History Review* (Online Advance – 18 May 2016). Available at www.tandfonline.com/doi/abs/10.1080/09612025.2016.1171103. Accessed 28 February 2017.

FCO Historians. 1994. 'Women in Diplomacy: The FCO 1782–1999'. *History Notes* 6. https://issuu.com/fcohistorians/docs/history_notes_cover_hphn_6. Accessed 1 February 2015.

Fischer, Joschka. 2015. 'Angela Merkel must Accept that her Austerity Policy is now in Tatters' *Guardian*, 31 January, available at www.theguardian.com/commentisfree/2015/jan/31/growth-decide-eurozones-future-greek. Accessed 1 February 2015.

Fritsche, Claudia. 2002. 'Opportunities and Challenges for Women in Diplomacy' Roberts Hall, Princeton University, 3 April.

Fukuyama, Francis. 1998. 'Women and the Evolution of World Politics' *Foreign Affairs* 77:5, available at www.foreignaffairs.com/articles/1998-09-01/women-and-evolution-world-politics. Accessed 28 February 2017.

G20 China. n.d. www.g20chn.org/English/G20Priorities/Engagement/201606/t20160628_2345.html. Accessed 14 February 2017.

Gould-Davies, Nigel. 2013. 'The Intimate Dance of Diplomacy: in Praise of Practice' *International Affairs* 89(6) November: 1459–1467. Available at www.chathamhouse.org/publications/ia/archive/view/195331#sthash.MsvvvdeA.dpuf. Accessed 28 February 2017.

Harris Rimmer, Susan. 2015. 'A Critique of Australia's G20 Presidency and the Brisbane Summit 2014' *Global Summitry* 1(1): 41–63. DOI: http://dx.doi.org/10.1093/global/guv004. First published online: 1 July 2015.

Iriye, Akira. 1979. 'Culture and Power: International Relations as Intercultural Relations' *Diplomatic History* 3(2): 115–128.

Mazurana, Dyan. 2005. 'Gender and the Causes and Consequences of Armed Conflict' in Dyan Mazurana, Angela Raven-Roberts and Jane Parpart (eds) *Gender, Conflict, and Peacekeeping*, 29–42. Boulder, CO: Rowman and Littlefield.

McCarthy, Helen. 2014. *Women of the World: The Rise of the Female Diplomat*. London: Bloomsbury Publishing.

McEnaney, Laura. 2009. 'Gender – Seeing Gender in Foreign Policy' in *Encyclopaedia of the New American Nation*, available at www.americanforeignrelations.com/E-N/Gender.html. Accessed 1 February 2015.

McEnaney, Laura. 2010. 'Gender Analysis and Foreign Relations' in Dennis Merrill and Thomas Paterson (eds) *Major Problems in American Foreign Relations, Volume II: Since 1914*, Volume 2, 14–17. Wadsworth: Cengage Learning.

McGlen, Nancy E., and Meredith Reid Sarkees. 1995. *The Status of Women in Foreign Policy*. Washington DC: Foreign Policy Association: Headline Series, No. 307.

Miller, Rachel. 2013. *Wife and Baggage to Follow*. Canberra: Halstead Press.

Morsink, Johannes. 1991. 'Women's Rights in the Universal Declaration' *Human Rights Quarterly* 13: 229–256.

Olsson, Louise, and Theodora-Ismene Gizelis. 2013. 'An Introduction to UNSCR 1325' *International Interactions: Empirical and Theoretical Research in International Relations* 39(4): 425–434.

Otto, Dianne. 2010. 'Power and Danger: Feminist Engagement with International Law Through the UN Security Council' *Australian Feminist Law Journal* 32(1): 97–121.

Pedersen, Susan. 2014. 'Women of the World: The Rise of the Female Diplomat by Helen McCarthy – review' *Guardian*, 27 June, available at www.theguardian.com/books/2014/jun/27/women-world-rise-female-diplomat-helen-mccarthy-review. Accessed 1 February 2015.

Pettman, Jan Jindy. 1996. *Worlding Women: A Feminist International Politics*. London: Routledge.

Piketty, Thomas. 2014. *Capital in the Twenty First Century*. Harvard, MA: Belknap Press.

Potter, Antonia, and Jaime Peters. 2008. 'International Women Leaders Global Security Summit Report', February, available at https://assets.aspeninstitute.org/content/uploads/files/content/docs/International_Women_Leaders_Global_Security_Summit_Report.pdf. Accessed 1 March 2017.

Reuters. 2016. 'IMF's Lagarde trial in Tapie case to begin December 12' *Reuters Business News*, 12 September, available at www.reuters.com/article/us-france-lagarde-trial-idUSKCN11I1S4?il=0. Accessed 1 October 2016.

Roberts, Yvonne. 2014. 'Women of the World Review – A Study of Female Diplomats that Lacks Class' *Observer*, 25 May.

Roosevelt, Theodore. 1899. *The Strenuous Life: Essays and Addresses*. Mineola, NY: Dover.

Schelling, Thomas C. 2008. 'The Diplomacy of Violence' in Thomas Schelling *Arms and Influence*, 1–34. New Haven, CY: Yale University Press.

Slaughter, Anne Marie. 2004. *A New World Order*. Princeton, NJ: Princeton University Press.

Sluga, Glenda, and Carolyn James, eds. 2015. *Women, Diplomacy and International Politics Since 1500*. London: Routledge.

Tickner, J. Ann. 1992. *Gender in International Relations: Feminist Perspectives on Achieving Global Security*. New York, NY: Columbia University Press.

Tickner, J. Ann. 1999. 'Why Women Can't Run the World' *International Studies Review* 1(3): 3–11.

The Economist. 2006. 'The Importance of Sex: Forget China, India and the Internet, Economic Growth is Driven by Women' 12 April, www.economist.com/node/6800723. Accessed 14 February 2017.

UNDP. 2014. *United Nations, Millennium Development Goals Progress Report*. www.un.org/millenniumgoals/2014%20MDG%20report/MDG%202014%20English%20web.pdf. Accessed 14 February 2017.

Yoon, Sangwon. 2014. 'UN Women Rise to Power; No Longer Mistaken for Prostitute' *Bloomberg*, 19 March, available at www.bloomberg.com/news/2014-03-19/i-m-not-a-hooker-and-other-tales-as-women-gain-un-power.html. Accessed 1 June 2014.

9 Becoming UN Women

A journey in realizing rights and gaining global recognition

Phumzile Mlambo-Ngcuka

Introduction

The pursuit of gender equality has become increasingly intertwined with the overarching goals of the United Nations, and stands as a centerpiece of the 2030 Agenda for Sustainable Development and its 17 Sustainable Development Goals.[1] Amongst other things, this pursuit serves as a signal to the international stage, that the realization of gender equality and women's empowerment is essential to achieving the sustainable development goals set forth by the United Nations and towards the creation of a just, peaceful, and equal world. In the diplomatic and international policy arenas in particular, the progress towards gender equality is viewed as an essential precondition to advancing these broader goals and objectives.

Over the past several decades, advances in gender equality in the diplomatic and international policy arenas have continued slowly but steadily, supported in part by more women entering the diplomatic arena, representing both their countries and gender, as heads of state, parliamentarians, and diplomatic actors. Indeed, these changes have taken place concurrently—the rise of women actors in diplomacy alongside the rise of gender equality and women's empowerment as preeminent considerations in international policy. While these changes have been essential to the fabric and pursuit of equality, the path to achieving them has proven difficult at best, with the right conditions being essential for them to flourish.

The United Nations General Assembly's creation of UN Women in 2010 was a vital step on this road to equality. For the first time in history, gender equality and women's empowerment went from being a marginal issue, discussed and deliberated within the contexts of other aims and interests to a recognized global priority in its own right. The establishment of UN Women validated the belief that to truly and permanently advance the space and role of gender within the diplomatic sphere, gender equality and women's empowerment needed to be prioritized at the highest diplomatic levels. Thus the establishment of UN Women's Executive Director at the level of Under-Secretary-General of the United Nations ensured that women's rights would be reflected in diplomacy and international relations, not just through the presence of individual women leaders, but by having the right institutions and structures at the highest levels.

Becoming UN Women 171

These achievements and the creation of such institutional structures, however significant, were not built overnight, and at times encountered defiant obstacles as the journey towards gender equality began and progressed. Moreover, this evolution is far from complete, and UN Women continues to work towards substantive equality through diplomatic channels, strategic partnerships, and grassroots engagement, based upon this solid foundation. Seeking to highlight the journey of UN Women in their quest to gain global recognition for the inalienable rights of women and girls worldwide, this chapter first considers and provides a historical context of the women's movement in the United Nations through three primary areas: the foundational Commission on the Status of Women, milestone conferences which have continued to impact the global agenda towards equality, and notable women diplomats whose presence altered the landscape for their successors.[2] Placed within this historical context, this chapter then moves to examine the current role of UN Women, offering positive and concrete examples of its work in the present day. The UN Security Council resolution 1325 is an illustrative case in point, which demonstrates how UN Women has successfully propelled gender equality into the top diplomatic channels and the international political sphere at large.[3] Finally, the chapter closes with policy recommendations on moving forward and the implementation of the United Nations 2030 Agenda for Sustainable Development, a landmark roadmap that has placed gender equality as a globally accepted key priority.

Shaping the world: the commission on the status of women

The understanding that securing human rights and individual well-being is the path towards a just and peaceful world has informed the UN from its earliest years. The preamble of the United Nations Charter (1945) refers to "equal rights of men and women" affirming signatories' "faith in fundamental human rights" and the "dignity and worth of the human person."[4] Of the 160 signatories to the UN Charter, only four were women, yet there already emerged an understanding that women needed their own separate body, one that was specifically dedicated to issues which affected them. Founded in 1946, that body came in the form of the Commission on the Status of Women (CSW), pre-dating the adoption of the revered Universal Declaration of Human Rights in 1948.[5] Members of the all-woman Commission succeeded in persuading the almost all-male group drafting the Declaration that "man" was not a synonym for "humanity" and in introducing for the first time, new, and more inclusive, language.[6]

Over the next five decades, the CSW served to address the concerns and issues of women, while evolving to become a significant and impactful component of the UN's architecture. From 1947 to 1962, the primary role of the Commission was to set standards and formulate international conventions to change discriminatory legislation and raise global awareness of women's issues. The Commission's research produced a detailed, country-by-country picture of women's political and legal standing.[7] Over time, this formed the basis for instruments setting out and safeguarding women's human rights, culminating in

CEDAW, the Convention on the Elimination of All Forms of Discrimination against Women, which the UN General Assembly adopted in 1979. CEDAW enshrined the concept that eliminating discrimination was a legitimate and vital aim of governments and institutions; "the Convention establishes not only an international bill of rights for women, but also an agenda for action by countries to guarantee the enjoyment of those rights."[8] CEDAW was a highly significant step for the United Nations in its pursuit of gender equality and justice, as it marked, for the first time, the need to go beyond the legal sphere and to look at socially constructed issues underlying gender-based discrimination, a challenge which remains prevalent today and has been taken forward into a new iteration in the 2030 Agenda for Sustainable Development, with its emphasis on universality and the interconnectedness of its development goals.

Strengthening the Convention's impact was its Optional Protocol, entering into force in 1999. At its core, the optional protocol reinforced the core message of the Convention, providing women with the right to petition, when they experience violations of rights protected under the Convention. It also created an inquiry procedure for situations of grave or systematic violations of women's rights.[9] Virtually all UN member states are now parties to CEDAW. Therefore, with its broad influence, notably in the CEDAW process,[10] the CSW could have been said to punch above its weight in the processes of the United Nations, contributing significantly to the achievement of gender equality and women's representation in the global sphere.

CEDAW, although highly significant, was just one part of the Commissions story. Through its work, both within policymaking and on the ground, the Commission helped guide and steer gender-related discussions at the United Nations throughout its history. For example, when the UN entered a period focused on development in the 1960s and 1970s, the Commission's research helped demonstrate both the contribution of women to development, as well as the disproportionate effect of poverty on women. Eventually, this work began to delve further into gender roles and eventually gave rise to a strategy called "gender mainstreaming," a strategy that works towards ensuring a gender-sensitive policy process from the outset. Furthermore, responding to the increasing size and self-confidence of women's organizations during the Decade for Women 1976–1985, the CSW also helped bring violence against women to the forefront of international debates. These efforts resulted in the Declaration on the Elimination of Violence against Women (1993). In March 1994, the Commission on Human Rights appointed a UN Special Rapporteur on Violence against Women with a mandate to investigate and report on all aspects of violence against women. This appointment reinforced the connection between the CSW and the Commission on Human Rights.

Landmark conferences

A second aspect worth exploring in the historical relationship of the women's movement at the UN, is the international conferences, which have marked turning points in the movement's pursuit of equality within the international fora. The first of these, the World Conference of the International Women's Year opened at the Palace of the Three Cultures in Mexico City in June of 1975. This conference marked a renewed spirit in how gender issues were treated in the global diplomatic architecture. Women made up 73 percent of the delegates and led 113 of the 133 national delegations. Even though men occupied the front seats in many delegations during the tense negotiations, the Mexico City conference was a breakthrough moment for gender equality and women's empowerment in the United Nations. Although women were, of course, on the political scene before the conference; this proved a milestone nevertheless, reflecting a change in the way the UN and the world considered gender and women's issues and embedding formal arrangements which continued to unfold and further normalize the evolving position of women within the global processes.

The Mexico City conference was also the starting point for the UN Decade for Women, and was the first of four world conferences on women, conferences which centered themselves on the themes of equality, development, and peace. Two subsequent conferences took place in Copenhagen in 1980 and in Nairobi in 1985, but it was the fourth and final one in Beijing which marked a significant turning point for the global agenda on gender equality.

The Beijing conference was significant, not only because the international women's movement was larger and more organized than ever before, but also because the movement and the conference began to work in synergy to develop, for the first time, a strategic approach towards influencing the international agenda. CSW preparations for the conference included 170 country reports and five regional preparatory meetings; the recommendations from these meetings then created the basis for the consensus document that eventually emerged. In addition to CSW-organized NGO meetings, many national and international civil society organizations also made their own preparations. In terms of attendance, the conference brought together the largest number of governments, NGOs, and media representatives ever before experienced at a UN conference up to that time.

The outcome of the conference cannot be underestimated in the historical narrative of the women's movement and its use of the United Nations as a strategic tool for the achievement towards gender equality. The Beijing Declaration and Platform for Action of 1995 was adopted by 189 Member States, firmly anchoring the struggle for gender equality within a human rights framework and making a clear statement about states' responsibility for delivering on their commitments. The Beijing consensus ensured that the agenda at the Millennium Summit in 2000, the next monumental collective milestone in multilateral policy, would also include discussions on gender equality and women's empowerment.

In development terms, the Beijing Platform for Action gave governments and international organizations detailed goals in 12 "Critical Areas of Concern." Many of these goals, particularly those regarding the girl child, education, health care (including sexual and reproductive health), the environment, and the economy, reflected long-standing UN priorities. Much of what came out of

Beijing also aligned with the outcomes of other international conferences held in the 1990s—on the environment, human rights, population and development, social development and human settlements. Together, the conferences laid out a roadmap for development in the twenty-first century. The major contribution of the Beijing Conference was to integrate a gender dimension into the broad concept of development. The creation of a UN entity dedicated to gender equality, as well as an Under-Secretary-General post expressly for this purpose, can be traced directly back to the success of the Beijing conference.

Leadership

As the four World Conferences on Women were taking place, a number of key figures were beginning to make their mark within the UN's official ranks and through their dedication and service act begin the long awaited normalization of women working as powerful diplomats. Notably, Helvi Sipilä, a skilled diplomat with a lifetime commitment to gender equality, led the Centre for Social Development and Humanitarian Affairs (which included the CSW secretariat) from 1972 to 1980. Appointed an Assistant Secretary-General at a time when 97 percent of the UN's senior staff were men, she steered the 1975 World Conference of the International Women's Year in Mexico City through the political shoals and secured some notable institutional advances. Among these was a new voluntary fund, which became UNIFEM (the UN Development Fund for Women), which was placed within the UN Development Programme in 1984. UNIFEM's primary purpose was to initiate and co-ordinate gender-related operational activities and to encourage action across the UN system. Also emerging from the conference was INSTRAW, the International Research and Training Institute for the Advancement of Women.[11]

The first woman to become an Under Secretary-General was Margaret Joan Anstee, who spent the majority of her career (1953–1993) far from UN headquarters in some of the most difficult and challenging assignments ever to face the UN. She was the first woman Head of Mission anywhere (and remained the only one for seven years). Anstee stated that,

> Governments always had to be cajoled into accepting my appointment as [UNDP] Resident Representative because they didn't want a woman ... In the first months I always felt I had to work much harder than a man to show I was up to the job.

On the other hand, she noted, "All were sorry to see me go when my tour of duty came to an end."[12]

Another pioneer for women in the diplomatic sphere, was Dr Nafis Sadik the first woman to head a major voluntary-funded United Nations programme. She was appointed Executive Director of the United Nations Population Fund (UNFPA) in 1987 and served as Secretary-General of the International Conference on Population and Development in 1994. From the time she joined UNFPA in 1970, to her retirement in 2000—and for many years afterwards—Dr Sadik called attention to the importance of addressing the needs of women and the necessity of involving women directly in making and carrying out development policy.

Through their combined commitment to gender equality and pioneering work, all of these women influenced the way gender was treated in international fora and helped raise the issues to where they are today—recognized at the highest levels of international diplomacy.

Becoming UN Women

The United Nations Entity for Gender Equality and the Empowerment of Women, UN Women, became operational in January 2011. However, the reform process began decades before, and required an array of individuals and strategic planning for its creation to first implemented.

Its beginning can be traced to the 1985 Third World Conference on Women Conference (in Nairobi), where it was noted that the UN's system for implementing the goals of the Decade for Women was fragmented, lacking a clear center for implementation. Five years later, at the Beijing conference, a related problem was highlighted with calls for the UN to "reform, renew and revitalise"[13] its mechanisms. These calls were echoed once again when, after Beijing, the UN's Joint Inspection Unit (JIU) criticized the low status and paltry resources of the UN's Division for the Advancement of Women (DAW), noting that "four world conferences on women have done nothing to move the staff resources devoted to the women's programme from the very bottom of the United Nations resource list."[14] Committing to reform in 2005, the General Assembly emphasized "system-wide coherence" and a closer relationship between the normative (DAW in the case of women) and operational (UNIFEM) activities.

Following up on reform efforts, UN Secretary-General Kofi Annan presented Member States with the "Delivering as One" report in 2006, which was prepared by a High-level panel of preeminent persons. It was a wide-ranging and ambitious proposal to reform UN system management and operations, which called for a single body to deal with issues of gender. It would be headed by an Under-Secretary-General and have "adequate, stable and predictable funding." This suggestion closely followed the recommendation submitted by a group of 50 women's organizations to the High-level Panel—a fact that underlines the unusually (for the UN) close relationship between the new entity and civil society. In creating the new entity, the UN General Assembly pulled together four distinct pieces from across the UN jigsaw: UNIFEM, INSTRAW, DAW, and the Office of the Special Adviser on Gender Issues and Advancement of Women (OSAGI). Thus, the normative, operational and system-wide co-ordination functions of the UN as they relate to gender were united under the same roof for the first time, with the backing not just of the UN, but of the women's movement which had fostered the strengthening of a unified voice for over half a century.

The significance of appointing an Executive Director at the Under-Secretary-General (USG) level was perhaps one of the most symbolic aspects of the organization's creation. It was considered a crucial diplomatic coup for women's rights. Appointment as a USG meant that the Executive Director would be a member of the Chief Executives Board (the Secretary-General's cabinet) on the same level as other heads of UN agencies, ensuring that the new entity's voice would be heard and its views given weight within and beyond the UN system. With the high-level rank of USG, the UN Women's leader could then seek meetings and appointments with top decision-makers and world leaders. In meetings with the private sector, CEOs would know that UN Women's Executive Director spoke for the system as a whole and had the backing of the Secretary-General, and the multilateral institution at large. For women's organizations, it was a vindication of their struggle since the earliest days. Their voices would be heard at the highest diplomatic levels. It was an evolution, which ensured gender equality, and women's empowerment could and would no longer be relegated; they were now top-level global priorities.

However, while the women's movement could celebrate the institutions creation from a diplomatic standpoint, and a vital step in the pursuit of gender equality, obstacles for the institution to achieve its full objective quickly emerged; particularly in relation to funding. UN Women received very limited funds from the regular Secretariat budget and was forced to raise the vast bulk of its operational funding through voluntary contributions from Member States. It was and is still well noted that despite the fact that gender equality has global consensus, there is a significant and chronic programmatic funding gap in making the aspiration a reality. A recent review of progress on implementation of the Beijing Declaration found that, often, the reason that advances towards gender equality have been slow and inconsistent is the fact of financing gaps. In some countries, these gaps are as high as 90 percent. More than ever, ambitious gender equality goals require the help of transformative financing, including gender responsive budgeting and strategic partnerships with the private sector.

First and foremost, UN Women works to support UN Member States at the global level in intergovernmental processes. The agency also supports other intergovernmental processes, in the UN General Assembly, Economic and Social Council, and Security Council, and engages with a broad range of intergovernmental processes, advocating for stronger attention to gender equality. UN

Table 9.1 What is UN Women? Policy objectives in the twenty-first century

With a universal mandate covering all countries, UN Women has three main functions:
- To support inter-governmental bodies, such as the Commission on the Status of Women, in their formulation of policies, global standards, and norms.
- To help Member States implement these standards, standing ready to provide suitable technical and financial support to those countries that request it, and to forge effective partnerships with civil society.
- To lead and coordinate the UN system's work on gender equality as well as promote accountability, including through regular monitoring of system-wide progress.

Women was actively engaged in shaping the 2030 Agenda for Sustainable Development, contributed to shaping the gender targets, and is closely involved in the development of the indicators through which implementation will be monitored. The entity also works on aligning sources of development funding—public and private, domestic and international—with gender equality goals, and promotes multi-stakeholder partnerships as key to ensuring adequate and robust financing. Second, UN Women helps countries translate international norms and standards into practices, which work towards achieving real change in women's lives. UN Women's programmes in 92 countries support women's leadership, strengthen women's economic empowerment, help end violence against women, promote women's participation in peace and security processes, and ensure that public planning and budgeting responds to the needs and rights of women.

Third, UN Women leads, coordinates, and promotes the accountability of efforts across the UN system to achieve gender equality. Of note, the UN System, which comprises 32 entities, has for the first time adopted a comprehensive action plan to increase accountability in regard to gender equality and women's empowerment called the UN System-wide Action Plan (UN-SWAP). This plan is stimulating mainstreaming of gender perspectives in the work of the United Nations at large through a common agenda and a common framework in which each entity can work in the years that lie ahead, and be tracked in their progress. With 15 Performance Indicators the UN-SWAP was the first unified framework to systematically revitalize, capture, monitor, and measure performance and accountability for the work of the UN system on gender equality and women's empowerment. Spearheaded by UN Women, its aim is to create a clearer picture of areas of strength and weakness and identify the human, financial, and knowledge resources needed to propel progress across all entities of the UN system. It requires annual reporting by each participating entity, department, and office, and has been remarkably successful in obtaining them and thereby holding the system to account: 90 percent of UN entities, offices, and departments regularly submit reports. As the performance indicators steadily climb, they record gradual systemic change.

Progress is tempered by challenges

UN Women's role in elevating gender issues in diplomacy and international policy has brought many positive changes, giving women's rights greater priority and visibility on the international stage and beyond. However, the fact that women's rights are continuing to lag in several key domains shows just how crucial it is that UN Women has a voice at the highest levels. Progress since Beijing has been tempered by significant work that still remains, as indicated by a number of distinct examples. For instance, while there has been an increasing willingness to legislate for gender equality and against gender-based violence, the World Bank reports that there are still 155 economies with at least one law impeding women's economic opportunities, and there continues to be weak enforcement of good laws.[15] Further to this, there have been notable increases in girls' enrolment in primary and secondary education, but school completion remains an increasing concern. In regards to maternal mortality, there has been a 45 percent decrease since 1990, but this remains well shy of the 70 percent target.

A similar picture of mixed results is reflected in the workplace. Efforts to improve women's educational attainment and growing participation in the labor market has not been matched with better conditions, better career prospects, fair remuneration or equal pay—globally, women are paid 20 percent less than men for the same work. Around the world, women work longer hours, do two and half times more unpaid care and domestic work than men, and are expected to care for children, the sick, and the elderly, even when they are also in paid employment. Existing data suggest that the majority of economically active women in developing countries are engaged in the informal sector and continue to bear a disproportionate share of unpaid work in family farms and businesses, with the additional penalty that they lack longer-term financial protection, such as pensions.

As other chapters in this volume have aptly demonstrated, in terms of women's leadership in the political sphere, female representation in national parliaments has doubled, from 11 percent in 1995 to 20 percent today. However, this figure is still well below the 50 percent figure that would mark parity. With relatively few women in global leadership roles, women continue to be excluded from decision-making at all levels, including peace and security, where their needs are most urgent and their contributions are irreplaceable (see below). At the current pace it could therefore take 50 years before we (or our great-grandchildren) see equal representation of women in parliaments and national governmental bodies.

Comparable results are evident in regards to women's health and well-being. Whilst women have gained better access to reproductive health information and services, the world is still far from the goal of universal access. Furthermore, countries have yet to make good on the promises that their governments made in Cairo and Beijing regarding women's sexual and reproductive health and rights. Although there is increased awareness in relation to the legal obligation toward gender-based violence and crimes, it is still endemic, and in all areas of life, women contend with pervasive and deep-seated discriminatory norms and stereotypes. In a number of countries, as many as 70 percent of women report having experienced physical or sexual violence from an intimate partner, whilst intimate partner violence accounts for between 40 and 70 percent of female murder victims. The persistently high numbers of women who live with this violence has prompted the World Health Organization to call it a global public health crisis of epidemic proportions.

UN Women remains committed to progressing on these familiar fronts, yet new challenges continue to emerge, increasing the need for young people to become engaged in this work, and to take ownership of the reforms and movements that will shape their world. Inequalities widen between and within countries. Global financial and economic crises, volatile prices, food and energy insecurity, environmental degradation, and climate change present challenges for everyone, but have specific impacts on women and girls. Women who face multiple and intersecting forms of discrimination, such as poverty, location, age, ethnicity, disability, sexual orientation, and social status are especially vulnerable. Many parts of this world are confronting violent extremism along with growing waves of conservatism, nationalism, and xenophobia and a backlash against women's rights that threatens fragile progress. Large-scale migration and an overall increase in the refugee population in developing countries, as well as in developed countries, has become one of the challenges of our time. In uncertain times, daily discrimination and violence intensifies, creating new threats such as trafficking and enslavement. UN Women has always, and continues to work towards overcoming these challenges and the creation of a just and equal world for all.

Case in point: women, peace, and security

This section closely examines a specific issue—women, peace, and security—and looks at how UN Women's positive diplomatic influence was able to elevate it to an area of global priority.

United Nations Security Council Resolution 1325 on Women, Peace and Security was adopted in 2000.[16] It is a three-page document that has been translated into more than 100 languages, and was born out of a truly global constituency of women's organizations and advocates. Resolution 1325 is based on the revolutionary idea that peace is inextricably linked with equality between men and women, an idea has since become both a global norm and the official policy of the highest body tasked with the maintenance of international peace and security.

Several subsequent Security Council resolutions, regional organizations' directives, and countries' national policies have since reinforced the importance of women's role in peace and security. As of the end of 2015, 55 countries had adopted national action plans on women, peace, and security. In October 2015, the Security Council unanimously adopted resolution 2242, which addresses substantive challenges such as integrating a gender analysis on the drivers and impacts of violent extremism, ambitious new targets for numbers of female peacekeepers, and the need for more senior women leaders in all levels of decision-making in peace and security. Resolution 2242 was adopted unanimously, co-sponsored by 71 Member States and had 113 registered speakers. With that, it became the most popular resolution in the Security Council's history, and its adoption was presided over by a head of government, a first for a resolution on women, peace, and security.

One of the greatest virtues of resolution 1325 is that civil society and women's organizations from all over the world have been able to leverage this resolution to attain political access and influence in their respective countries. It has proven a tool to raise consciousness and awareness about women's rights, to build coalitions and networks across the globe, and to hold governments and the international community's interventions accountable.

But it has been a long journey. When UN Women was created in 2010, the international community was celebrating ten years since the adoption of resolution 1325, but the lack of progress in women's leadership in diplomacy, peacemaking, and conflict resolution was alarming. UN Women specifically committed to using the normative power of resolution 1325 to advocate for increased participation of women in the halls of government, in the diplomatic corps and international civil service, in the military, in formal peace negotiations, in post-conflict governance bodies, in international organizations, and in all centers of power where decisions were being made. For example, in 2012, a UN Women study indicated that in peace talks over the two previous decades only 2 percent of chief mediators and 9 percent of negotiators were women. Compare the figures that 97 percent of our blue helmets are men, as are 80 percent of our special envoys.

Since then, we have seen a welcomed increase in the overall participation of women in peace processes. In 2014, women in senior positions were found in 75 percent of peace processes monitored by the UN; and in recent years, peace talks to resolve conflicts in Georgia, Colombia, and the Philippines have seen more women participating as negotiators or as signatories. For example, in Colombia, where UN Women invested in women's activism and supported the government's efforts to increase women's representation, women have, to date, made up to one-third of the delegates on each side in the Havana peace talks, and at least half of the participants in all public consultations relating to the peace negotiations.

However, as any UN organization is aware, progress is often slow and full of setbacks, and that our advances toward equality are not yet irreversible. In 2014, for the first time, women filled over a third of the Council's 15 seats, making history at the venerable institution, and in 2015, women led almost 40 percent of UN peacekeeping missions. In the short time since, many of these positive gains have unraveled with men replacing outgoing women representatives. Furthermore, for the election of the new Secretary-General in September 2016, only one woman representative had the power of a vote in the Security Council.

The reality is that as long as the overwhelming majority of policymakers, diplomats, military leaders, combatants, and official mediators and negotiators in peace talks are men, engaging men will remain a necessary and inevitable strategy to change gender inequality in peace and security matters. Men must be made aware of and proactively promote women's positive role in peacebuilding. A recent in-depth analysis of 40 peace processes since the end of the Cold War shows that, in cases where women were able to exercise a strong influence on the negotiation process, there was a much higher chance that an agreement would be reached—in fact, an agreement was almost always reached. The role of women in the negotiation processes was positively correlated with a greater likelihood of implementation of such peace agreements, and this had an impact on the effectiveness of commissions set up to monitor ceasefires or disarmament, seek truth and reconciliation, or write a new constitution. Similarly, a recent statistical analysis based on a dataset of 181 peace agreements signed between 1989 and 2011 showed that peace agreements that included women had a 35 percent increase in the probability of lasting 15 years. In 2011, only 36 percent of peace processes had specialized gender expertise, and this percentage has more than doubled in the last few years. Similarly, almost all peace processes in which the UN plays a role now include regular consultations with women, although these meetings are often more symbolic than meaningful.

Yet, despite this evidence, there are still implicit or open questions and doubts about women's leadership leading to better outcomes and more peace. In peace processes, including in recent conflicts like Mali, Myanmar, Syria, and South Sudan, the low levels of representation of women in formal negotiations is still shocking,. The international community must recognize the often invisible and informal role that women and girls play in conflict prevention and resolution, from peace activism to day-to-day intra-family and inter-community mediation and reconciliation.

In Mali, after Malian women's impressive mobilization and exceptional acts of courage, the formal negotiations marginalized women. Among the 100 delegates from the three negotiating groups at the talks, there were only five women, and the international diplomatic teams were mainly men. In Burundi, UN Women supported local women mediators in 129 municipalities, and helped manage hundreds of small conflicts in just a few months in 2015. Staff sensitized demonstrators to ensure that demonstrations were non-violent; advocated for the release of demonstrators and dissenters; promoted tolerance by initiating dialog between security forces and protesters, and among divided ethnic groups and communities; and countered rumors that were causing unnecessary fear, instability, and displacement.

In the case of Syria, women often negotiate cessations of hostilities and humanitarian access at the local level, but they remain virtually excluded from formal attempts to end the war. Instead, the international community pays attention to mostly male political and military elites and neglects the local and subnational processes where women are already brokering peace and strengthening community resilience. In this regard, UN Women has welcomed that the UN Special Envoy for Syria's, Mr Staffan de Mistura, established the historic Syrian Women's Advisory Board, which is made up of 12 independent civil society representatives who contribute to peace talks. This is the first time that a UN Special Envoy has formally established a Women's Advisory Board, and it is hoped such a precedent will create further change in this vein. UN Women can and will continue to advance critical action in the area of women, peace, and security, and ensure that gender equality and women's empowerment are a part of the global conversation at the very highest levels, especially in the wake of new global security challenges.

A new agenda

The convergence of an array of United Nations processes in 2015 offered a unique opportunity to reinforce global commitments to gender equality and women's empowerment. These processes included the twenty-year review of the implementation of the Beijing Declaration and Platform for Action; the end of the Millennium Development Goals and the adoption of a 2030 Agenda for Sustainable Development; the Third International Conference on Financing for Development; high-level reviews of United Nations peace operations and peace building architecture; high-level reviews of the implementation of Security Council resolution 1325 and attendant resolutions; and a new international climate agreement.

In 2015, UN Women also published a landmark report[17] showing that "economic and social policies can contribute to fairer and more gender-equal societies, as well as stronger and more prosperous economies, if they are designed and implemented with women's rights at their centre."[18] The report came with recommendations for specific actions. For example:

- governments' economic and social policies can generate decent jobs for women and ensure that unpaid care work is recognized and supported;
- the business community can ensure full and equal participation of women in decision-making at all levels, enact flexible leave policies and close the gender pay gap;
- civil society, including women's organizations, must act as a watchdog and move women's rights higher up the agenda for policy and action;
- mass media and developers of web content can represent women and women's lives without distortion, give equal time and consideration to women's stories and perspectives, and put aside once and for all stereotyped and objectified images—not only of women, but of men too.

UN Women has taken every opportunity to encourage the world to live up to the commitments made more than twenty years ago in the Beijing Declaration and Platform for Action. In 2014, 167 countries undertook national stock-taking of their implementation of their gender equality commitments in a review of unprecedented scale. This process has led to firmer commitments to take transformative actions before 2020, with the aim of a "Planet 50–50 by 2030."

UN Women's diplomacy at the United Nations and within Member States today has ensured that the 2030 Agenda for Sustainable Development reflects gender equality, the empowerment of women, and the human rights of women and girls across 17 Sustainable Development Goals. Furthermore, as women's economic empowerment can play such a unique role in accelerating progress on the 2030 Agenda for Sustainable Development, the Secretary-General established a High-Level Panel for Women's Economic Empowerment in 2016. Along with prioritizing equal pay and the care economy, the Panel focuses on best practices that will work towards removing discriminatory legislation, calibrate levels of informal work, ensure digital and financial inclusion, and support women's entrepreneurship. UN Women's flagship programme "Empowering Women and Powering Economies: Gender-Responsive Procurement" also responds to many of these areas, with the aim of fostering women's empowerment on both the supply and demand sides to boost profits for women-owned businesses and spur growth in the small and medium sized business sector. UN Women is also directly addressing the gender pay gap through its Equal Pay Coalition, a global call to action to galvanize multi-stakeholder commitment and multi-stakeholder action on equal pay for work of equal value.

Efforts have also been made towards ensuring that strong accountability mechanisms are in place so that actions match intentions, and all responsible make good on their commitments. We saw such commitments from more than 90 Heads of State and Government following UN Women's Global Leaders' Meeting at the United Nations on September 27, 2015. Indeed, it was the first time in history that leaders at the highest levels made personal commitments to take action for gender equality and women's empowerment in their countries, building on the knowledge gained through the review of implementation of the Beijing Platform for Action. One year later, UN Women was able to follow up with leaders to monitor and pursue those commitments. It is this kind of direct, high-level engagement that the creation of UN Women has made possible and will continue to drive in the next decades and beyond.

Indeed, part of the significance of UN Women elevating gender equality to high-level diplomatic channels is that it has helped public opinion evolve beyond the view that women's rights are merely the purview of women themselves. Truly transforming the way the world views gender equality and women's empowerment demands that both women and men take responsibility for change, with the understanding that gender equality benefits all of society; women and men, boys and girls. We know that social and cultural expectations shape male decisions and behaviors from an early age, with many boys finding themselves in gender roles that come with emotional constraints and expectations to exert power and control. They may grow up to believe that "being a man" calls for dominant, even violent behavior towards girls and women. In these circumstances, admitting uncertainty or questioning prevailing norms is translated as "weak." Transformation requires that, from an early age, both boys and girls learn values of equality, respect for diversity, empathy, paying attention to the needs of others, solidarity, and partnership. Motivated by such cause, UN Women has committed to finding ways to reach out to non-traditional audiences including men and boys, which led to the launch of UN Women's *HeForShe* movement in September 2014. In addition to this highly successful campaign, the initiative "IMPACT $10 \times 10 \times 10$," launched in January 2015 at the World Economic Forum, engages HeForShe Champions within governments, corporations, and universities by securing firm gender equality commitments in each sector. These commitments include using technology creatively to meet gender goals, encouraging financial inclusion, quotas for political representation and wage parity, and working toward the elimination of gender-based violence. In an unprecedented move, our corporate IMPACT champions released their own workforce gender diversity figures, including details on leadership roles and board membership, in UN Women's inaugural HeForShe Corporate Parity Report launched January 2016. In September 2016, they were joined by the programme's ten university champions who, in addition to sharing data on gender equality in their institutions, each pledged to take on the monumental task of ending gender-based violence on campus.

Civil Society is also a key actor for UN Women, and the organization is committed to engaged with it in the form of young people, religious actors and private sector leaders. Civil society, including trade unions and workers' movements, remains a bedrock partner for all of UN Women's endeavors. They provide the everyday voice of conscience and action, and the essential "feet on the ground," particularly in times of humanitarian crisis. Civil society organizations form part of a complex response to the growing number of interconnected threats to international peace and security—in particular the emergence of a rising wave of violent extremist groups that are directly and explicitly targeting women and women's rights.

Finally, working with the media, a tool which has enormous power to transform stereotypes by offering accurate and balanced portrayals of women's stories, is another way that UN Women seeks to overturn out-dated norms. UN Women's *Step It Up* for Gender Equality Media Compact is a coalition of media organizations committed to changing the industry by covering gender equality issues, increasing the number of women as news sources, training reporters on gender-sensitive reporting, and promoting gender equality in the news room.

By working with these actors and organizations on the international stage, UN Women's aim is nothing less than full equality by 2030 with substantial progress over the next five years. The only way to achieve a 50–50 Planet is to correct the global balance of power, resources, and opportunities that perpetuate gender inequality. This requires greatly increased understanding and commitment in all areas and at all levels, and unified action on a scale never before seen in the 70 years of the United Nations. This is a major task, and it demands a commitment to nothing less than a complete transformation, a new vision of the meaning of gender equality and women's empowerment, the political and intellectual leadership to provide it, and renewed belief among women and men in all countries that they can achieve it.

Moving forward

This chapter has explored the historical journey of UN Women from its foundation to its current incarnation. Through case studies, and discussion, it examined the changing landscape of the women's movement within the UN system and how some pivotal moments and key players worked towards the evolution of the organization to its current form. Highlighting some of the challenges, including the discriminatory laws and barriers which continue to impede women's economic empowerment and often hit the poorest and most marginalized the hardest, this chapter sought to craft a narrative of the obstacles which confront the full implementation of UN Women's work toward realizing their fundamental and immoveable goal of gender equality for all. Through a case study on women, peace, and security, the chapter explored the vital role women play at the peace table, the importance of Security Council Resolution 1325 in advancing the women, peace, and security agenda, and the need to ensure women's inclusion in peacekeeping missions and peace building efforts. Finally, this chapter concluded with a look at where UN Women is going as an organization, and its vital work in collaboration with new partners and constituencies.

With that said, it is to made clear that there is still a long road ahead toward realizing women's full human rights. Resistance to change is built into all institutions, and the United Nations is no different. This is why UN Women will continue to work with a host of local and international partners and advocate for action, collect quality data, and monitor results. This includes working for parity within the UN's own ranks, and engaging with the Secretary-General designate to ensure the women's rights agenda remains a top priority for the UN's future. UN Women's diplomatic authority in global fora has been hard-won with promises made and laws enacted at the highest levels. Now it must be strengthened by forging strategic partnerships and reaching new and non-traditional constituencies. Marginal progress will not suffice; it is the norms themselves, which must change. UN Women must, and will, use its unique position to transform our societies into places that work for women, men, girls, and boys alike, both in the domestic and the political realms. Progress to date on internationally-accepted norms on gender equality and women's empowerment, have evolved through collective commitment and the passion of pioneers, early women diplomats and politicians who paved the way for those to follow. In the words of one of those pioneers and the driving force behind the Universal Declaration of Human Rights, Mrs Eleanor Roosevelt, "One thing we know beyond all doubt: Nothing has ever been achieved by the person who says, 'It can't be done'."[19]

Notes

1 The Sustainable Development Goals (SDGs), otherwise known as the Global Goals, are a universal call to action to end poverty, protect the planet, and ensure that all people enjoy peace and prosperity: www.undp.org/content/undp/en/home/sustainable-development-goals.html (Accessed November 20, 2016).
2 The Commission on the Status of Women (CSW) is the principal global intergovernmental body exclusively dedicated to the promotion of gender equality and the empowerment of women. A functional commission of the Economic and Social Council (ECOSOC), it was established by Council resolution 11(II) of June 21, 1946: www.unwomen.org/en/csw (Accessed November 20, 2016).
3 The Security Council adopted resolution (S/RES/1325) on women and peace and security on October 31, 2000. The resolution reaffirms the important role of women in the prevention and resolution of conflicts, peace negotiations, peace-building, peacekeeping, humanitarian response, and in post-conflict reconstruction and stresses the importance of their equal participation and full involvement in all efforts for the maintenance and promotion of peace and security: www.un.org/womenwatch/osagi/wps/ (Accessed November 20, 2016).
4 www.un.org/en/charter-united-nations/ (Accessed November 20, 2016).
5 www.un.org/en/universal-declaration-human-rights/ (Accessed November 20, 2016).
6 www.un.org/womenwatch/daw/CSW60YRS/CSWbriefhistory.pdf (Accessed November 20, 2016).

7 www.unwomen.org/en/csw/brief-history (Accessed November 20, 2016).
8 www.un.org/womenwatch/daw/cedaw/text/econvention.htm#intro (Accessed November 20, 2016).
9 www.un.org/womenwatch/daw/cedaw/protocol/text.htm (Accessed November 20, 2016).
10 For a detailed account of CSW and CEDAW, see Jain, 2005, 87–88.
11 www.un.org/womenwatch/daw/news/helvi.html (Accessed November 20, 2016).
12 Maslin (2005) 42.
13 Platform for Action Para. 309 www.un.org/womenwatch/daw/beijing/pdf/BDPfA%20E.pdf (Accessed November 20, 2016).
14 Report of the Joint Inspection Unit, The Advancement of Women Through and in the Programmes of the United Nations System: What Happens after the Fourth World Conference of Women, note 66, para. 210. Quoted in Chinkin and Charlesworth (2013) 10.
15 http://wbl.worldbank.org/~/media/WBG/WBL/Documents/Reports/2016/Women-Business-and-the-Law-2016.pdf (Accessed November 20, 2016).
16 UN Security Council, Security Council resolution 1325 (2000) (on women, peace, and security), 31 October 2000. S/RES/1325 (2000), available at www.refworld.org/docid/3b00f4672.e.html. Accessed February 4, 2017.
17 UN Women 2015–2016. http://progress.unwomen.org/en/2015/pdf/UNW_progress report.pdf (Accessed November 20, 2016).
18 Ibid., 3.
19 Roosevelt (1960) 168.

References

Chinkin, Christine, and Charlesworth, Hilary. 2013. "The Creation of UN Women," LSE research paper http://eprints.lse.ac.uk/53605/. Accessed February 6, 2017.
Jain, Devaki. 2005. *Women, Development and the UN*. Indiana University Press.
Maslin, Anna. 2005. *Women at Work: Perspectives, Experiences and Tips*. Northumbria University Press.
Roosevelt, Eleanor. 1960. *You Learn by Living: Eleven Keys for a More Fulfilling Life*. Westminster John Knox Press.
UN Women. 2015–2016. "Progress of the World's Women 2015–2016." http://progress.unwomen.org/en/2015/pdf/UNW_progressreport.pdf. Accessed February 6, 2017.

10 Unprecedented

Women's leadership in twenty-first century multilateral diplomacy

Jessica Fliegel

Introduction

> Might I, to begin with, express my gratitude to those male members of the General Assembly who have so warmly supported of this motion ... many of you might point out that this is still a man-built world and that women feel strangers as soon as they venture into it. This is true in a way. I must say that men have built this world quite impressively and that we feel duly impressed at first. After a certain time, however, some of us feel inclined to say: Is that all? ... From that moment we feel quite capable of playing our part.
>
> (Mrs H. Verwey, Delegate from The Netherlands, addressing the first UN General Assembly meeting in 1946 (cited in Boutros-Ghali 1996, 35))

In a globalized era, where seemingly trivial decisions and interactions can affect countries and the world on a grand scale, the role of the diplomat is of utmost importance. As the responsibilities of diplomats have been reshaped to account for changing global dynamics and widely accessible means of technology and transportation, the composition of foreign services has changed as well. Whereas women were largely marginalized from leading diplomatic posts throughout much of the twentieth century, in the twenty-first century women have reached unprecedented levels of representation in diplomatic corps and esteemed international organizations worldwide, including within the United Nations (UN). While men currently hold approximately 80 percent of UN permanent representative posts (the top diplomatic appointment within each mission), the number of women permanent representatives has steadily risen to reach a rate of unprecedented representation. Today, of the 193 recognized UN member states, there are 41 women permanent representatives from every region of the world serving as Heads of Missions (Permanent Missions to the United Nations, June 2016). In 2014, there were six women permanent representatives serving on the UN Security Council, meaning that for the first time in history women held more than one-third of the seats within the UN body that is "responsible for the maintenance of international peace and security" (Bryant 2014; United Nations Security Council, 2015). Additionally, while the 2016 campaign to elect the

Ninth Secretary-General of the United Nations included seven qualified women candidates, Antonio Guterres was ultimately selected, meaning that the highest position within the UN still remains exclusively held by men (1For7Billion, 2016). As the number of women permanent representatives appointed to the UN has reached unprecedented levels, and the scope of their portfolios and responsibilities continues to expand, leading women diplomats have an unparalleled opportunity to influence the dynamics of UN processes and international relations like never before. To enhance understanding of women's diplomatic leadership, this chapter seeks to answer the question: how do women permanent representatives to the UN exercise leadership in the twenty-first century? It is argued that while there are key characteristics of successful ambassadorial leadership[1] in the UN, there are also factors that influence how envisaged and embodied leadership translates into concrete action. How women permanent representatives assert their leadership, and the factors that influence their ability to do so, impacts their individual effectiveness in their capacities as well as their collective influence on shaping international policies and relations worldwide.

In this chapter, a representative sample of 15 women permanent representatives to the UN from Australia, Belgium, Bosnia and Herzegovina, Czech Republic, Hungary, Jordan, Kiribati, Lithuania, Micronesia, Nauru, Panama, Romania, Singapore, St. Lucia, and Timor-Leste participated in qualitative interviews to provide first-hand perspectives and experiences of leadership. Interview responses are used to identify key characteristics and factors influencing women's ambassadorial leadership in the UN. Factors are identified and assessed through three scopes: character, contingency, and contextual dimensions. The *character dimension* consolidates cross-cutting leadership characteristics, traits, and behaviors that are personified and enacted by women ambassadors to examine the attributes of successful diplomatic leaders. The *contingency dimension* evaluates factors to uncover if, and how, women's ambassadorial leadership roles are complemented or challenged by dynamics outside of their immediate control. The *contextual dimension* examines organizational and structural factors, including the UN diplomatic culture, to evaluate how the UN system has responded to women's increased representation in leading diplomatic posts. Constitutive theorizing is employed throughout the chapter to understand the conditions within which women ambassadorial leaders operate and to account for the elements that comprise women's ambassadorial leadership in the UN, rather than attempting to unearth causal variables to explain it and its effects (Carlsnaes 2002: 58).

Through this framework, this chapter attempts to address a profound gap in the existing literature on women in leadership. To date, no comprehensive global studies on women's leadership in multilateral diplomacy settings exist. Further, while there is a vast existing literature that discusses the UN's efficacy in ensuring that the organization's mission and agenda are gender conscientious, there is a lack of wide-ranging literature on women in UN diplomatic leadership—the women driving the policies and resolutions being drafted—specifically at the ambassadorial level (Pietila 2007: vi). To respond to these gaps, this chapter provides empirical insight into the UN system and how it accounts for women's increased representation in the highest diplomatic ranks. Finally, through showcasing the progressive nature of the UN's diplomatic culture, this chapter seeks to improve understanding of women's ambassadorial leadership in the twenty-first century.

In the following section, a brief historical overview of women's participation in multilateral diplomacy is provided for contextual reference. Existing theories of women in leadership, primarily focused on women in foreign policy, are then introduced through a survey of the extant literature on the subject. An explanation of the research methodology and framework follows. Responses from the interviews are then presented in a composite manner and analyzed through the character, contingency, and contextual dimensions. In closing, the chapter lays the groundwork for future research on the effects of women's increased representation in leading diplomatic posts while referencing practical recommendations for the continued advancement of women's leadership in multilateral diplomacy settings.

The history of women's leadership in multilateral diplomacy

While the twentieth century brought with it significant changes in the composition of many countries' foreign services, and women's diplomatic presence in international organizations has steadily increased over the course of time, the most prominent capacities in many diplomatic services and postings are still largely held by men (McCarthy 2014: 344). In addition, a genuine belief that women and men have different capacities to successfully fulfil foreign policy roles has persisted over time, particularly surrounding women's ability to hold diplomatic postings (McCarthy 2014). As McCarthy states, "It is arguably only since ... the 1990's that it has become possible to talk seriously about gender diversity as a genuine asset rather than a threat to the effectiveness of the ... diplomatic workforce" (McCarthy 2014: 345).

The historical ostracism of women in diplomatic service stems in part from early barriers to their public and political participation. As Towns explains, up through the early twentieth century, the inclusion of women in formal political spheres was seen as unthinkable in many societies (Towns 2010: 79). Further, societies began to perpetuate stark contrasts between women and men, which led to women being characterized as the antithesis of what the state (as progressive, strong, scientific, and modern) signified (Towns 2010: 66). Consequentially, societies and, therefore, states were thought to flourish when "each sex devoted its energies to appropriate tasks," whereby appropriate tasks came to include public, political, and business-oriented capacities for men, and homecare and familial responsibilities for women (Towns 2010: 80).

Widespread isolation from public life would eventually serve as a platform for motivated and courageous women to coalesce and demand their rightful inclusion through suffrage movements (Pietila 2007). In many countries, alongside these suffrage movements were activist-led efforts calling for women's inclusion in another official state capacity: serving in the Foreign Service. While women's access to political and diplomatic arenas varied by country, global events of the early twentieth century led to the formation of national and transnational women's movements advocating for women's inclusion in international peace-building processes (Pietila 2007). Prior to and during the Paris Peace Conference in 1919, the Inter-Allied Suffrage Conference, an international coalition of women, lobbied the governments of the 14 Allied States to call for women's inclusion in decision-making positions in the League of Nations (Pietila 2007: 2). Despite these efforts, the League of Nations had just one woman delegate who held the rank of ambassador, Elena Vacaresco of Romania (Worldwide Guide 2015). The Covenant of the League of Nations did, however, include "provisions that all positions in the League of Nations, including the secretariat, should be open equally to men and women" (Pietila 2007: 3). Following the collapse of the League of Nations and the eventual conclusion of World War II, many women used their experience to call for women's engagement in post-war international peace-building processes (Pietila 2007: 9). As a result, at the founding of the UN in 1945, women representatives were sent directly as official delegates of their countries (Pietila, 2007).

In total, 17 women were sent as representatives from 11 countries to the first General Assembly (GA) meeting of the UN in 1946 (Boutros-Ghali 1996). In the spirit of collaboration to strengthen and promote a cohesive women's voice, the women delegates drafted and signed an "Open Letter to the Women of the World" in advance of the meeting (Boutros-Ghali 1996: 11). During the first GA meeting, Eleanor Roosevelt, representative of the delegation of the United States of America (US), read excerpts from the letter to fellow delegates representing 51 countries worldwide (Boutros-Ghali 1996). Roosevelt stated in her remarks:

> In view of the variety of tasks which women performed so notably and valiantly during the war, we are gratified that ... women representatives ... are taking part at the beginning of this new phase of international effort. We hope their participation in the work of the United Nations Organization may grow and increase insight and in skill. To this end we call on the Governments of the world to encourage women everywhere to take a more active part in national and international affairs ...
>
> (Boutros-Ghali 1996: 94)

Roosevelt's remarks, along with the many voices before her, were realized when Article 8 of the UN Charter was drafted to state that "The United Nations shall place no restrictions on the eligibility of men and women to participate in any capacity and under conditions of equality in its principal and subsidiary organs" (Charter of the United Nations 2015). Ultimately, 160 signatories signed the UN Charter. Four of these signatories, or approximately 2.5 percent, were women delegates (Pietila 2007: 9).

Despite Article 8 of the UN Charter, and the introduction of Article 8 of the Convention on the Elimination of All Forms of Discrimination Against Women (1979), the responsibility to decide if women will ascend within foreign services remained with governments worldwide. As such, in many countries throughout the twentieth century, women were marginalized from holding official diplomatic roles in Foreign Ministries. Further, even when women diplomats received UN postings, traditional gender-roles were perpetuated through subtle means such as committee appointments. Tickner (2001) claims that since the founding of the UN in 1946, those select women who have been sent to represent their countries have been placed on committees that deal primarily with women's initiatives, and social and humanitarian issues. This reality, specifically as it relates to the Commission on the Status of Women, still exists today, though gender-balance has become more prevalent in the main GA committees as substantiated through interview responses discussed in this chapter.

A review of existing theories on women and leadership

The word *leadership* has various meanings and usages. As Sadler (2003) explains, the term can be applied to social processes, it can be embodied through personal characteristics, it can be singular or collective, and it can involve one actor or many actors. As the ability to assert leadership is largely contextual, Sadler explains that leaders must account for various factors, such as culture or the specific attributes of the task, to fulfill their role in an influential way (Sadler 2003: 171). Accordingly, to achieve goals, certain characteristics are embodied by leaders or enacted through leadership initiatives (Keohane 2010). Leadership is individualized, however, and is leveraged differently based on a leader's circumstance, audience, and objective. As Keohane explains "Individual women display different styles of leadership, just as men in such positions have always done" (Keohane 2010: 128).

While individuals lead in distinct ways given varying circumstances, the question arises: do women and men have distinctive leadership styles or characteristics? In an indirect response to this question, Mary Robinson, the first female President of Ireland, stated:

> As women lead they are changing leadership ... When women lead and articulate their purpose, it seems to me that they work together, not as individuals, but with a sense of community and networking in a healthy way. Women have fresh and imaginative skills of dialogue and are setting a more open, flexible and compassionate style of leadership.
>
> (Cork Federation 1995)

In addition, Nye states that women may generally have a greater mastery of employing soft power skills than men do, which may result from "A lower need to demonstrate command and greater patience" (Nye 2008: xii). Nye later explains that the ability to effectively use soft and hard power is equally important for men and women, and both are equally capable of utilising these skills (Nye 2008). To do so, however, it is essential that stereotypes are not perpetuated by gendered expectations of leadership.

Building off existing theories of women and leadership, McGlen and Hardees (1993) introduce two divisive theories related to women in foreign policy capacities. The first, which they refer to as 'the maximizer feminist' theory, argues against negative implications perpetuated by gendered differences (McGlen and Sarkees 1993: 6). Maximizer feminists claim that "any gender differences" that exist between men and women's leadership in foreign policy make women more suited to manage foreign affairs, not less suited as commonly misconceived (McGlen and Sarkees 1993: 11). Alternatively, the "minimizer feminists dismiss the existence of differences, arguing that women (and men) both have a right to make foreign policy decisions" and any expectations of how women and men will act in this respect is a result of cultural and social constructs, not the individual's capacity (McGlen and Sarkees 1993: 11). In light of this, they claim that by actively moving towards the promotion of a "culture" where gender-distinctions are not correlated with difference in capacity to lead, this "will eliminate the few remaining artificial differences" (McGlen and Sarkees 1993: 11). Interview responses unveil validity in the maximizer and minimizer theories as they relate to women's ambassadorial leadership in the UN in the twenty-first century.

As women have been marginalized from leadership capacities in political, diplomatic, and international institutions throughout history, some theorists have argued that to be successful within these institutions today leaders must now fit traditionally-defined masculine molds (Duerst-Lahti and Kelly 1995). According to Keohane, the very gender stereotypes, bias, and assumptions that are traditionally held regarding women in leadership evolved in support of "a world view in which leadership is a man's job and women do their part through caring, mothering and providing services to men" (Keohane 2010: 127). It is this line of thinking that grounds the "assumption" that women who do ascend to leadership capacities will lead in ways that are associated with femininity, despite the fact that perspectives of successful leadership can be largely linked with masculinity (Keohane 2010: 127). Alternatively, theorists argue that a leader's ability, whether woman or man, is not fully contingent on their own characteristics, or response to context. Rather, they argue that a leader's success will only be hindered insofar as others—including peers, colleagues, and followers—enable a leader's gender to affect the ways in which they choose to interact with or respond to their leadership. According to Genovese and Thompson, a leader's strategy will be "influenced by society's definitions and expectations of gender," and for a woman this may mean learning to succeed in what society promotes as being a "man's world" (Genovese and Thompson 1993: 7).

Lastly, Holsti and Rosenau (1981) draw two hypotheses from studies they conducted to understand societal perceptions of American women in foreign policy leadership capacities. The first hypothesis is that "the foreign policy beliefs of women in leadership positions differ significantly from those of their male counterparts" (Holsti and Rosenau 1981: 328). This hypothesis is founded on the belief that women generally hold a more optimistic view of the international system, they tend to focus their efforts strongly in the social, humanitarian, and economic spheres, and they are more hesitant to seek military responses for managing global crises (Holsti and Rosenau 1981: 328). The basis of this preconceived notion implies that traditional gender-stereotypes do shape societal attitudes surrounding women in foreign policy leadership positions. The second hypothesis states that "the foreign policy beliefs of women in leadership positions do not differ significantly from those held by men in comparable roles," promoting the perspective that leaders in similar capacities will share commonalities with one another, regardless of gender (Holsti and Rosenau 1981: 329).

Overall, a large proportion of the studies that have been conducted on women and leadership in foreign policy-related positions have culminated with similar conclusions: that expectations of gendered-differences may be more significant than any actual differences between women and men in foreign policy leadership (Keohane 2010: 146), that leadership by its nature is highly individualized, and that the effects of time, socialization, and cultural shifts will continue to reshape and potentially eliminate existing gendered expectations (Keohane 2010: 154). While these overarching conclusions are largely applicable to aggregated interview responses shared in this chapter, additional insights on women in ambassadorial leadership are drawn from responses received.

Insights into women's ambassadorial leadership at the UN

Moving beyond theory to strengthen understanding of women's ambassadorial leadership in practice, the following sections examine how current women permanent representatives to the UN exercise leadership through experiential insights gathered through interviews conducted with 15 women permanent representatives to the UN. Since all 193 member states have at least a basic form of diplomatic representation within UN headquarters in New York, ranging anywhere from two staff members working within a nation's mission up to 157 staff members working within the United States Mission to the UN, evaluating women's ambassadorial leadership at the UN allowed for a concentrated yet global study of women's diplomatic leadership within a universally esteemed and prestigious posting (Permanent Missions to the United Nations, June 2016). The UN also has built-in indicators for successful diplomatic action as it is founded on principles of consensus-building and global cooperation. At the time of initiating the research through to conducting the interviews, all then-serving women permanent representatives were indiscriminately invited to participate in the study. For those who agreed to participate, one-on-one semi-structured interviews were conducted at participating permanent representatives' missions at UN headquarters in New York to observe the ambassadors in their professional operating environment.

Respondents are considered to be experiential experts throughout the chapter, which is comprised of what Trochim (2006) refers to as "phenomenological research," meaning that samples and responses shaped by the experiences of these experts are used to draw conclusions about women's ambassadorial leadership in the UN without generalizing about the applicability of these responses to a larger population (Rudestam 1992). This approach is taken because leadership, as previously discussed, is largely individualized and UN dynamics are distinct from most other diplomatic postings. Additionally, arguments made throughout the chapter are, as previously mentioned, derived through constitutive theorizing. As introduced by Alex Wendt and employed by Lauren Wilcox (2010), constitutive theorizing focuses on raising questions surrounding what makes a phenomenon possible rather than why it happened or unfolded in the manner in which it did. As such, this chapter accounts for the significance of structures within and beyond the UN system, but does not seek to identify causal variables to explain women's increased ambassadorial representation. Through the constitutive theorizing lens, factors are identified and assessed through character, contingency, and contextual dimensions to understand the key characteristics of, and factors influencing, women's ambassadorial leadership in the UN in the twenty-first century.

The character dimension

Context

The *character* dimension of leadership focuses on an individual's skills, behaviors, and attributes that enable them to effectively lead in varying circumstances. According to Sadler (2003), cognizance of the situation and understanding the skills and behaviors to employ given the circumstance is crucial for leaders to be effective in their capacities. Supporting this argument, Gertrude Bell, one of Britain's earliest official female diplomats, stated "Occasionally, too, specialist knowledge and sheer force of character could catapult an exceptional woman" into leadership capacities within the Foreign Service (Pedersen 2014). While character dimensions of leadership theory emphasize the importance of an individual's skills, traits, and behaviors, the question of universality must be raised. Hartog, *et al.* (1999) explain that although societies may have distinctive cultures and therefore may emphasize dissimilar attributes for successful leadership, there exists universality in various characteristics that make for successful leaders. This research supports the claim that characteristics of successful leaders are crosscutting and universally endorsed within the UN organizational system. In implicit agreement with this perspective, Ambassador Don Mills provided an overview of the key characteristics of diplomats who are "best suited" to work in a multilateral organization, such as the UN (Mills 2009: 38). According to Mills, these characteristics include: the ability to coordinate effectively, having prior experience working in an international or multilateral environment, serving "country interests," recognizing regional needs as well as those of the international community, being out-going and skilled in relationship-building, and having a willingness to be both "student" and "researcher" as required (Mills 2009: 39–40). Through findings applicable to the character dimension, these traditional characteristics of diplomats in a multilateral environment are re-evaluated in light of perspectives and insights gained from women permanent representatives to the UN.

Findings

Throughout the interviews conducted for this research, respondents were asked to identify the key characteristics that they believe make for a successful diplomatic leader in a multilateral environment based on their first hand experience. Responses are categorized and reported based on frequency. All 15 permanent representatives interviewed responded to this question, and the following key findings were identified.

- The most frequently discussed response, referred to by 12 permanent representatives, included the importance of being *friendly*, fostering friendships, and *building relationships* within the UN (Permanent Representatives, 2015, pers. comms.). Respondents further emphasized the importance of *working with regional networks* as well as *establishing contacts*, and *building personalized relationships* beyond the formalized relationships mandated by the UN system's consensus-building culture (Permanent Representatives 2015, pers. comms.).
- The second most discussed response was the importance of *listening* (Permanent Representatives, 2015, pers. comms.). The majority of respondents who referenced listening as a key characteristic focused on the need for ambassadors to be effective listeners. However, this was also referenced in relation to the need to be persuasive in order to encourage others to listen to you and to understand your position.
- Equally referenced was the importance of ambassadors being *passionate about the initiatives* that they work towards fulfilling. Within this umbrella category, respondents referenced the importance of *passion for issues* and *country*, having a *respect for differing ideas* and contributions, being *dedicated* to both individual initiatives as well as serving the people that they are there to represent, and lastly, the importance of *enjoying the work* that they do as diplomats (Permanent Representatives 2015, pers. comms.). According to Ambassador Edita Hrda of the Czech Republic, "You have to be dedicated. It is very much seen if you don't like the job … it must be fun for you, you have to find something that [you enjoy doing]" (Hrda 2015, pers. comm.).
- Also referenced by respondents was the importance of being a *strong and effective communicator* (Permanent Representatives 2015, pers. comms.). Other key characteristics that were cross-referenced by respondents included the need for ambassadors to be *patient, respected, credible*, and *trustworthy*. Respondents also emphasized the importance of being *understanding* and *empathetic, working hard, being open to others* (including different ideas, contributions, cultures, and topics), being *knowledgeable, well-informed*, and having a keen *ability to prioritize* (Permanent Representatives 2015, pers. comms.).

All 15 women permanent representatives were also asked to provide concrete examples of when they successfully employed these characteristics to exercise ambassadorial leadership at the UN. Examples provided were vast and distinctive, though one cross-cutting categorization was exemplified by most respondents. This was the ability to *successfully lead a group*. The groups that the ambassadors led varied immensely, including, but not being limited to, serving as Acting President of the GA, leading regional bodies, leading a coalition of member states advocating for UN reform, and leading their countries' missions to the UN (Permanent Representatives 2015, pers. comms.).

Speaking from her past experience chairing a main UN GA committee, Ambassador Miculescu of Romania stated:

> That is when I had a revelation about the qualities of women in mastering something like this. First of all, what the member states liked very much about my chairmanship, to quote them ... [was] the way I was chairing made them [attend] with interest. It is about the atmosphere that you create as a woman.... We have a hospitable way of embracing an audience that I think makes a difference ... the way that they described me was that "I am a steel hand in a velvet glove." I was very structured in committee ... [I led with] discipline, but also availability ... [I] listen and communicate ... this again is a major quality ... that I think distinguishes women.
>
> (Miculescu 2015, pers. comm.)

Based on their experiences, the permanent representatives were further asked to consider whether women ambassadors in the UN assert leadership distinctively from fellow, male ambassadors. Responses to this question are aggregated as follows.

- Approximately 46 percent of respondents believed that women and men ambassadors assert leadership distinctively, while 54 percent of respondents believed that there is either no gendered-difference, or no explicitly notable difference, in the way that leadership is asserted between women and men ambassadors to the UN.
- Aligning closely with the "maximizer feminist" theory as discussed by McGlen and Hardees (1993), the seven women permanent representatives who responded that there is a gendered difference in the way that leadership is asserted supported their claims by highlighting differences that make women more suited than men to manage foreign affairs.

When asked to support the claim that women ambassadors in the UN assert leadership distinctively from male ambassadors, the following responses were provided:

- Women ambassadors in the UN tend to be more *open to listening*, may be *stronger communicators*, more *empathetic* and *sympathetic*, *seek a deeper understanding* of not only the issues but also of who they are working with, *promote constructive dialog*, are *willing to make compromises* to reach agreement, are *passionate, organized, less confrontational,* more *analytical, driven to find solutions,* may appear more comfortable when discussing certain (namely gender-specific) topics, can be more *willing to take initiative* and not wait, employ a more *holistic and pragmatic approach,* and are *peacemakers, mediators,* and *problem solvers* (Permanent Representatives 2015, pers. comms.). Many of these distinctions were made with a sense of caution, though, as many respondents believed that leadership is individualized, and just as men may hold these traits, some women may not.

In addition to highlighting the positive distinctions between the ambassadorial leadership of women and men at the UN, several negative distinctions were made as well.

- Two respondents expressed the idea that women ambassadors have to do more, work harder, or behave differently in order to be taken seriously by their own governments as well as by colleagues within the UN (Permanent Representatives 2015, pers. comms.).
- Lack of recognition and visibility of women permanent representatives' efforts was discussed by more than one respondent.
- Referenced by several respondents, there was also a belief that women permanent representatives may be disproportionately affected by the stringent work–life balance within the UN system, particularly due to cultural assumptions about family life and added pressure for women to deliver on personal, familial, and professional levels (Permanent Representatives 2015, pers. comms.). However, the demanding commitment that it takes to be a successful permanent representative while balancing a social and family life was predominantly described as gender-neutral, and pressures to deliver in all realms were described as largely equal for women and men diplomats alike (Permanent Representatives 2015, pers. comms.).

Further discussing the distinctions between how women and men ambassadors assert leadership at the UN, Ambassador Miculescu stated:

> You always have to prove … you are just a serious partner who wants to have discussion on a certain issue for your country. When there are a few women in a male environment, sometimes people tend to treat this superficially, they are cautious and nice but they don't trust you much until you prove that you are a reliable partner, that you can make a gentleman's agreement.
>
> (Miculescu 2015, pers. comm.)

Alternatively, the women permanent representatives who responded that women ambassadors in the UN do not assert leadership distinctively from men ambassadors largely dismissed the existence of differences in leadership style. Aligning with the "minimizer feminist" theory of McGlen and Hardees (1993), eight respondents believed that there was either no difference, or no notable difference, in the way that women and men ambassadors lead at the UN.

- To support their claims, respondents referred to the individualism prevalent in leadership styles, the inclusive nature of UN diplomatic culture, the unequivocal support and equal treatment of women and men diplomats in their country's foreign ministries, the reality that women have proven themselves and therefore gender-distinctions are no longer relevant, and the dangers of perpetuating male and female differences in diplomatic leadership (Permanent Representatives 2015, pers. comms.).
- Respondents claimed that "professionalism is uni-sex" and permanent representatives were appointed to their capacities because they are their country's best, regardless of their gender (Miculescu 2015, pers. comm.). Further, it was discussed that all permanent representatives are professionals with equal importance in the UN system, and therefore they are viewed not as gendered beings but rather as representatives of their countries (Permanent Representatives 2015, pers. comms.).

While embodied and enacted leadership characteristics proved to be significantly important in the way that women permanent representatives assert leadership at the UN, it is also important to understand how external factors may influence efficacy in asserting leadership.

The contingency dimension

Context

Looking beyond the character dimension, the *contingency* dimension focuses on external factors to display how the ability to effectively lead can be complemented or challenged by influencers outside of the leader's immediate control (Deckard 2009). Fielder's contingency theory, the first-ever established, was largely built around organizational leadership (Deckard 2009). Though Fielder's model is a cornerstone of the leadership contingency theory, his application is not employed in this research as it focuses primarily on the relationship between leader and supporter within an organization. The research in this chapter instead focuses on the relationship between leaders and sending governments, and ambassadorial leaders with others within the UN system. A second contingency theory, House's 'Path–Goal Leadership Theory', is comprised of four components (Deckard 2009: 190). One of these components, the environmental contingency factor, is used in this research, as it examines the "external dynamics" that shape leadership styles (Deckard 2009: 191). Factors of this type, which are considered "outside of the control and influence" of the leader, are evaluated including support and resources provided by sending governments and how this impacts permanent representatives' abilities to fulfill mission objectives, and the role that the UN Secretariat plays in supporting women's diplomatic leadership in the UN (Deckard 2009: 191).

Findings

During the interviews conducted, the importance of *receiving support from home governments* was specifically mentioned by 40 percent of respondents (Permanent Representatives 2015, pers. comms.). For example, one respondent had to challenge traditional gender-norms and ask for an accommodation never before considered by her country's foreign ministry to successfully fulfill her capacity. She explained that whereas diplomatic spouses would traditionally fill the role of hostess and housekeeper for their diplomatic husbands, as the first woman ambassador for her country serving as permanent representative to the UN, and without a spouse accompanying her to take care of these responsibilities, she had to ask her home government for additional resources (Permanent Representative 1 2015, pers. comm.). After presenting a case to the foreign ministry, her sending government took account of the unique circumstance and provided the ambassador with the support needed for her to successfully fulfill her diplomatic responsibilities without the traditional support that a diplomatic spouse might provide (Permanent Representative to the UN 1 2015, pers. comm.).

Another permanent representative interviewed spoke about the need to compete with other diplomatic missions for ministerial resources. The ambassador explained that taking initiative to lead, chair, and even establish new regional bodies assisted her in gaining attention from her home government, therefore resulting in the government's enhanced trust in her abilities, recognition of the importance of her role, and support for her and her initiatives (Permanent Representative to the UN 2 2015, pers. comm.). Further, in response to receiving comparatively limited resources from their home governments as compared to other missions, several respondents spoke about the importance of being creative and cooperative in their efforts at the UN. For example, Ambassador Rambally (2015, pers. comm.) of St. Lucia discussed the heightened significance of the UN posting for her country, as foreign ministerial resources and limited personnel do not enable the country to have bilateral missions in all countries throughout the world. Speaking to the effects of limited resources on her ability to assert leadership, Rambally stated:

> It is challenging, but it forces you to rise to the occasion ... from time to time, where I am tempted to advocate to my country for maybe greater support staff like some other offices have, I am [forced] to take a pause, a step back, and reflect on the reality that we are limited in resources and so we have to find creative ways. One of the ways we do this ... we work together to advance and to advocate on behalf of our individual countries more as a region.
>
> (Rambally 2015, pers. comm.)

Additionally, one permanent representative (Permanent Representatives 2015, pers. comms.) also spoke about the importance of innovation in overcoming limited resources from the home government through the example of establishing an internship program. According to the Ambassador, she successfully lobbied her home government to establish an internship program, which has proven to have multiple benefits. The internship program provides two aspiring individuals with a short-term opportunity to learn about and work in the UN, establishes a pool of early-trained potential future diplomats, and provides additional support for the country's modestly-staffed Mission (Permanent Representatives 2015, pers. comms.).

In addition to the importance of support from home governments, *support from the UN Secretariat* was also discussed. Approximately 47 percent of respondents stated that UN Secretary-General Ban Ki Moon has played a significant role in recognizing and accounting for women's increasing diplomatic leadership in the UN (Permanent Representatives 2015, pers. comms.). For example, Ambassador Bogyay of Hungary, who was appointed in January 2015, stated that:

> Here I was the 34th [woman permanent representative] to arrive and I remember when I arrived the Secretary-General said "I am so happy a new woman becomes ambassador," because Ban Ki Moon's legacy is very much of creating UN Women, giving a chance for women ...
>
> (Bogyay 2015, pers. comm.)

Additionally, one respondent spoke of a time when she seized an opportunity to speak directly with Secretary-General (SG) Ban Ki Moon to ask him to visit the Asia-Pacific region (Permanent Representative 2 2015, pers. comm.). As a sitting SG had not visited the Pacific region in more than 60 years, she recalled being strong and assertive in a conversation with him, while highlighting the importance of seizing opportunities as they arise (Permanent Representative 2 2015, pers. comm.). As a result of her efforts, SG Ban Ki Moon visited the Pacific in 2011 (UN News Centre 2011). This visit led to two highly significant outcomes: first, it made climate change a priority issue for the SG and has since influenced the UN agenda's focus on this topic, and second, the high visibility of this visit led to the Ambassador's sending government, for the first time ever, allocating the necessary resources to establish a Permanent Mission to the UN in 2013 (Permanent Representative 2 2015, pers. comms.).

Overall, the role that sending governments and the UN Secretariat play in enabling, and at times challenging, women's ambassadorial leadership is important to account for when examining how leadership is exercised within the UN. While not all factors influencing leadership are directly in the control of leaders themselves, respondents displayed that being assertive, creative, and innovative can assist in influencing home governments and the UN Secretariat to garner immediate and/or future support. Respondents also provided recommendations for how sending governments and the UN secretariat may further continue to strengthen women's ambassadorial leadership at the UN. Pointing to the reality that sending governments have the power to select who to send to leading diplomatic posts and how to position their diplomats for success, several respondents to the study recommended that Governments should undertake assessments within their foreign ministries to examine the representation of women in all diplomatic ranks. They explained that while diplomatic corps in their countries have approximately equal representation of men and women at the entry level, at the middle and high-ranking capacities women's inclusion steadily tapers off. Finding out the levels of women's representation within all diplomatic ranks in foreign services, and understanding the reasoning behind lower representation at certain levels, is essential for establishing applicable prescriptions for addressing any barriers to women's inclusion that may be uncovered.

Another recommendation for increasing women's representation in ambassadorial leadership included that governments should make a conscious effort to appoint qualified women to high-ranking diplomatic capacities, and quotas should be considered by foreign ministries to ensure that women are included in all diplomatic ranks. While instituting legally-binding gender quotas within foreign ministries may be worth aspiring to (although gender quotas, too, have their limitations) it was recommended that willing countries should set target goals for women's representation within all diplomatic ranks. Even if they will not be legally binding, setting target goals may have an effect on encouraging greater and more conscientious efforts around including qualified women in diplomatic leadership capacities.

The contextual dimension

Context

While understanding the contingent role that sending governments and the UN Secretariat play in how women permanent representatives assert their leadership at the UN is important, of equal significance is the *contextual* dimension of leadership, which focuses on the context or operating environment within which individuals assert their leadership and utilize their innate and acquired skills to respond accordingly to organizational and situational factors. As Rumsey explains, leadership is highly "complex," and therefore it is essential to account for social, cultural, and circumstantial factors that may influence a leader's response (Rumsey 2013: 1–2). Nye also explains that "contextual intelligence" is required of those who seek and/or assert power as leading requires both an ability to strategize and discern while mitigating situations as they arise (Nye 2008: 85–88). Osborn, Hunt, and Jauch further argue that leadership is largely shaped by context. Leadership, they claim, should be operationalized through a theory of complexity, meaning that when assessing or attempting to understand effective leadership, researchers and practitioners should consider the context to develop more robust models and understanding (Osborn, Hunt, and Jauch 2002). Within this study, the contextual dimension of leadership accounts for situational, cultural, and organizational factors within the UN to understand how women ambassadors respond to these factors, thus shaping how leadership is asserted. The contextual dimension examines the UN diplomatic culture, the diversity of representation on UN committees, and the informal and formal networks that have formed to foster relationship-building amongst women diplomats in the UN in the twenty-first century.

Findings

Diplomatic culture plays a significant role when understanding the operating environment within the UN. As Paul Sharp explains, "a diplomatic culture arises out of the experience of conducting relations between peoples who regard themselves as distinctive," yet through continual interactions establish certain shared values, communication methods, and interaction techniques (Sharp 2004: 361, 371). When asked to identify aspects of the UN diplomatic culture that are either ideal or adverse for women ambassadors in the twenty-first century, many positive responses were provided.

- The UN diplomatic culture was overwhelmingly acclaimed for its acceptance of diversity, including the increasing representation of women in leading diplomatic ranks (Permanent Representatives 2015, pers. comms.). Ambassador Kawar of Jordan, for example, noted that it has become "a taboo *not* to discuss or respect women and women's issues" in the UN in the twenty-first century (Kawar 2015, pers. comm.).
- Others also noted that the UN is more women-friendly than many other institutions and that there has been a mainstreaming of thinking when it comes to the inclusion of both women in decision-making positions as well as including women-specific topics on the UN agenda (Permanent Representatives 2015, pers. comms.).

Ambassador Flores of Panama noted:

> It is true that women in leadership positions are held to very different standards, more rooted in traditional gender stereotypes, but here [at the UN] I haven't seen that ... it is much more equal ... the people who work [here] are very culturally and politically aware.
>
> (Flores 2015, pers. comm.)

Generally, respondents believed that the diplomats who comprise and shape the UN diplomatic culture tend to be progressive in their thinking, and therefore support for women's diplomatic inclusion both in leadership capacities and on the agenda has become customary within the institution, although not necessarily within each individual mission (Permanent Representatives 2015, pers. comms.).

While there was an overwhelmingly positive response regarding the diplomatic culture as it relates to the increased representation of women in ambassadorial postings, responses also alluded to challenges within the diplomatic culture.

- Though women comprise many entry or assistant/secretary-level postings within various UN missions, and the number of women permanent representatives is incrementally increasing, ambassadors spoke of a need to see more women diplomats in middle-ranking and expert-level positions since many of these women will go on to either lead in the UN or in diplomatic missions worldwide (Permanent Representatives 2015, pers. comms.).
- Additionally, there was also brief reference to the culture being intrinsically masculine. As one respondent stated, "I hope a time comes when there are more women and we don't have to assume masculine roles to succeed" (Permanent Representative 3 2015, pers. comm.).
- Several respondents also noted that there needs to be greater gender diversity on certain UN committees. For example, as of January 2015, of the six main GA committees, only one committee was chaired by a woman, while women diplomats held 9 of 15 vice-chair positions (UN General Assembly 2015).

When asked about her experience serving as the only woman permanent representative chairing a main UN committee at the time that the research was conducted, Ambassador Borges of Timor-Leste stated:

> I have been chairing the third committee, and from feedback that I have received it has been a very successful chairmanship ... the third committee ... [can have] very divided discussion when it comes down to human rights.[2] Last night I was at a dinner where I was told ... [by] a male colleague who is also chairing one of the committees, that I got away with so much that he could not get away with, the things I said in the room and the way I drove the meetings, and my persistence about being disciplined about time ... keeping the room focused ... I assume he said that because I am a woman. I think women always look for consensus, we always reach out and that's what I did ... not being shy about being the one to make the first move ... [my style] enabled people to focus on substance rather than the tension.
>
> (Borges 2015, pers. comm.)

While at the time of conducting the interviews there was only one woman ambassador serving as the chair of a main committee, representation within most main GA committees was described as gender-balanced by respondents. Committees such as the Commission on the Status of Women, however, remain dominantly comprised of women diplomats, whereas peace-keeping initiatives, committees, and missions tends to remain very much a "man's world" (Permanent Representative 3 2015, pers. comm.). Overall, respondents observed that women and men's representation across main committees is generally mixed and equal.

To garner a better understanding of the nature of interactions amongst women permanent representatives in the UN diplomatic environment, respondents were asked to describe the collegiality between themselves and other women permanent representatives. Responses to this question largely revealed that while women seem to have an "instantaneous understanding," "instinctual solidarity" and "connection" with one another, and interactions and collegiality between men and women permanent representatives tend to be the same or very similar (Baaro 2015, pers. comm.; Miculescu 2015, pers. comm.). Respondents felt that they received an equal reception from male and female permanent representatives upon their arrival to the UN, and that interactions are based on professionalism and how an ambassador carries out instruction without consideration of gender (Permanent Representatives 2015, pers. comms.). Despite this reflecting the majority of responses, one ambassador noted that she feels a need to be more cautious when interacting with male colleagues, as intentions and interactions can be viewed differently amongst men and women colleagues rather than amongst women colleagues (Permanent Representatives 2015, pers. comms.). Overall, responses indicated that all permanent representatives are expected to prove themselves as reliable partners, regardless of gender, and all interactions and relationships in the UN are of strategic importance and remain largely gender-neutral.

While formal networks, specifically regional blocs and topic-specific groups, were continuously referred to as being the most important networks that exist within the UN system, there are many informal networks that also play a role in building relationships and influencing how leadership is exercised. Specifically, there are several women's networks that exist within the UN system. When asked if there is a women's caucus or group within the UN, all 15 respondents unanimously replied yes. Ambassador Miculescu of Romania, who was noted by several respondents as serving as the chairwoman of the group, referred to the group as the "Women Diplomats Network" (WDN) (Miculescu 2015, pers. comm.). By compiling responses about the network, the following information was gathered.

- The WDN is an informal assembly that invites all currently serving women permanent representatives, as well women diplomats at all levels and from all missions across the UN, to participate in the group (Permanent Representatives 2015, pers. comms.).
- The network meets several times a year and does not abide by a set schedule. The format of meetings traditionally remains consistent including having a prominent speaker address the group followed by a question and answer session, and an opportunity for dialogue and networking.
- Since the group coalesces women diplomats at all levels within the UN, it provides an opportunity for mentorship, encouragement, networking, and experience sharing.
- While UN Women has worked with the WDN, women permanent representatives have initiated many of the meetings.
- Respondents believed that the strength of the network is in its informality. Since most other aspects of engagement in the UN are structured, participation in an informal forum was noted as being welcomed. Further, as the

women diplomats in the UN represent greatly diverse countries with distinctive policies, it was stated that the network has not, and likely will not, serve as a platform for advocacy or discussion of official agenda items. Despite this, however, the WDN can provide opportunities for women diplomats to acquire additional face time with important stakeholders (Permanent Representatives 2015, pers. comms.).

While there is no known date for when the WDN was formed, accounts from as early as 1983 reveal that there was already a group of women permanent representatives who met for lunch regularly to discuss similar informal items (Permanent Representative 4, 2015, pers. comm.). According to Madeleine Albright, former US Ambassador to the UN, in 1993:

> When I just arrived at the UN ... I said to my assistant, invite the other women permanent representatives [for lunch] ... I get there and there are 6 women of 183.... So being an American I decided to set up a caucus, and so, we set it up, and we called ourselves the G7, "Girls 7," and we lobbied on behalf of women's issues.
>
> (Albright 2010)

While there is no direct link between the G7 and what today exists as the WDN, it can be deduced that women permanent representatives, no matter how limited in number, have taken initiative to coalesce as early as the mid-1980s (Permanent Representative 4, 2015, pers. comm.). Approximately 40 years later, with 41 women permanent representatives currently serving in the UN, the network continues to grow in size, diversity, and complexity.

Beyond the WDN, the Women's International Forum (WIF) has been in existence since 1975 (Women's International Forum 2014). Established during the UN's International Women's Year, the WIF was initiated by diplomats' wives who, as a result of being excluded from formal participation in international politics, decided to collectively establish a forum for keeping informed of world affairs through lectures and discussions surrounding UN agenda items (Women's International Forum, 2014). The WIF also served as a forum for informal information sharing about establishing a New York lifestyle including where to send children to school, what physicians to see when medical attention was needed, and how to manage household responsibilities (Women's International Forum 2014). The WIF has greatly evolved over time. Today, with more than 300 members, including both women and men, the WIF hosts meetings at UN Headquarters and invites all UN diplomats to attend (Women's International Forum 2014). The UN Secretary-General's wife is the overseer of the Forum, and all currently-serving women permanent representatives to the UN serve on the WIF Honorary Board (Women's International Forum 2014).

Overall, organizational and relational factors within the UN were examined through the contextual dimension. The UN diplomatic culture, which plays a prominent role in shaping interactions amongst diplomats, was noted as being progressive in regards to its respect for, and response to, women's ambassadorial leadership. This may be the case for several reasons. Unlike most foreign ministries worldwide, which were established as exclusively male domains, the UN's founding Charter and GA enabled women's representation in all UN capacities since its inception (Charter of the United Nations 2015). Second, as a global institution that is founded on liberal democratic principles through a one vote per country and consensus-building model, diversity and respect for diversity is required to be successful in the UN system. Since every GA vote matters equally, diplomats are obliged to respect permanent representatives, regardless of gender, in order to garner support for initiatives. Accordingly, collegiality amongst women ambassadors is predominantly noted as being highly comparable to that between women and men ambassadors, with many respondents observing no differences at all, though several nuances were discussed. Over time, various informal networks have been established to provide forums for experience-sharing, networking, and relationship building. Although these forums are not said to be used for substantive discussion of UN agenda items, they do have the potential to serve as platforms for acquiring additional face-to-face time with important stakeholders, and can assist with exercising ambassadorial leadership.

Conclusion

To date, women's representation in ambassadorial leadership at the UN has reached an unprecedented level. Whether this will have significant or long-term implications on the way that diplomacy is conducted depends on how women permanent representatives exercise their leadership, and the factors that influence their ability to do so. Responses from interviews with 15 women permanent representatives of the UN provided insight into women's ambassadorial leadership in the UN in the twenty-first century. Through the character, contingency, and contextual dimensions, the argument has been advanced that while there are key characteristics of successful ambassadorial leadership, there are also factors within the UN system that influence how envisaged and embodied leadership translates into concrete action. Through the character dimension, respondents provided a composite list of the key characteristics of successful diplomatic leadership in a multilateral environment. Examples of specific leadership initiatives were presented to solidify how these characteristics are embodied and employed to achieve concrete results, and distinctions between women and men's ambassadorial leadership were discussed. Assessing factors external to the permanent representatives' control, the contingency dimension uncovered the importance of support from home governments and the UN Secretariat in contributing to ambassadors' successful assertion of leadership within the UN. Lastly, the contextual dimension examined factors within the UN system that either complemented or challenged women's ambassadorial leadership, including how the UN diplomatic culture has adapted to women's increased representation in leading diplomatic postings, the nature of interactions amongst women and men permanent representatives in the UN system, and the significant role that informal networks play in fortifying diplomatic relationships beyond the confines of the UN structure.

Overall, the UN has proved to be a comparatively progressive culture, and this has had a constructive effect on the ways that women permanent representatives exercise leadership in the twenty-first century. As we look to the future and the representation of women in ambassadorial postings continues to rise, it is essential that further research is conducted to understand what larger implications this may have both within and beyond the UN. Research questions that may build off this study include, do women and men lead distinctively in ambassadorial leadership capacities, and if so, is diplomatic practice being reshaped by women's increased representation? Finally, and perhaps most importantly, how is diplomacy—both as a profession and a practice—being reshaped by women's increased diplomatic leadership, and what will this mean for the conduct of international relations in the twenty-first century?

Notes

1 The concept of ambassadorial leadership is undefined insofar as it relates to diplomatic practice. Coalescing aspects of various leadership theories, as discussed throughout this study, I define *ambassadorial leadership* as: inherent traits, targeted behaviors, and skills that are embodied and employed by high-level diplomats with the intention of influencing and actualizing foreign policy objectives through bilateral and/or multilateral diplomatic engagement. This term will be employed throughout the chapter, specifically as it relates to women permanent representatives' leadership in the UN.
2 The Third Committee of the General Assembly of the United Nations is the Social, Humanitarian, and Cultural Committee. For more information about the Third Committee visit www.un.org/en/ga/third/.

References

1For7Billion Campaign. www.1for7billion.org/. [Accessed October 8, 2016].
Albright, M. (2010). "On being a woman and a diplomat." TEDWomen www.ted.com/talks/madeleine_albright_on_being_a_woman_and_a_diplomat?language=en. [Accessed February 9, 2017].
Baaro, Ambassador Makurita. (2015). Permanent Representative to the UN. Interview. March, 25, 2015. Personal communication.
Bogyay, Ambassador Katalin. (2015). Permanent Representative to the UN. Interview. March 26, 2015. Personal communication.
Borges, Ambassador Sofia Mesquita. (2015). Permanent Representative to the UN. Interview. March 18, 2015. Personal communication.
Boutros-Ghali, B. (1996). *The United Nations and the Advancement of Women: 1945–1995*. New York: United Nations Department of Public Information.
Bryant, N. (2014). "At the UN, women play increasingly powerful roles." *BBC News Magazine*.
Buchan, J. (2003). "Miss Bell's lines in the sand." *Guardian*, March 12, www.theguardian.com/world/2003/mar/12/iraq.jamesbuchan. [Accessed March 15, 2015].

Carlsnaes, W. (2002). *Handbook of International Relations.* United Kingdom: Sage Publications.

Charter of the United Nations. (2015). www.un.org/en/documents/charter/3.shtml. [Accessed March 1, 2015].

Convention on the Elimination of All Forms of Discrimination Against Women. (1979). United Nations Women. www.un.org/womenwatch/daw/cedaw/text/econvention.htm. [Accessed May 19, 2015].

Cork Federation of Women's Organizations. (1995). *Women and Leadership: Redefining Power.* Cork: Bradshaw Books.

Deckard, G. J. (2009) "Contingency Theories of Leadership" in Nancy Borkowski, *Organizational Behavior, Theory and Design in Health Care*, 185–202. London: Jones and Bartlett Publishers.

Duerst-Lahti, G. and R. M. Kelly. (1995). *Gender Power, Leadership and Governance.* Ann Arbor, MI: University of Michigan Press.

Flores, Ambassador Laura. (2015). Permanent Representative to the UN. Interview. March 20, 2015. Personal communication.

General Assembly of the United Nations, Social, Humanitarian, and Cultural – Third Committee. (2016). www.un.org/en/ga/third/. [Accessed October 10, 2016].

Genovese, M. and S. Thompson. (1993). *Women as National Leaders.* Newbury Park, CA: Sage Publications, Inc.

Hartog, D., R. J. House, P. J. Hanges, S. A. Ruiz-Quintanilla, P. W. Dorfman, I. A. Abdalla, B. S. Adetoun, *et al.* (1999). "Culture specific and cross-culturally generalizable implicit leadership theories: Are attributes of charismatic/transformational leadership universally endorsed?" *The Leadership Quarterly* 10 (2): 219–256.

Holsti, O.R. and J. N. Rosenau. (1981). "The foreign policy beliefs of women in leadership positions." *Journal of Politics* 43 (2): 326–347.

Hrda, Ambassador Edita. (2015). Permanent Representative to the UN. Interview. March 26, 2015. Personal communication.

Kawar, Ambassador Dina. (2015). Permanent Representative to the UN. Interview. March 20, 2015. Personal communication.

Keohane, N. (2010). *Thinking about Leadership.* Princeton, NJ and Oxford: Princeton University Press.

McCarthy, H. (2014) *Women of the World: The Rise of the Female Diplomat.* London: Bloomsbury Publishing.

McGlen, N. E. and M. R. Sarkees. (1993). *Women in Foreign Policy.* New York: Routledge.

Miculescu, Ambassador Simona. (2015). Permanent Representative to the UN. Interview. March 24, 2015. Personal communication.

Mills, D. (2009). "The Diplomat at the United Nations: Yesterday and Today" in J. P. Muldoon, E. Sullivan, J. F. Aviel, and R. Reitano (eds), *Multilateral Diplomacy and the United Nations Today,* 23–41. Boulder, CO: Westview Press.

Nye, J. (2008). *The Powers to Lead.* Oxford and New York: Oxford University Press.

Osborn, R. N., J. G. Hunt, and L. R. Jauch. (2002). "Toward a Contextual Theory of Leadership." *The Leadership Quarterly* 13 (6).

Pedersen, S. (2014). "Women of the world: the rise of the female diplomat review." *Guardian,* June 27. www.theguardian.com/books/2014/jun/27/women-world-rise-female-diplomat-helen-mccarthy-review. [Accessed March 15, 2015].

Permanent Missions to the United Nations (Blue Book) No. 306, June 2016. Protocol and Liaison Services. www.un.int/protocol/sites/www.un.int/files/Protocol%20and%20Liaison%20Service/bb305.pdf. [Accessed October 8, 2016].

Permanent Representative to the UN 1 (Anonymous). (2015). Interview. March 2015. Personal communication.
Permanent Representative to the UN 2 (Anonymous). (2015). Interview. March 2015. Personal communication.
Permanent Representative to the UN 3 (Anonymous). (2015). Interview. March 2015. Personal communication.
Permanent Representative to the UN 4 (Anonymous). (2015). Interview. March 2015. Personal communication.
Permanent Representatives to the UN (Anonymous, Multiple Compiled Responses). (2015). Interviews. March 2015. Personal communications.
Pietila, H. (2007) *The Unfinished Story of Women and the United Nations.* New York and Geneva: UN Non-Governmental Liaison Service.
Rambally, Ambassador Menissa. (2015). Permanent Representative to the UN. Interview. March 17, 2015. Personal communication.
Rudestam, K. E. (1992). *Surviving Your Dissertation: A Comprehensive Guide to Content and Process.* London: Sage.
Rumsey, M. G. (2013). *The Oxford Handbook of Leadership.* Oxford: Oxford University Press.
Sadler, P. (2003). *Leadership.* London: Kogan Page.
Sharp, P. (2004). "The Idea of Diplomatic Culture and its Sources" in H. Slavik (ed.), *Intercultural Communication and Diplomacy*, 361–371. Malta and Geneva: Diplo-Foundation.
Tickner, A. (2001). *Gendering World Politics.* New York: Columbia University Press.
Towns, A. (2010). *Women and States: Norms and Hierarchies in International Society.* Cambridge: Cambridge University Press.
Trochim, W. M. K. (2006). "Research methods: knowledge base." www.socialresearchmethods.net/kb/qualapp.php. [Accessed April 1, 2015].
United Nations General Assembly. (2015). United Nations General Assembly Main Committees. www.un.org/ga/maincommittees.shtml. [Accessed May 18, 2015].
United Nations Member States. (2015). www.un.org/en/members/. [Accessed January 5, 2015].
United Nations Security Council: UN Department of Public Information. (2015). www.un.org/en/sc/ [Accessed January 15, 2015].
UN News Centre. (2011). "UN Chief and Kiribati leader warn over climate change threat to the Pacific Islands." *UN News Centre*, September 5. www.un.org/apps/news/story.asp?NewsID=39449#.VWJILBZyQds. [Accessed May 18, 2015].
Wilcox, L. (2010). "Gendering the Cult of the Offensive" in L. Sjoberg (ed.), *Gender and International Security: Feminist Perspectives*, 61–83. London: Routledge.
Women's International Forum. (2014). "Who We Are." http://womensinternationalforum.org/about/. [Accessed April 23, 2015].
Worldwide Guide. (2015). Worldwide Guide to Women in Leadership: "Female Permanent Representatives and Ambassadors to the League of Nations and the United Nations." www.guide2womenleaders.com/UN_Representatives.htm. [Accessed April 4, 2015].

11 Conclusion

Progress and policies towards a gender-even playing field

Jennifer A. Cassidy

This volume has theorised and empirically demonstrated the gendered nature of diplomacy as a practice and study. By bringing together established scholars and seasoned practitioners of diplomacy, this volume has provided a detailed discussion of the often-overlooked historical role of women in politics and their ever-increasing involvement in modern diplomatic practice. At its centre, the discourse of this volume has endeavoured to move beyond the naïve notion that considers the entering of women into the diplomatic corps a unique or novel phenomenon; it has, rather, attempted to generate much needed discussion surrounding the nature of the roles which women occupy upon entering the diplomatic sphere. Further, this work has explored the individual and collective power women hold within their respective ministries and international diplomatic bodies at large, their agency for change within them, and the obstacles they continue to face – both institutional and normative – as they continue the fight for gender parity within the diplomatic corps.

This volume has addressed three themes in particular. First, while the nominal participation of women within the diplomatic sphere may be increasing, the substantial nature of their role within the service has not progressed at the same pace. Each chapter in this volume has paid homage to this theme, with a strong consensus from all of the expert contributors that diplomacy, both as a profession and practice, remains sculpted by strict gendered norms. So long as the image of the typical diplomat remains so resolutely masculinised, women active in the diplomatic sphere will continue to appear as the exceptions and, as such, unable to escape reference to their gender. In their chapter 'Gender, status, and ambassador appointments to militarized and violent countries', Ann Towns and Birgitta Niklasson drew firmly upon this theme by addressing some fundamental questions regarding ambassadorship appointments; specifically, the authors delineated the extent to which gender invariably influences the type of appointments that women receive compared to their male constituents. Their data is clear: female ambassadors are more likely to be posted in states of lower military and economic standing compared to their male counterparts, who are overrepresented in states of greater military and economic clout. The reason for this is that traditional gender roles associate women with vulnerability, weakness, and peace – characteristics that are not valued in war. Concerns that women may not function as effective representatives in violent contexts – together with beliefs that women should be protected from war rather than be overtly exposed to it – partially underpin the aforementioned gender bias in ambassadorial roles. Towns and Niklasson rightly note that while such a gender pattern could be seen as an advantage to female ambassadors (i.e. being posted away from war-afflicted areas), previous research has also indicated that experience gained through postings in countries which suffer armed conflicts can serve as stepping-stones in diplomatic careers. Indeed, diplomats who experience service in challenging (even life-threatening) environments acquire skill sets and develop a level of professional competence that often amount to an acceleration in career path. Thus, if women are systematically overlooked when it comes to postings in militarised and violence ridden countries, as direct consequence of adherence to gender norms, they are potentially being robbed of career advancement opportunities. Susan Harris Rimmer's chapter, which centred on the role and narrative of women participating in the sphere of global economic governance, also drew strongly on the aforementioned theme. Using a feminist approach, she analysed the lived experiences of women working in economic summitry, whilst firmly interrogating how masculine values and worldviews have shaped this area of diplomacy, as evidenced by the assumptions of mainstream economics

The second theme to emerge is the recognition that, although gender and its role within the diplomatic realm is becoming an increasing topic for discussion within MFAs and diplomatic studies at large, the analysis surrounding this discussion has been limited in quantity and quality. Existing discussions continue to centre around the narrow belief that gender equality will be achieved once nominal equality is achieved. Through its varied discussion and analysis, this volume has sought to highlight that true gender equality can only be achieved once the gender *of* diplomacy is confronted and addressed explicitly. Furthermore, discussion of gender equality within the diplomatic sphere should avoid emphasis on a limited set of women's experiences, – namely those of white, Western, women – and instead expand to include, without delay, the diverse range of voices, backgrounds, and historical experiences of female practitioners across the globe. In her chapter 'Women of the South: engaging with the UN as a diplomatic manoeuvre', Devaki Jain draws a welcomed distinction between the historical journeys of the women of the South and North, and their role within the initial construction of the United Nations. Tracing the major ideas that shaped the UN's engagement with women, Jain highlights the various strategies used by the women of the South to negotiate their ideas and proposals to an international bureaucratic system; a system which consistently overlooked their calls for equality.

This distinction between the varying historical experiences of the women of the North and South, and the appropriate contextualisation, should serve as a template to guide inclusive and informed discussions of women's contributions to diplomacy. By emphasising the value of historical and sociocultural idiosyncrasies in shaping women's stories and struggles within the diplomatic sphere, this volume challenges the 'one size fits all' narrative and mitigates for this pitfall within existing literature.

The third and final theme to emerge from this unique compilation is one centred on the institutional origins relating to the obstacles women continue to face whilst working in the diplomatic realm. These obstacles span everything from the initial hiring process to competing for the most senior diplomatic posts. From a historical perspective, Anne Barrington spoke of the experiences of women diplomats who entered the Department (Ministry) of Foreign Affairs in Ireland from 1970 to the year 2000 onwards, illuminating the various barriers and challenges these women faced during this time frame. These include, and are not limited to, workplace sexism, an institutional 'marriage bar', and strict institutional policies which affected the personal lives of many female workers: maternity leave, career breaks, and inflexible working hours. Since then, the Department has made significant progress in working towards gender equality in the workplace, but many obstacles remain firmly in place. Barrington's chapter does not stand alone in highlighting these challenges, but was echoed in all chapters, which addressed institutional practices, both historical and present. Such persisting institutional roadblocks to equality are a continued area of discussion for policy makers and practitioners alike, and one that needs greater expansion if gender equality is to be realised within the diplomatic realm.

Each of the contributors to this volume highlighted, to varying degrees, aspects of the three thematic dimensions and found areas in which they converge. They have self-reflectively placed their perspectives within the broader debates about the role of diplomacy in international politics and the traditional paradigms of international relations theory. Through their own narratives and analytical approaches, they have questioned the reigning archetypes that plague diplomacy to this day and have probed the validity of diplomacy's invention and reinvention on the basis of strict gender norms. Rather than provide summaries of the findings and contributions of each, the aim of this chapter is to highlight a research and policy agenda for the 'role' of gender moving forward and recommend ways in which policy makers can acknowledge its impact and work towards making meaningful policies concerning it. Reflecting on these themes is a crucial exercise in determining how the study of gender and diplomacy, and the gender *of* diplomacy, will progress in the future in terms of making actionable policy recommendations.

The gender of diplomacy: future scholarly endeavours

Through this concerted effort to systematically expose the gender of diplomacy, more questions have been raised than answered. Indeed, the contributing authors have put forth a number of timely and pertinent arguments with respect to women's role and place within the diplomatic service, which have the potential to guide future research and policy-making in the field.

Chief among these arguments is the acknowledgement that *an increase in number does not translate to an increase in power or meaningful, impactful, representation*. Whilst numbers reflect a degree of progress, albeit largely superficial, real progress cannot be attained with the existing and persisting imbalance of power in a gendered international political system. As Claire Annesley writes,

> gendering policy does not refer merely to the inclusion of women's ideas or issues onto the mainstream policy agenda but to the renewal of the whole policymaking process to give men and women real and equal access and influence at each stage.
>
> (2010: 334)

This volume has demonstrated the complexity of renewing policies concerning gender equality, with the primary obstacle to this renewal emerging from the normative nature of diplomacy. Through their individual chapters Anne Barrington, Jane Marriott, and Phumzile Mlambo-Ngcuka demonstrated that challenging prevailing gender norms has never proven easy – and that the challenge is amplified when these norms are silent and unspoken. As a whole, this volume has illustrated that the hidden life of institutions and their unwritten rules have proven highly resistant towards change.

Of course, acknowledgement of the gendered nature of diplomacy and the long road ahead to alter such an archaic infrastructure should not deter future policy makers from continuing the quest for greater numerical parity. Improving the gender composition of diplomatic bodies may not be enough on its own when dealing with seemingly gender-neutral norms, but it does help challenge the more overt sexism that prevails within in these institutions. Moreover, increasing the percentage of women within the diplomatic sphere brings with it the potential to disrupt these embedded practices. Disruption through numerical alteration is necessary, because it allows for the questioning of assumptions about what matters, who carries authority, and what an acceptable institutional make-up consists of. Increasing the numerical representation of women therefore enables new norms to emerge. So while future leaders and policy makers should continue to work towards increasing women's numerical representation, their efforts need to be equally focused on restructuring the system to allow for proportionality between numbers and authority.

A central point of this volume that may also inspire further research is the recognition that is there exists *no steady upward trajectory* for women who serve the diplomatic corps. This volume has drawn attention to a number of straightforward explanations as to why it has been harder for women to decide to enter the diplomatic sphere: namely reasons on the 'supply side', with the supply side referring explicitly to the challenges women face when deciding to enter the diplomatic sphere itself (Norris and Lovenduski 1995). Here we see that time continues to be at a premium for women compared to their male counterparts because they are the gender who continue to assume the bulk of caring responsibilities and this is why achieving work/life balance – something of importance to both sexes – is of particular urgency for women (LSE 2015: 28). Unlike their male counterparts who may have children or elderly parents, women frequently have to choose between their care responsibilities and a diplomatic career. In fact, women are actively discouraged from a life in politics by gendered practices and assumptions and the routine disparagement of their knowledge and abilities. The representation of women politicians (and, to a lesser extent, diplomatic agents) in the media, including the irrelevant continuous scrutiny of hairstyle or dress, continues to play a role in how we view gender within these professions. Therefore, the supply side, and the challenges it continues to perpetuate for women entering the diplomatic profession, is certainly an area that needs increasing exploration and study.

This recognition; that is there is *no steady upward trajectory* for women in diplomacy is also expanded to include the recognition that *there is no one single experience* which women share once they enter the diplomatic realm. This volume has attempted to unveil and expand upon this key element within gender studies and feminist analytics through the uniqueness and complexity of its contributing authors and the broad range of topics which they have covered. This commitment to diversity has been a central discourse of this volume, and it acknowledges that within the current literature and discussion, this theme needs increased recognition and substantially more work within the field. The story of women cannot – and should not – be constructed on a single race, religion, or creed.

From these themes and questions for future research, we are now pressed to develop a concrete set of policies, which work towards not only increasing the numerical representation of women within the service, but also a renewal of the gendered institution itself.

Moving forward: recommendations for policymakers

This volume will now conclude with several recommendations for policy makers based on the preceding analysis by its contributors.

i The burden of representation must now shift

The burden of equality must now shift from the underrepresentation of women to the overrepresentation of men. Taking a lead from the LSE's *Commission On Gender, Inequality And Power* (2015), this volume recommends that diplomatic bodies establish a ceiling gender quota: a maximum of 70 per cent of either sex should be hired and present within their institution. This is the most controversial of any recommendation because it involves a mandatory quota. Although perhaps contentious and challenging for some Ministries, the LSE study notes that shifting the burden of representation is, however,

> an increasing practice across Europe, including now in Ireland, and reflects frustration with the history of failed promises and insincere commitments by parties that do not yet regard the homogeneity of their representatives as a serious concern. Current improvements in gender balance are almost entirely due to those parties that have chosen, voluntarily, to act on this issue.

While this recommendation seeks to address the issue of gender equality in terms of a ceiling as opposed to a floor, shifting the burden of the argument from the underrepresentation of women to the unjustifiable over-representation of men, this is not to say the issue of minimum quotas in a Ministry is distinct or contradictory to this claim. Both recommendations and practices are to work in unison to address the issue of gender equality in the diplomatic sphere. It is to be seen as a two-pronged strategy working towards the same goal of nominal and substantive equality.

ii Gender audits

The second recommendation is a call for the introduction of gender audits for national ministries and international diplomatic bodies. While women's role in diplomacy is ever-growing, the archetypal structure of diplomacy, developed on the basis of gender norms, remains solid. To facilitate an alteration of the reigning archetype, this volume recommends that MFAs should be required to carry out gender audits of all the policies they propose to introduce. Like everything in international politics, gender audits provide no guarantee: they can easily degenerate into a 'tick-box' approach, and often do when carried out by people who have no vested interest in their outcomes (LSE 2015). That said, the central motive behind an implementation of gender audits is that they require policy makers to address explicitly the likely impact of a policy on women and men, and to demonstrate that they have considered and provided justification for whether the opportunities and burdens will be distributed differentially between the sexes (Ibid., 7). Given that so much of what sustains power inequalities are the unspoken assumptions, hidden principles, and taken-for-granted parameters with which policy is currently made, requiring MFAs and international diplomatic institutions to think consciously about the gender impact of their initiatives opens up the space for what researchers call a 're-gendering' of diplomacy and policy (Ibid.).

iii Quotas

While this volume has frequently presented the case that numbers do not translate to authority and agency, still, the numeric inferiority of women to men is a systemic problem. It matters because of the messages conveyed about women as second-class citizens, better suited to the 'private' world of family and household than to 'public' political life. As a number of the contributors have noted, although modernity continues to challenge archaic patriarchal infrastructures, diplomacy – as a profession and practice – remains adherent to conventional notions of gender. As a result, diplomacy continues as a sphere rife with power dynamics, serving only to reinforce gender inequality and perpetuate the historical 'otherisation' of women.

This volume therefore recommends that MFAs introduce minimum quotas for women for all internal positions. The use of gender quotas for internal positions will ensure that men and women alike gain political experience and are able to contribute to policy formation. Though any kind of quota can, on occasion, be cumbersome or feel overly mechanical, evidence suggests that this is the only way to ensure that questions of equality and diversity are taken seriously within a diplomatic institution (Pande and Ford 2011; Freidenvall 2003). Whilst quotas are not a perfect solution, they do help make questions of inclusion and exclusion more visible, and widen awareness of the issues that need to be addressed in policy development.

Finally, in amendment to the quota system, policy makers must also recognise that the frequently cited 'one in three' objective – a regular numerical target put forth by policy makers when it comes achieving gender and racial equality – is quite simply a flawed objective. Its primary flaw stems from the valid belief that whilst changing the gender composition of an organisation enables different voices to be heard and new agendas to be addressed, it is clear that needs, interests, and experiences do not vary by gender alone, but by location within a range of power hierarchies, structured by race, ethnicity, age, sexuality, religion, culture, and disability (LSE 2015: 28). Speaking with regard to the political sphere, Preethi Sundaram (Fawcett Society) frames the issue as follows:

> the women who have made it to public office are remarkably similar – white, middle class, well-educated and within a narrow age range. BME [Black and Minority Ethnic] women are still under-represented at all levels, as are women from lower socio-economic backgrounds and both older and younger women. The diversity of women's voices is not proportionally represented within the political realm.
>
> (2012: 18)

The same is true for the diplomatic sphere, requiring us then to reevaluate the 'one in three' target so frequently cited, and work towards a composition which captures the diversity of experiences, campaigns, and concerns.

iv Achieving work–life balance

It is clear from the narrative voiced within this volume, that the personal life of women who have served and are currently serving the diplomatic corps, plays a substantial role in the trajectory of their diplomatic careers. Although men and women both juggle the competing demands of work and family, the problems of balancing these responsibilities does not fall equally on both sexes (Lewis 1999). Indeed, the common understanding today is that women's disproportionate share of domestic and caring tasks directly relates to discrimination against women in the labour market and subsequent gender inequalities in pay and quality of jobs (Budig and England 2001; Ferree 1991; Gornick et al. 1998). As Lewis noted 'women, and during recent decades, mothers in particular, have increased their participation in the labor market greatly, but men have not increased their participation in unpaid household work to a matching degree' (Lewis 1999: 1). Issues underlying work–family balance are those of the gendered divisions of paid and unpaid work, and have long served as a fundamental source of gender inequalities within the workplace and at home.

From a policymaker's perspective, this issue cannot be solved by MFAs alone, but must incorporate central state bodies. Here the institution and the state must work in synergy if gendered divisions of labour are to be adequately addressed. Reforms have already been introduced in a number of ministries which target both the work and family side of the equation; extension of maternity leave, creation of onsite nurseries, arranging sessions around school terms, and the development of more flexible working patterns as a whole. Parental leave has also become an emerging policy initiative, but substantial improvement in terms of policy creation and its implementation remains a prominent concern. Increasing paternal leave would not only serve to reverse the burden of childcare on the female worker, but also grant fathers a healthier and more equitable work–life balance. Such reforms must be built upon by both the state and the diplomatic institutions which serve them, if the burden of domestic responsibilities is to shift or balance between sexes.

Conclusion

Revealing diplomacy as an inherently gendered practice and profession is in its relative infancy. But, by all measures, we are on a steady path towards non-gendered diplomacy despite various obstacles which persist to this day. These play a wide-ranging prohibitive role which spans everything from complete absence of female participation in some countries to an absence from highest political office in other nations and virtually every scenario in between. While eliminating these obstacles is one way towards achieving equal involvement and representation of women in the diplomatic sphere, such a strategy would depend largely on the open-mindedness of men, by whom the barriers were set up in the first place. The timeliness of this topic is not only linked to issues of equality and justice, but also about expanding the pool of talented people necessary to tackle today's complexities and challenges. Indeed, according to the mantra of UN Women: women's full participation as leaders, advocates, and agents of change is necessary in every regard, if we are to achieve the universal ideals of the United Nations – peace, justice, and equality for all. Progress in each of these areas is therefore highly dependent upon the support of national ministries, international diplomatic bodies, and, equally, non-governmental actors.

This volume has not represented a form of appeal to those who would prefer a state of perpetual isolation of women from diplomacy. Rather, it has attempted to bring to the mainstream the often downplayed and underreported role of women in governance and policymaking. More importantly, it has strived to showcase the inevitability of increased female representation in the realm of diplomacy, and the impact that this increased representation (in all areas of diplomatic practice) will have on the practice of international politics in the twenty first century.

References

Annesley, C. 2010. 'Gendering Politics and Policy', *Policy and Politics* 38(3): 333–336.

Budig, M. J. and P. England. 2001. 'The Wage Penalty for Motherhood', *American Sociological Review* 66(2): 204–225.

Ferree, M. 1983. 'Housework: Rethinking the Costs and Benefits' in *Families, Politics, and Public Policy: A Feminist Dialogues on Women and the State*, ed. I Diamond. New York: Longman, 148–167.

Freidenvall, L. 2003. 'Women's Political Representation and Gender Quotas – the Swedish Case' www.niyf.org/wp-content/uploads/2016/05/zipping.pdf. Accessed 20 November 2016.

Gornick, J. C., M. K. Meters, and K. E. Ross. 1998. 'Public Policies and the Employment of Mothers: A Cross National Study', *Social Science Quarterly* 79(1): 34–54.

Lewis, J. 2009. *Work–Family Balance, Gender and Policy*. Massachusetts: Edward Elgar Publishing Limited.

LSE. 2015. *Confronting Gender Inequality: Findings from The LSE Commission On Gender, Inequality And Power* http://eprints.lse.ac.uk/66802/1/Confronting-Inequality.pdf. Accessed 20 November 2016.

Norris, P. and J. Lovenduski. 1995. *Political Recruitment: Gender, Race and Class in the British Parliament*. Cambridge: Cambridge University Press.

Pande, R. and D. Ford. 2011. 'Gender Quotas and Female Leadership: A Review' http://scholar.harvard.edu/files/rpande/files/gender_quotas_-_april_2011.pdf. Accessed 20 November 2016.

Sundaram, P. 2012. 'The Power Gap: Why we Are at a Watershed Moment for Women's Rights', *Fabiana – The Fabian Women's Network Magazine* https://fabianwomensnetwork.files.wordpress.com/2013/03/fabianawinter2012.pdf. Accessed 20 November 2016.

Index

Africa 35–6, 38, 39, 49, 54, 66–7, 69, 75, 108–9, 126, 130, 134, 136
Albright, Madeleine 149, 150, 205
ambassador 6, 8–10, 16–17, 19–27, 34–5, 37, 39–41, 43–4, 48, 50, 52, 55, 60, 74, 86, 100–5, 107–17, 119–27, 129–31, 133–4, 136–9, 145, 146, 149–50, 153–5, 167, 188–90, 192–3, 211
Association of Southeast Asian Nations (ASEAN) 156
Australia 24, 126, 147, 149, 151, 153, 162, 188

Beijing Conference 74, 149, 173–8; Platform for Action 149, 164, 182, 184
Belgium 146, 188

Canada 24–5, 100, 148, 162
Caribbean Community (CARICOM) 77
China 16–17, 104, 106, 126, 151, 160–3
civil service 23, 25, 41, 50, 52, 55, 61, 63, 180
civil society 27, 71, 74, 88, 132, 151, 153, 161, 173, 175–6, 179, 181–2, 184
Clinton, Hillary 7–8, 28, 83–8, 90–9, 146
Convention on the Elimination of all forms of Discrimination against Women (CEDAW) 73, 149, 172
Copenhagen conference 71, 74, 75, 193

democracy 17, 87, 93
Denmark 19, 24–5, 101, 108, 114, 145
developing countries 68, 71, 72, 75, 76, 143, 163, 178–9
development 15–16, 49, 53–6, 62, 65–6, 69, 72–4, 77, 85, 88, 93, 102, 141, 144, 146, 149, 152, 155–6, 159, 160–1, 166, 173–5, 182, 217; Sustainable Development 9, 165, 170, 171, 172, 177

Development Alternatives for Women Networks (DAWN) 72, 75–6

Europe 15, 19–20, 22–3, 35, 48, 51, 108–9, 214; European Union 67, 126, 158

feminism 71, 76, 88, 91
foreign policy 3, 6, 15–16, 18, 20–1, 27, 50, 59, 85–8, 95, 141–2, 150, 153, 189, 193
France 19, 20, 23–4, 34, 106, 126, 156, 162

gender 1–10, 15–24, 28, 32–3, 35–6, 38–44, 48–63, 71–4, 76, 78, 80, 83–8, 90, 91, 91, 94–7, 100–19, 121, 122, 124–33, 137, 140–4, 147–50, 157–66, 170–85, 188–90, 191–3, 196, 197, 198–9, 201–4, 206, 208–17
Geneva 25, 90, 91, 153, 155
globalisation 77, 147
governance 5, 9, 7, 140, 151–2, 157, 159–60, 164, 165, 180, 211, 217
Group of 7 (G7) 151, 153, 157, 158, 205
Group of 8 (G8) 151, 153–4, 158, 166
Group of 10 (G10) 126
Group of 20 (G20) 9, 105–6, 110, 115, 140–1, 144–5, 152–4, 156–66

Hague 17, 48, 52
human rights 17, 62, 66, 71, 90, 95–6, 144, 148–9, 153, 160, 164–5, 171–4, 177, 184, 203

India 67, 71, 75, 106, 11, 113, 149, 162
Indonesia 67, 69, 162
international women's movement 7

Index

Iraq 95, 121, 131, 133
Ireland 6, 48, 50–3, 56–7, 63, 148, 191, 212, 214
Israel 106, 108, 111, 163
Italy 106, 162

Japan 6, 24, 54, 106, 162
Jordan 188, 202

Latin America 75, 146, 158
League of Nations 25–8, 145, 190
liberal 22–4, 51, 87, 94, 96, 206

Malaysia 135, 156, 163
Middle East 108–9, 117, 123–5, 128, 136
Ministries of Foreign Affairs (MFA) 7, 27, 63, 101, 121, 128, 140, 151, 158, 160, 191, 198, 201, 214–15, 217
multilateral 10, 55, 75, 149, 153, 173, 176, 187, 188, 189, 194–5

Nairobi Conference 73–6, 173, 175
NATO 125, 136
negotiation 7, 9, 19, 20, 72, 76–7, 83, 87, 142, 148, 149, 152, 173, 180–91, 185
Netherlands 24, 187
New Zealand 114
Non-Aligned Movement (NAM) 66–70
Non-Governmental Organisation (NGO's) 27, 74, 142, 173

Pakistan 88, 105–7, 110, 111, 115
Palestinan 74
peacekeeping 55–6, 180, 185

policymaking 5, 155, 172, 213, 217
poverty 50, 75, 165, 172, 179

refugee 107, 179
regional 7, 16, 72, 74–7, 108, 134, 159, 161, 173, 179, 194–6, 199, 204
Russia 19, 22–3, 85, 92, 106, 108, 126, 131, 145, 151, 153, 162

Secretary General 9, 35, 74, 148, 157, 159, 170, 170–6, 180, 180, 182, 185, 188, 200, 205
Secretary of State 7, 9, 28, 68, 83, 84–8, 90, 91–3
sherpas 9, 140, 141, 151, 152–5, 157–8, 165
South Commission 72
Spain 19, 24–5, 145–6, 155, 158, 165
summit (summitry) 9, 68, 140–2, 148–9, 151–4, 158, 161, 164, 166, 173, 211
Sweden 23, 100, 101, 145–6

transnational 28, 142, 152
Turkey 145, 151, 153, 154–7, 160–2

United Kingdom 123, 125–6, 135, 146
United Nations 7, 9, 27, 37, 48, 62, 65–7, 70–3, 77–8, 136, 142, 148, 159, 164, 170–5, 177, 179, 181–8, 193, 206, 211
United States 2, 6, 24, 32–3, 40, 43, 83, 85–7, 95, 100, 126, 217, 144, 145, 149, 190, 193

Yemen 8, 121, 123–7, 130, 132, 133